POSTHUMOUS KEATS

Also by *Stanley Plumly*

. . .

W. W. NORTON & COMPANY

new york   london

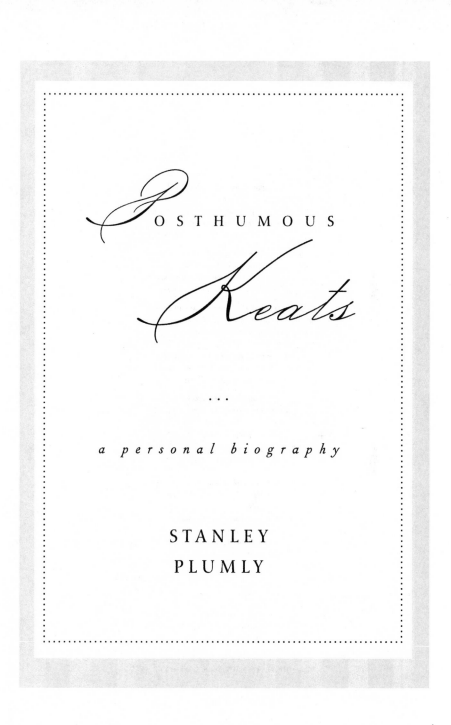

POSTHUMOUS

Keats

...

a personal biography

STANLEY
PLUMLY

Copyright © 2008 by Stanley Plumly

For information about permission to reproduce
selections from this book,
write to Permissions, W. W. Norton & Company, Inc.,
500 Fifth Avenue, New York, NY 10110

For information about special discounts for bulk
purchases, please contact W. W. Norton Special Sales at
specialsales@wwnorton.com or 800-233-4830

Manufacturing by Courier Westford
Book design by Barbara M. Bachman
Production manager: Julia Druskin

LIBRARY OF CONGRESS
CATALOGING-IN-PUBLICATION DATA

Plumly, Stanley.
Posthumous Keats : a personal biography / Stanley
Plumly. — 1st ed.
p. cm.
Includes bibliographical references and index.
ISBN 978-0-393-06573-2 (hardcover)
1. Keats, John, 1795–1821. 2. Keats, John,
1795–1821—Influence. 3. Poets, English—19th
century—Biography. I. Title.
PR4836.P68 2008
821'.7—dc22
[B]
2008002681

W. W. Norton & Company, Inc.
500 Fifth Avenue, New York, N.Y. 10110
www.wwnorton.com

W. W. Norton & Company Ltd.
Castle House, 75/76 Wells Street, London W1T 3QT

1 2 3 4 5 6 7 8 9 0

For

WILLIAM MATTHEWS

Acknowledgments

. . .

VERSIONS OF THE FIRST THREE CHAPTERS WERE PUBLISHED in *TriQuarterly* ("On He Flared"), *The Virginia Quarterly Review* ("Cold Pastoral"), and *The Kenyon Review* ("This Mortal Body"). Thanks are due the editors. Versions of parts of the chapter "Season of Mists" first appeared in sections of *Argument & Song: Sources & Silences in Poetry* (2003).

Very special thanks to Megan Riley and Elizabeth Countryman, whose help in the preparation of this book was invaluable.

Also special thanks to Christina Gee and Roberta Davis, stalwarts of the Keats House, without whose help the making of this book would have been impossible.

To Jill Bialosky, Evan Carver, and Paul Whitlatch, my editors at Norton, admiration and warmest appreciation.

To friends Michael Collier, Howard Norman, and David Wyatt, steadfast and true, my greatest thanks.

To Daniel Halpern, whose patience and support have mattered most, my heartfelt thanks.

And to Deborah Digges a debt of gratitude for introducing me to Keats's *Letters* by quoting whole passages from memory.

And appreciation to Hawthornden Castle, the Bellagio Study and Conference Center, and the University of Maryland for their support.

*We with our bodily eyes see but the fashion
and Manners of one country for one age—
and then we die—*

—LETTER TO THE GEORGE KEATSES

DECEMBER 31, 1818

CONTENTS

...

℘REFACE

· · ·

BOOKS THAT MATTER THE MOST TO THEIR AUTHORS OFTEN acquire a considerable longevity, even history, as part of their making. I first got the notion for *Posthumous Keats* from a poem of mine of the same title—well, not directly from the poem but from a commentary I wrote about the poem in *Singular Voices* (Avon Books, 1985), a collection of such commentary edited by Stephen Berg. My brief essay reads, in retrospect, like a summary of what brought me to the idea—now some twenty years ago—that certain connections and crossovers in the John Keats story had not fit the profile of strict biographical narrative, of which, in Keats's case, there is an abundance, notably the great 1960s biographies by Walter Jackson Bate (1963), Aileen Ward (1963), and Robert Gittings (1968). The inciting incident at the heart of my poem involves an extended moment concerning Keats's land journey along the coast from Naples to Rome, his last journey. His friend Joseph Severn is traveling with him, and will become not only Keats's nurse but the biographer of the young poet's final months. I write that

Keats is in a hired carriage, a vettura, *on his way from Naples to Rome. He has less than four months to live. It is November*

1820, warm, wildflowers everywhere. Severn, his companion, thinking to make more room for his sick friend and tired of the rough ride, decides to walk. His painter's eye cannot help but be attracted to the color in the day—mountains, the sea, the Italian sky, the fencerows of the vineyards, and, almost at their feet, blue and white and yellow flowers. After the long, claustrophobic, tubercular, and stormy voyage on the Maria Crowther, *six weeks from Gravesend to the Bay of Naples; after a typhus quarantine of more than two weeks in a lie within teasing distance of their destination; after the long-suffering realization that Keats is deeply and irrevocably ill; after the sea-cold and the damp and the smell of death, the autumn countryside feels like spring. The land trip north, in slow motion, will take yet another week. Keats and Severn are tourists, but broke. They won't eat well, they won't ride well, but they will see—at one point, improbably, a cardinal, with two footmen also dressed in red, shooting songbirds. And they will see, daily, as if wildflowers were the motif of the mortal world, spread after spread of floral color, right up to the Campagna. Severn can't keep his hands off the flowers. Nor does he know what to do with them once he's picked them. So he puts them, by the handful, in the small carriage with Keats, like company. This goes on, off and on, for days. By the time they reach the outskirts of Rome, Keats is witness to his own funeral.*

Keats's story is replete with moments and meetings such as this funeral-carriage example. But as crucial as they are, examples are texture: They do not structure a text. The last thing I wanted, as I began to imagine what *Posthumous Keats* might look like, was a book built on linearity—a narrative line of rescued biographia. The many biographies and studies of Keats had already straightened that line perfectly. The problem, as I saw it, was point of view: Who, in what voice, would speak what I wished to say? After different tries, I realized I could not write this book in limited first person or omniscient third person, in a strictly subjective or objective voice, the one being too familiar, the other too distant. I had to find a middle way of discovering and articulating Keats in his possible and potential afterlife, not only his life. I needed to be able to think with a warm mind through the mortality—and its meander—that helped bring about his ultimate immortality. The power of Keats's story is so wrapped up in his young, drawn-out, painful death that it is almost impossible to separate that fact from the power of the poems. Much of my point in this book is that they should not be separated, nor should their vital connection be exaggerated. The death of Keats, in his despair, is to him the death of his poetry. The apparent decline in his attitude toward his work can be measured in his statement to his brother George, in 1818, that he would be among the English poets after his death compared to his request to Severn, in 1821, that his epitaph should read that here lies one whose name was writ in water. For Keats, in his final year and a half—his "posthumous existence," as he sometimes called it—mortality was total. It would be years before his real posthumous life would take hold, though it begins the morning he is buried.

I needed to find a voice, in Keatsian terms, that could deal with the biographical issues with "disinterestedness" and the poems with selection and passion. The voice needed to be convicted in its opinions and thoughtful in its musings. In the end, this is a book of reflection, contemplation, mediation. Thus the structure of its thinking tends to be circular rather than linear. I wanted to walk around in Keats's life and art, not simply through them; I wanted to process how, in the exemplary instance of Keats, the mystery of immortality becomes manifest. Each chapter, then, is formed

from a single image, theme, or object relative to Keats's vulner-
abilities as an individual and his strengths as an artist. Reiteration
and juxtaposition become the means of letting the afterlife—and
life—of Keats "greet" the reader. Keats is not a poet one reads in
half-portion, nor a man one comprehends without love. I needed
to find the tone of voice that listens as well as speaks. I needed to
find a little bit of Keats in myself. I could not help, over these last
years of writing *Posthumous Keats*, but think of my friend Wil-
liam Matthews, whose own posthumous life has barely begun.

January 26, 2007
KENTLANDS

POSTHUMOUS KEATS

ON HE FLARED

...

His flaming robes streamed out beyond his heels,
And gave a roar, as if of earthly fire,
That scared away the meek ethereal Hours,
And made their dove-wings tremble. On he flared

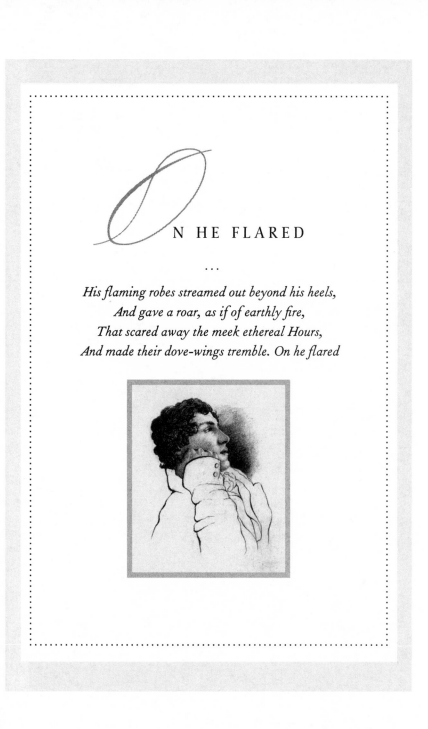

1

ONCE, WHEN HE STILL HAD NINE MONTHS TO LIVE AND WAS living alone, really alone, for the first time, he found himself at tea with a certain Mr. and Mrs. Gisborne, who were introduced as friends of Shelley and who, like the expatriate poet, had decided to settle in Italy. This was at Leigh Hunt's new place on Mortimer Terrace, in Kentish Town. The Hunts had recently moved from the Vale of Health, on Hampstead Heath, and had located rooms for the itinerant Keats just around the corner—"a sort of compromise," Hunt later noted, "between London and our beloved Hampstead." Both Hunt and Keats had moved for the usual economic reasons. It was Thursday, June 22, 1820, and one of the warmest days in anyone's memory. All that morning Keats had been spitting blood, a painful fact of life that had become if not routine then all too common. By early afternoon, with the second-day-of-summer heat building in his upstairs bedroom, he had to get out. One possibility—no, necessity—was to take the day coach out to Walthamstow to see his sister, who had been begging him for weeks to visit. Fanny Keats was the youngest of the four Keats children and the only one who had actually had to live with their guardian Richard Abbey, in a life she had long since begun to think of as a kind of imprisonment. But at the coach stop Keats could feel a small issue of blood start to move from his lungs up into his throat, and fearing another all-out hemorrhage he returned to his Wesleyan Place residence.

He lay there on the floor of the second story in the heat, with the rust taste of blood in his mouth, for most of the rest of the day, late afternoon and the closeness of the humidity and the weight of the ceiling pressing down on him. That is when he decided to try to make his way around the corner to the Hunts, with whom he had an open invitation and with whom, soon enough, once it was determined he could not be alone, he would move in. The Hunts had five wild children, and neither Hunt nor his neurasthentic wife, Marianne, seemed interested in or capable of exercising control. Keats must have thought twice about this visit, but it was better than being ill by himself. The visiting Gisbornes were a surprise, yet they were at least adult company. They had heard of Keats and heard that he was not doing well. They must have been, therefore, equally surprised. Keats's third, and last, book of poems would appear in a matter of days, with work he had done his best—under the circumstances—to revise. It would be the book that would make his reputation, containing all the great odes and *Lamia, The Eve of St. Agnes,* and *Hyperion: A Fragment.* It was a measure, however, of how far removed he was from any sense of the literary value of the moment—a moment he had struggled his whole life, it seemed, to come to—and how far removed from any sense of posterity or personal future—a future that meant to place him "among the English poets" and at the side of Fanny Brawne—that what was probably most on his mind was the residual taste of blood in his mouth.

His new book was never mentioned. Instead the conversation went here and there, and he said little. In addition to the fire-and-char sensation throughout his thorax, his throat felt inflamed. Finally the talk came around to Mrs. Gisborne's favorite subject, which the lyrical Hunt also enjoyed: singing. Mrs. Gisborne, first thing the next morning, wrote in her journal that "Yesterday evening we drank tea at Mr. Hunt's . . . Mr. Keats was introduced to us the same evening; he had lately been ill also, and spoke but little; the Endymion was not mentioned, this person might not be its author; but on observing his countenance and his eyes I persuaded myself that he was the very person. We talked of music, and of Italian and English singing; I mentioned that Farinelli had the art of taking breath imperceptibly, while he continued to hold one single note, alternately swelling out and diminishing the power of his voice like waves. Keats observed that this must in some degree be painful to the hearer, as when a diver descends into the hidden depths of the sea you feel an apprehension lest he may never rise again. These may not be his exact words as he spoke in a low tone."

Keats likely hardly pronounced the words at all; they must have come out of his mouth almost involuntarily, considering the narrative of the day so far. That night, back in the isolation of his rooms, which still felt airtight even with the windows open, he had his second major pulmonary attack. This time, unlike the winter hemorrhage at Wentworth Place, the blood was coagulate and dark and boiled in his throat in such a way that he was afraid he might suffocate or drown. The convulsions, which came in waves, seemed to shake his very heart loose from its foundations. He survived the night, though more than ever "under sentence of death from Dr. Lamb."

2

MRS. GISBORNE, WITH HER POLITE BUT OBJECTIVE EYE, ADDED as a postscript to her journal entry that Keats looked "emaciated" —from the Latin emaciatus, meaning to waste away, which, in the early nineteenth century, meant consumption. The wasting diseases covered just about every form of slow death, including various cancers, syphilis, ulcers, bronchitis, depression, and generic nervous disorders. It was not until the 1840s—decades after Keats's death—that consumption and the symptoms of tuberculosis became synonymous, though the tubercle bacillus itself was not identified until 1882. The emaciation usually registered first in the face. Mrs. Gisborne, new on the scene, could see in the ghost face of Keats the consequence of a year or more of wasting, whereas it might have been less obvious to someone seeing Keats on a more or less daily basis. Even so, in his worst moments, when the blood seemed literally to drain from his look, friends including Joseph Severn, who had drawn and painted Keats more than once, and Charles Brown, who had drawn him best, were concerned at his alternately flushed and blanched appearance. They had been concerned for some time. As early as the autumn before Keats's last summer, in London, Severn had noted that he "seemed well neither in mind nor body."

And as early as the summer before the encounter with the Gisbornes, the summer "o'er-brimmed," the summer of 1819, between the great spring odes and the great ode "To Autumn," Charles Brown, in his famous accurate rendering of Keats's right profile, with a full pugilist's fist tucked at the cheek, captures something of the fatigue that was already starting. It is typical of the story of Keats's immortality that this drawing—beautiful in its neutrality, thoughtful in its likeness—was unknown for more than a hundred years, when, in 1922, Brown's granddaughter sent it from New Zealand to Sidney Colvin, one of Keats's first biographers. "Keats and my grandfather were out sketching together," she says in a late interview. "When they came in Keats was a little tired, and he half-reclined in a couch or easy chair. My grandfather opened his portfolio and made this pencil copy. He was pleased with the result and kept it. Then it passed on to my father; and after his death my mother gave it to me." Keats's own version of the general moment, in a letter dated July 31, 1819, praises, sort of, Brown's draftsmanship: "The other day he was sketching Shanklin Church and as I saw how the business was going, I challenged him to a trial of Skill—he lent me Pencil and Paper—we keep the Sketches to contend for the Prize at the Gallery—I will not say whose I think best—but I really do not think Brown's done to the top of the Art." These Isle of Wight pencil landscapes are lost. Brown's "pencil copy" of Keats, in which the amateur artist is at the top of his art, not only survives but has become the indelible honest modern face of Keats—pensive, care-worn, a little flushed, yet luminous and alert with intelligence. It stands alone against the beautification of Keats that would compromise later renderings by professional artists. It, along with the life and death masks and a few depictions by Robert Benjamin Haydon, stands in distinction to the long, chronological gallery of drawings and paintings and other renderings purported to be Keats—Keats alive and Keats posthumous.

In the Shanklin narrative, Keats and Brown are on a working visit to the Isle of Wight in order to collaborate on the now infamous Covent Garden–variety *Otho the Great*, a highly theatrical tragedy intended to be both barn burner and moneymaker. Keats, at the same time, is working on *Lamia*, perhaps his most serious and successful poetry romance. Part of the day is devoted to art, the rest to commerce—an average of twenty couplets of *Lamia* and a hundred lines of *Otho*. No wonder he seems tired. Keats is penniless; the collaboration is a sign of just how desperate he has become. "Brown and I are pretty well harnessed again to our dog-cart," he writes in the same July 31 letter. "I mean the Tragedy which goes on sinkingly—We are thinking of introducing an Elephant but have not historical referance within reach to determine us as to Otho's Menagerie. When Brown first mention'd this I took it for a Joke; however he brings such plausible reasons, and discourses so eloquently on the dramatic effect that I am giving it a serious consideration." Taking time off for sketching contests and landscape painting ("Brown . . . says plainly that he cannot see any force in my plea for putting Skies in the back ground—and leaving indian ink out of an ash tree") is only one of Keats's and Brown's diversions. Visitors are another, one of whom is the "sensible and wise" James Rice, a good friend but also a sick one. "He was unwell and I was not in very good health." Keats adds, without a trace of irony, that "I confess I cannot bear a sick person in the House . . . I think Rice is in a dangerous state." Keats may be talking about Rice, but he must as well be thinking about his own brother Tom, whom he has nursed and watched die of consumption only months before, in a room as confining as it was, from a communicative point of view, dangerous.

Brown's drawing of this time, of this busy and difficult moment in the Keats biography, is not only beautiful but dispassionately natural, beautiful perhaps because it is so natural. It catches Keats at the edge of his outward makeover. If you go to the National Portrait Gallery in London, you will see bicentennial Keats brought to life in present-tense terms, as if his vitality were at once being summoned yet questioned. The witnesses say he was tired; he says he was not in very good health. In the July 31 letter—which, by the way, is being written to Keats's and Brown's mutual friend Charles Dilke—Keats refers to his "lounging habits," and in an instance of irritation worries aloud about the proximity of "irretrievable" illness in a not-so-subtle reference to the visitor Rice. In less than a year, the strong, fatigued, aloof face of Keats—as brought to life by Brown, with the eyes not quite sure as they gaze off into the uncertain future—in less than a year this face will be the ghost of itself that Mrs. Gisborne looks upon. Still, Brown's drawing is so draftsman-like, so confident, with Keats's firm fist anchored at the cheek, that what is sensitive in the rendering could be interpreted as aggressive. The ambiguity of apparent square-shouldered robustness versus the potential, inevitable destruction going on inside Keats's body, the contradiction of his history of dynamic personal beauty as opposed to the months of emaciation—this seeming physical paradox of health and illness mixed helps contribute, in his last two years, to the confusion of many, including himself, as to what, until it is far too late, is wrong with him. Keats and his circle could see the consumption in Rice and the "palely loitering" Tom, but until Keats was irretrievably caught "between despair & Energy," his ups and downs were assigned to temperament, mood, nerves, poetry.

Brown, of course, has the advantage of a living subject, the model himself posing in front of him, even though the fruit of his labor will not be brought to life for a hundred years. This theme of posthumousness, of the afterlife of the life, is obviously larger than the chronology of Keats's changing, and declining, appearance. It is at the heart of how his reputation as a poet came into being, of how his name, apparently writ in water, eventually "traveled in the realms of gold." But reputation is directly connected to how few likenesses—almost none actually—we have of a contemporary Keats. Outside of his circle, he was, in effect, invisible or mocked. "We venture to make our small prophecy that his bookseller will not a second time venture 50 on anything he can write," commented the reviewer in the infamous *Blackwood's* notice of *Endymion*, 1818. "It is a better and wiser thing to be a starved apothecary than a starved poet. So back to the shop, Mr. John, back to 'plasters, pills and ointment boxes.'" And indeed, Keats's first publisher, Olliers, dropped him, and his second, Taylor and Hessey, sold copyright to the poems and unpublished manuscripts for exactly fifty pounds, less than twenty-five years after his death, because of a lack of readership. In addition to the sketch by Brown, the best of the other contemporaneous renderings are the life mask of 1816 done by epical artist Haydon and the deathbed drawing in 1821 by Severn, in London and Rome, respectively. In between these two examples are various silhouettes, light fragmentary drawings, and a miniature by Severn that all too typically puffs the poet's face. There is also a remarkable profile detail of Keats of an on-he-flared quality in Haydon's monumental *Christ's Entry into Jerusalem*, a wall-wide painting that employs perspective. Keats's head resides in the upper right-hand corner just above Wordsworth's devout pose, next to which stand Voltaire and Newton. There appears to be a cast of hundreds in the painting, most of whose heads trail off into the background like distant treetops in a landscape. Recognizable foreground figures are adoring or at least curious of Christ's passage. In the fierce profile of Keats, however, with eyes and mouth wide open, he looks to be interested in something else. The look is wild eyed, if not agnostic.

Haydon's life mask of Keats and the fiery representation of his left profile in the wall painting reveal profound opposites of mood: one, the cool repose of a sculpted facade in which the eyes and mouth are keenly closed, the mind behind them secret in its own long thought; the other, brilliant in burning color, completely porous and exposed, the eyes and mouth on the verge of shouting. One image in plaster, like stone; the other in paint, wet with intensity. Then reverse the images and imagine Keats's face a month after his first hemorrhage, in February 1820, and compare it to the 1817 version of himself on canvas when Haydon's epic picture finally goes on display in the Egyptian Hall in Piccadilly in late March 1820. The three-year difference must have been obvious to everyone at the opening, though "obvious" may be too strong a word, since on the day of the exhibition the weather had warmed and Keats felt he "was getting better every day." As if to prove it, he walked all the way back to Hampstead, some four city miles. The face in the life mask, whose subtext is facial structure, and the face in the painting, whose subtext is flesh and color, are starting places in the chronology of Keatsian portraiture. The ending place is Severn's well-known candlelit deathbed drawing that views the subject in a three-quarters profile and from a little above. This just five years later, and less than a year after the Egyptian Hall showing of a living Keats on fire. A month after Severn's drawing and the day following Keats's death, the maskmaker Gherardi is called in to do the mask of a face wasted to the bone.

3

KEATS HAD A MARVELOUS FACE. "HIS FACE WAS THIN WITH prominent cheek bones, a well-formed nose—Forehead rather receding, characteristic more of the Poet than the Philosopher," says Henry Stephens, a fellow medical student at Guy's Hospital. "A painter or sculptor might have taken him for a study after the Greek masters," says G. F. Mathew, another medical school classmate. Benjamin Bailey, who was close to Keats at the time he was writing *Endymion*, says that "Indeed the form of his head was like that of a fine Greek statue." Brown and Severn, at different times in various Keatsian descriptions, focus on the eyes: "His full fine eyes were lustrously intellectual"; "I can never forget the wine-like luster of Keats's eyes, just like those of certain birds which habitually front the sun"; "he had the hazel eyes of a wild gipsy set in the face of a god." These, along with most of the details, verbal portraitures, notational accounts, and romantic depictions of Keats, are remembered representations, usually long after the visual experience, in that posthumously open time when the scales of immortality are being weighed. Keats made a vital impression on almost everyone he met, but too often the record got postponed, elevated, or distorted by memory, even grief. He did, in fact, have an arresting head on broad shoulders, dynamic yet sensitive facial features, and a carriage that suggested a military bearing. His light eyes must have seemed like sources of light, his auburn hair golden. He had a temper and a keen sense of justice, qualities that must have underscored his intensity as well as his warmth. He gave off an energy much larger than his size, which was, by measure, sixty and a half inches.

Such impressions reinforce the value of Brown's Shanklin drawing and Haydon's studio life mask and painted profile; they help flesh out the mortal record, the singular moment. They not only render but enhance the life at hand, and evoke the "high-mindedness" and the "terrier courage" that so many of his early friends speak of. Keats's younger brother George, some while after his death, writes of him as a hero: "John's eyes moistened and his lip quivered at the relation of any tale of generosity or benevolence or noble daring, or at sights of loveliness or distress—he had no fears of self thro interference in the quarrels of others, he would at all hazards, without calculating his power to defend, or his reward for the deed, defend the oppressed."

Memoir memory, however, is no substitute for the living picture, the eidetic image of Keats at rest or in motion, whether at the beginning, with Haydon's renderings, at the midpoint, with Brown's, or at the close of his life, with Severn's firsthand study of the final days in Rome. Severn's journal prose sets the scene that has been replayed in every biography since the middle of the nineteenth century. "He remained quiet to the end, which made the death-summons more terrible . . . He died with the most perfect ease. He seemed to go to sleep. On the 23rd, Friday, at half-past four, the approach of death came on. 'Severn—I—lift me up, for I am dying. I shall die easy. Don't be frightened! Thank God it has come.' I lifted him up in my arms, and the phlegm seemed boiling in his throat. This increased until eleven at night, when he gradually sank into death, so quiet, that I still thought he slept. . . ." Somewhere in those empty, sleepless hours between late night and the hour before dawn, Severn did his charcoal drawing of the slightly propped head of Keats, a rendering remarkable enough on its own but made infinitely more so when compared to Severn's other, and later, attempts to create a Keats from memory.

One key to the drawing, whose original hangs in the Keats-Shelley Museum in Rome, is that it is not immediately clear whether Keats is sleeping or in fact has passed. The ambiguity, by Severn's own testimony, serves the power of the moment. Keats is certainly dying, but the event of it has been extended in time, through months and months of fever and recovery, hemorrhaging and bloodletting, relapses into indolence and resolutions to live, confused diagnosis and clear manifestation. The event of his death has been so long in coming, as if it had been postponed as a test, that here at the last, in what seems the final, incremental hour, it feels wholly internal, invisible, mysterious, like a state between life and death. The intimacy, the silence, the imperceptibility of the corporeal crossover, the secrecy with which the breath, the spirit, escapes the body—all of this unspoken and unspeakable quality enters into Severn's deathbed portrait. And it is as graphic as it is lyric—the night sweats, the dampness of the bedding, the way Keats's dark hair drapes his forehead. Although he does not say so, Severn must have made the drawing in part because he did not know what else to do that night and in part because art was his first—for better or worse—language. He claims he drew the picture in order "to keep me awake." The source of light in the cell-like bedroom is of course a candle off to the left, leaving the artist in shadow, like a witness. The peace on Keats's face is both fatal exhaustion and acceptance. And though death, on February 23, is still three weeks away, he looks, after his terrible literal and figurative journey, to have arrived, even disappeared into arrival. The artist in Severn creates a large black sun to relieve the face against in order to emphasize the angle of the resting, lifted three-quarters profile. This circular backdrop is massive in its animation, dramatic in its contrast. Sleeping or dead, Keats seems to be dreaming. Two floors down, where the waterfall of the Spanish Steps spills into the Piazza di Spagna, a true fountain—Bernini's *Barcaccia*—is flowing. The bedroom ceiling is festooned with motifs of roses, as are the little fireplace and the woodwork, the high papered walls forming a narrow rectangle. Severn and Keats, in their candle dark, are closed in, embowered, both windows likely closed.

In the warp and woof of fame after his death, Keats's friends, and later his admirers, were at pains to resurrect his face, his presence, in innumerable "memory paintings," miniatures, engravings, alleged versions, woodcuts, busts, and in innumerable copies of these. Severn's deathbed portrait itself offers alternate versions, by Severn and imitations by others, including the Marquess of Crewe and T. G. Weatherbee incarnations at the Keats Museum in Hampstead, the Pierpont Morgan Library incarnation in New York, and the engraving after Severn by W. B. Scott (published by Reeves & Turner, London) in 1883. Any resemblance once captured by Haydon or Brown or even Severn becomes not only diluted through imitation and time but distorted by assumption. This, in fact, is more true of the living Keats than the dying

Keats. Death demands a certain reality; the life of the individual, though, invites projection. Keats's posthumous face, therefore, becomes more and more anonymous under a palimpsest of erasure and approximation, intention and attenuation, so that by the end of the nineteenth century it is not so much Keats who is being represented in the Mary Newton "portrait" and the Edmund Sullivan engraving or the George Henry Harlow Lawrence School portrait and the W. L. Colls or H. Davidson engraving of Severn's so-called "Lost Portrait" as it is an idealization of the sensitive, dew-eyed poet, generic and salable, an imposed Victorianized idea of what a poet should look like. The various heads and busts of Keats, leading well into the twentieth century, achieved by such artists as Patrick MacDowell, Sidney Waugh, Anne Witney, and Malvina Hoffman, are no less problematic if sometimes more effective: In some hands Keats looks like a child, in others a man well past Keats's twenty-five years. Each of them, like the posthumous drawings, etchings, and paintings, perpetuates an immortalized, generalized Keats.

There is no substitute for the living model or an alternative to talent. Sometimes even a good artist reads too much into his subject. Compare, for example, the several engravings based on the now lost chalk drawing sketched from life by William Hilton in 1819 in Keats's publisher's office. Severn, Hilton's contemporary and competitor, never liked the "sneaking fellow" it made of Keats's honest face. Because we do not have the original drawing to collaborate, we have to rely on the imitators—Charles Wass, F. Croll, and P. Kramer—whose versions are consistent one to the other but totally out of sync with the eventual portrait that Hilton completed some ten years later. The engravings give Keats a precise and pretty look, a Byronic lordly elegance he never had or wished to. Hilton's painting, which hangs like an official portrait in London's National Portrait Gallery, shows

Keats as a studious thinker, chin resting in his left hand anchored to a table with a book opened doubtless to poetry. Keats's fair face is untouched by disease or mood or sorrow. It not only disresembles the engraved copies of Hilton's original sketch, it parodies, through boyish innocence, the living, vital renderings of Haydon, Brown, and the death watch of Severn. It is curious that Hilton's pose is identical to Severn's inferior minature of Keats, executed as early as 1818 and itself imitated by Severn and others. Once again, Keats, as a visual memory, becomes a rumor of himself, passed along into immortality through central casting.

4

THERE ARE WELL OVER A HUNDRED SEPARATE RENDERINGS OF Keats's face—that is, drawings, paintings, engravings, and sculptings by some forty separate artists. Because almost all of them are posthumous, they are almost all secondary, sometimes tertiary, in their sources. *After* is a popular designation, "after Severn" is the most popular. Severn, first and foremost, becomes Keats's visual biographer, though "foremost" is misleading. Both Brown and Severn served crucial roles at different times as Keats's nurses when the poet was near death; both created for the record the two most singular images of the living and dying Keats. Severn, however, because of his vocation and proximity to the subject, had the most opportunity to assay the look, the decline, the reality of Keats. An ordinary draftsman or amateur sketcher might have done better. But Severn was a young man of ambition. Although he starts out as a miniaturist—and one of his most famous and imitated versions of Keats is a miniature first hung in 1819 at Somerset House, now at the National Portrait Gallery, London—his star is set on becoming an important thematic painter, primarily of set pieces from myth, literature, and history, such as *The Death of Alcibiades*, *Rescue of Lorenzo di Medici from Assassination*, and *The Cave of Despair*. One of his unvarnished motives for accompanying Keats on his journey to Italy is the hope of winning a Royal Academy traveling fellowship. He does, in fact, achieve his goals, including the Academy's Gold Medal, a fellowship, and, ultimately, the British Consulship to Rome.

In the process, Keats inevitably becomes his favorite mythic, literate, historical subject, which is to say a confusion of all three modes, as if, in memory, a posthumous Keats needed amending, elevating, or hyping in order to sell him to the future. The painting—the portrait that Severn is working on the day he dies, August 3, 1879—is called simply *Keats*. As late as 1863 he publishes his most visible article in the American magazine the *Atlantic Monthly* entitled "Vicissitudes of Keats's Fame." Somewhere in the makeup of his multiple anxieties, Severn did not trust the final verdict on Keats's reputation. Whether from lack of talent, therefore, or an inability to separate himself from his subject, or a need to "adonize" (Keats's word) his "beloved Keats" (Severn's phrase), his portraits of the posthumous Keats become more and more unreal one from the other and completely perfected and abstracted from the source. They become "the poet" Keats through numbing imitation, repetition, self-reflection. In the better known renderings, Keats is reading in his reading room at Wentworth Place or sitting at a table with a book (vis-à-vis Hilton) or lounging on the Heath listening to a nightingale, as if he were a prop in a fantasy of what a poet should be doing as he contemplates great art and immortality. Only Haydon, Brown, Hilton, and, yes, Severn took the chance at the living, relatively obscure Keats, the sick Keats, the dying Keats. The portraits after death depend on invention or Severn. The reality of the poet becomes compromised by a good many things, including friends' reactions to his health, reviewers' responses to his poems, and Keats's own late doubts and anger about whether he really would be among the English poets. Severn's frankly well-intentioned yet finally self-serving picturing of Keats, over the course of a long, long life, may be but a part of the fantasy that became Keats's "fame" immediately and well after his death; Severn's posthumous pictures do, nevertheless, reinforce the image of a being too sensitive for this world, or of a being who has already left it.

In the Dulwich College Picture Gallery of Paintings in London hangs a *Portrait of a Young Man, Rembrandt School.* The young man is said to be Philip Wouwerman, an artist and contemporary of Rembrandt. An old catalog copy states that the figure in the painting is "Turned to the left, full face, long fair hair, short mustache, about 25 years of age, black cap, white under garment, reddish brown coat lined with fur; hands not visible, dark background . . . The picture is not well preserved. Painted by a pupil or imitator of Rembrandt. It used to be called 'Portrait of Wouwerman by Rembrandt' and was highly esteemed by Hazlitt. Nothing can be richer than the colouring, more forcible and masterly than the handling, and more consistent and individualized than the character of the face. It is one of those portraits of which it is common to say—'that must be a likeness of someone.' "

Not long after Keats's death, his former school friend Charles Cowden Clarke and Clarke's father-in-law, Vincent Novello, visited the Dulwich Gallery. Novello, whose house Keats had been a guest at many times, recalls that "I was particularly struck with the portrait of Wouwerman, which is so extraordinary a likeness of Keats that if his name had been inserted in the catalogue, no one could have doubted it had been painted for him instead of the Flemish artist." Later on, in his *Recollections of Writers*, Clarke seconds this impression, but with qualification. Clarke is in the middle of a passage discussing and evaluating who thus far has best "got" Keats in a portrait: "There is another and curiously unconscious likeness of him in the charming Dulwich Gallery of Pictures. It is the portrait of Wouwerman by Rembrandt. It is just so much of a resemblance as to remind friends of the poet, although not such a one as the immortal Dutchman would have made had the poet been the sitter." Clarke is assuming that Rembrandt himself painted the portrait, which may be why he adds that "It has a plaintive and melancholy expression which, I rejoice to say, I do not associate with Keats."

There is, of course, no accounting for the eye of the beholder, and even less for the hand of the artist. We see, more often than not, what we want to see, and make of it what we can. Clarke, Keats's oldest friend and defender, rejoices in remembering Keats without melancholy. Novello, older as well as more objective, sees Keats exactly in the melancholy—sees the large dark eyes, the large straight mouth, the strong nose; sees the distracted look that Brown got in his drawing and the silent intensity that Haydon got in his. Both Clarke and Novello use the word "likeness," meaning compared with the actual, the living presence, though more likely the remembered living presence. Nevertheless, it was not an approximation or a version, and certainly not a copy, but a likeness, a quickness—even if the "likeness" is like someone else, another likeness, "a young man." Clarke, still so soon after the death, needs to see Keats in a special way, the very young Keats. Novello, an artist in his own right and at best an acquaintance of the poet, sees a face of likeness with darkness in it. Both see a young man of twenty-five. The disparity of renderings in the meander of time following Keats's death—a disparity afflicting copies and copies of copies as much as original pieces—suggests that different people had a different person in mind or differing agendas. After the first miniature, Severn painted full-form versions of Keats in any number of remembered or imaginary poses—sitting, reclining, indoors, out-of-doors—but each of them "capturing" a different, if variant, face; each of them, perforce, "historical" or what later came to be known, by Whistler's time, as "memory work." Sometimes, in the Severn variations, Keats's hair is flat, sometimes curly; sometimes the cheeks are puffed, sometimes severe; sometimes the eyes dominate, sometimes they withdraw. Brown himself falls prey to Severn's sentimental distortions when he, too, in 1820 decides to imitate the miniature in an India-ink copy of his own, which in no way resembles his from-life drawing of some years before. The result is a darker parody of Severn's already much-imitated pretty little portrait. Likeness may not be so much the question here as life-like. The entombing of Keats's face, whether through idealization, incompetence, or imitations, implies a misreading of the man himself as well as an insecurity about the visage of his reputation. Of course, save for the hopes of a few friends, who knew what would become of him? What choice, then, but to paint him as an afterlife? The chameleon poet, as Keats once referred to himself, might or might not disappear into fame. Might or might not be melancholy or healthy, pensive or passionate, important or perhaps permanent. At some point the face of the poet becomes the face on the poems, and then the mask takes over.

5

SHELLEY, FOR EXAMPLE, WHOSE REPUTATION AT THE TIME HARDLY exceeded Keats's, has an official posed-for portrait hanging in the National Portrait Gallery. It was painted by Amelia Curran in 1819, the year Keats wrote his greatest work. Byron's National Portrait Gallery portrait, by Thomas Phillips in 1814, is not only official but perfect Byronic hype; the lord is dressed in exotic Albanian costume, with appropriate headgear and either a smoking instrument, a sword, or a gun draped in his arms like a favorite pet. He looks noble and revolutionary at once, a poster-boy Romantic as opposed to the eighteenth-century poet he was. He is posing, for sure, and knows he is filling the picture. Shelley, on the other hand, in his portrait looks white as a ghost, "vegetarian," about to float out of the frame. From all reports, he was in life wraith-like, tall, thin, on the run. Keats's official portrait was painted by Severn in Rome right after the poet's death, though the portraiture setting is Wentworth Place, thousands of miles and an eternity away: The thoughtful Keats is reading a book, sitting on a chair, with another chair, at perpendicular, placed as a prop for his left arm. His right hand holds the pages open, his left supports his head. If we replaced the right hand with the fist in Brown's rendering and forgot the book in this one, Keats would be, anachronistically, the thinker. The pose, in other words, is familiar, classical. Even if Severn observed Keats in this mode—which, apparently, he did many times—the painting feels contrived and, even by artificial drawing-room standards, unreal, dioramic, funereal. Shakespeare's portrait on the wall above Keats's head does not help, nor does the floral garden stage left just outside the window. Severn doubtless is doing his best, but he has overdressed Keats, again, in the role of sensitive, effeminate genius, and created an impression of the figure as far from the fierce, strong profile in Haydon's *Christ* painting as possible.

Wordsworth and Coleridge, as first-generation Romantics, naturally receive the best on-site attention as compared to their young counterparts. Among the living portraits of Wordsworth, the 1806 and 1818 drawings by Henry Edridge and Haydon, respectively, stand out, as well as sittings by Richard Carruthers (1817) and William Shuter (1798). What is impressive about Wordsworth's face in all of his poses is the consistency with which, from artist to artist, youth to age, the Wordsworth look comes through: the clarity and conviction of the gaze, the Nordic majesty of the brow, the hauteur of greatness in the bearing— whether at rest or standing; the poet of *Lyrical Ballads* and the posthumous *Prelude* is present and aware of himself. These are portraits without apology, as is the first painting of Wordsworth in 1798 by William Shuter, with the nose and the forehead prominent, which can be found now in the Wordsworth Collection at Cornell. Washington Allston's 1814 portrait of Coleridge (which, like the Edridge *Wordsworth*, is part of the Granger Collection) may make the poet-philosopher look like a president—Allston is American—yet it does, as art, reveal the white-haired, jowled, heavy, full-faced, aging Coleridge who will not write poetry again and whose single-mindedness will be to attempt to remember, as *Biographia*, everything. Coleridge has a small piece of paper in his left hand, as if it were a note of permission. Coleridge is imposing, dignified, but on the edge. Just eight years earlier, in Rome, Allston paints an incredibly younger Coleridge—same bright, big face, same expression—with hair as dark as a crow's wing. Thomas Phillips's *William Blake* (uncompromising at age fifty) and Alexander Nasmyth's *Robert Burns* (expectant at age twenty-eight) are no less accurate.

The living Keats, however, remains a figure in the landscape, a face in the crowd. His present-tense portraits are accidents of timing, performed by friends on the spur of the moment. What they offer in vitality and intimacy they lose in the planned patience of detailed study. For all his quick-take preliminary drawing, Haydon's left profile of the fiery Keats in *Christ's Entry into Jerusalem* is blessed with a sense of spontaneity over accuracy, perspective over close-up. For all its feeling for the moment, Brown's 1819 right-side profile pencil sketch is only that, a sketch. By the time posterity's schedule calls for an old-fashioned, full-fledged portrait of Keats, it is too late—too late to supersede memory, impression, invention, intention. Keats had once said that he had no use for poetry with "palpable designs" on the reader; he would have certainly had no use for portraits with palpable designs on the viewer, particularly in the projection of his own face. Thus in his posthumous portraits Keats either resembles the effeminate innocent that the bad reviews kill, the poverty overwhelms, the disease ravages, the "poor Keats" cast in soft focus, or he turns into the ideal handsome poet no mere mortal harm can come to. At the close of the "Indolence" ode, he writes that "I would not be dieted with praise, / A pet-lamb in a sentimental farce!" There is something unnecessarily compensatory in the general artistic attitude toward Keats after his death: He needed to appear, apparently, either as a victim or valiant. And because he was unavailable to correct or give realism to such an attitude, artists tended to paint, draw, sculpt the myth, the easier story. Severn, for all his virtues as a friend, facilitated, for the remainder of his long life, the poeticizing of the poor Keats.

6

FIRST EXHIBITED AT THE ROYAL ACADEMY IN 1856, IN THE EARLY years of the Victorians and six years after the death of Wordsworth, *The Death of Chatterton* by Henry Wallis presently hangs in the Tate Gallery, along with a number of other examples of Pre-Raphaelite art. Thomas Chatterton died by his own hand from a potion of water and arsenic in 1770, the year Wordsworth was born. Wordsworth, like many poets, including Keats, remembers Chatterton as

> *the marvelous Boy,*
> *The sleepless Soul that perished in his pride;*

then goes on to add the sad example of Robert Burns, who died at thirty-six of drink,

> *who walked in glory and in joy*
> *Following his plough, along the mountain-side:*

and concludes that

> *By our own spirits are we deified;*
> *We Poets in our youth begin in gladness;*
> *But thereof come in the end despondency and madness.*

Spirits self-deified or deified by others often come, from posterity's point of view, to the same thing. Coleridge, remembering Chatterton, writes that

> *we, at sober eye, would round thee throng,*
> *Would hang, enraptur'd on thy stately song,*
> *And greet with smiles the young-eyed Poesy*
> *All deftly mask'd as hoar Antiquity.*

Even Keats laments

> *O Chatterton! how very sad thy fate!*
> *Dear child of sorrow—son of misery!*
> *How soon the film of death obscur'd that eye,*
> *Whence Genius mildly flash'd and high debate.*

And Shelley, anticipating the Wallis painting, sees, in the illustration of Chatterton's death, his face "Rose pale, his solemn agony . . . not / Yet faded from him."

Chatterton elegies, in both poetry and commentary, come,

naturally, well after his death, in a posthumous period we still think of in terms of Romanticism and Victorianism—Chatterton reconsidered, revalued. If the Romantics honor him, the Victorians make him famous. As a struggling adolescent eighteenth-century poet, he was a wunderkind for sure, on track to be as visionary as Blake, as church-mouse poor as Burns. He was a fantast in extremis who imagined a whole lost world of poetry by inventing, quite convincingly, a medieval identity for himself in the person of a fifteenth-century priest-poet named Thomas Rowley. More to the point, he "invented" Rowley's language ("Thou seest this Maystrie of a human hand / The Pride of Brystow and the Westerne Lande / Yet is the Buylders Vertues much moe greete / Greeter than can bie Rowlie's Pen be scande—"). Because he was just seventeen and a half when he killed himself, because he fit so apparently the role of young, afflicted genius, the reflected light on Chatterton tends to be forgiving, warm. ("Last Verses": Farewell, Bristolia's dingy piles of brick,

> *Lovers of Mammon, worshippers of Trick!*
> *Ye spurned the boy who gave you antique lays,*
> *And paid for learning with your empty praise.*
> *Farewell, ye guzzling aldermanic fools,*
> *By nature fitted for Corruption's tools!*
> *I go to where celestial anthems swell;*
> *But you, when you depart, will sink to Hell.*
> *Farewell, my Mother!—cease, my anguished soul,*
> *Nor let Distraction's billows o'er me roll!—*
> *Have mercy, Heaven! when here I cease to live,*
> *And this last act of wretchedness forgive.*)

Chatterton's playing of the impostor-poet is usually laid to the fact that he was born posthumously—that is, fatherless. His father died three months before the birth, engendering, in psychoanalytic parlance, an eventual identity crisis in a young man overwhelmed by his mother. By rhyming "gladness" with "madness" in his tribute, Wordsworth not only celebrates poets in their youth but implies that it may be best to die before the demons arrive. In a very real sense, Chatterton's example is the template for the gifted, oversensitive young writer ignored by an indifferent world, a genius—like a lover—spurned. The template graduated quickly into a cultural cliché—in Keats, an "involuntary" suicide, in the "confessional" generation of American poets nearly two hundred years later, post–World War II, a mass suicide. The Wallis painting, done some eighty-five years after Chatterton's death, is a summary as well as a *tableau vivant* of extreme typecasting.

John Ruskin said of the Wallis painting that it is "Faultless and wonderful: a most noble example of the great Pre-Raphaelite school. Examine it well inch by inch: it is one of the pictures which intend and accomplish the entire placing before your eyes of an actual fact—and that a solemn one." "Actual fact" is a loaded phrase, for in actual fact when one dies of arsenic poisoning the body convulses into something like a fetal position and the mouth emits a kind of white vomit. Moreover, the view from London's 39 Brooke Street, right off Gray's Inn Road, where the suicide took place, would not have been permitted the soft sighting of St. Paul's let alone a direct sunrise. The poetic license is further compounded by the fact that Chatterton had already been gone for almost a century, thus could not have posed for his own death scene, forcing Wallis to use as a model another bright young poet, George Meredith, whose flowing auburn hair and dramatic, balletic draping off the bed sets the standard. Meredith, as poser, becomes himself impostor. The painting, all in all, in a gorgeous Pre-Raphaelite sort of way, is beautiful, with just enough mood brocade to give it an otherworldly, mythic-sacred, lost-in-time glow. The dead figure is attached at the edge of the small bed, above which is a half-opened window looking out on a golden, distant London. Morning sun is the only source of light, and it bathes "Chatterton" as if the viewer, at this one moment, had discovered the body. The boy's red hair dominates but is somewhat balanced by his waistcoat—another red—tossed on a chair to the right. There are, like spilled money, scraps of paper, suggesting torn manuscripts, littering the floor not far from where the poison vial has rolled from the suicide's right hand, which is resting between paper and vial. There is even a wisp of smoke rising from a candle, adding to the sense that we have come upon the scene immediately. A rose on the window seat is fading.

The stylistic signature of most Pre-Raphaelite figure painting is the dramaturgical pose, the definitive outline, the absence of shadow, the decorative detail, a wallpaper range of color—russet, wheat, reds and blues, muted and blended tones—and lots of moody weather. The color is often like Technicolor in early color movies, brighter or quieter depending on the subject. The major "characters" in Pre-Raphaelite paintings tend to project innocence, heightened by the color scheme and the stiff arrangement of positions. The Pre-Raphaelite penchant for matters medieval or classical adds to the posed sense of things, an art based on art, ancient art. These values mark the work of John Everett Millais, William Holman Hunt, and Dante Gabriel Rossetti, the movement's founders, who at the time were younger than Keats when he died. Wallis was a second-tier Pre-Raphaelite but no less committed to the one aspect that all the movement's ideas and techniques gravitate toward, which is that the language of painting must translate first as symbol. It must speak immediately and primarily as one thing representing another. Hence, in

Chatterton every object, each detail means something more than itself, though what that might be is suggestive, symbolist, rather than specific or exactingly emblematic: the silken texture of Chatterton's clothes, the tossed torn manuscripts, the open pose of the body, the open window, the rose, the gold morning light, the whole feeling of a life spilled, poured out, wasted, the empty vial almost casually rolled to the center of the picture. What the Pre-Raphaelites were generally after, and what Wallis achieves here, is an illustration of an idea, a scene, a "freeze" of an event already enacted from a real or an imagined established text—historical, biblical, literary. Even Chatterton, by the time he appears in paint, has become a text, a text of imagined majesty invested in both the texture and the tone of the picture, an art for theme's sake that necessarily turns personal tragedy into sentimentality.

Illustration, by its nature, depends on a frozen action tableau that may well be appropriate for scenes from the Bible, literature, or didactic texts, whether it is *Jesus Washing Peter's Feet* (Ford Maddox Brown, 1851–56), *Claudio and Isabella* (W. Holman Hunt, 1850–51), or *The Woodman's Daughter* (J. Millais, 1850–51). A flushed intensity of color may vivify imagined yet illustrative landscape scenes, such as Brown's *The Hayfield* (1855–60) and Holman Hunt's *Sunlight on the Sea* (1852–54) or Millais's *The Rescue* (1855). But the Rossetti series of women's portraits, notably those of Jane Morris and Annie Millar, and Edward Burne-Jones's highly decorative rendering of *Sidonia von Bork*—all from the same period—are no less stylized, no less form-set than these landscapes and dramas, and certainly no less than their own illustrations from myth and passages in literature. Whatever the historical claims—post-Romantic, pre-Symbolist—it is hard to view the Pre-Raphaelite Victorians, in terms of any one of the variety of their beautifully illustrative pictures, and not think of a world burdened by brocade and heavy silks, gingham and gossamer, furniture and finery, and faces filled with high purpose, even when the theme is dark. Because of the pointed heightening of effects, because of the potential for reducing or distorting the energy of a moment in order to fit the frame, illustration sacrifices spontaneity for the sake of construct, manipulation, moral instruction. It looks to paraphrase dynamic image into static narrative: to costume the subject. The Pre-Raphaelites perfected illustration.

7

IT IS POSSIBLE TO ARGUE THAT ILLUSTRATING KEATS IS INDIrectly responsible for the meeting that led Holman Hunt and Rossetti, and later Millais, to form what came to be known as the "Pre-Raphaelite Brotherhood." At the 1848 Royal Academy annual exhibition, Holman Hunt's contribution was a fair-size picturesque version of the penultimate stanza of *The Eve of St. Agnes*, in which Madeline and Porphyro sneak past the sleeping drunken porter and his vaguely alert bloodhounds. "The sacredness of honest responsible love" and "the weakness of proud intemperance" were meant to be related themes of the picture, a picture that was mostly ignored. Someone who did notice it was Rossetti, who had just completed a Keatsian illustration of his own for the Cyclographic Society—*La Belle Dame sans Merci*. It was, as Keats might have said, a greeting of two lost spirits. Holman Hunt had suggested that "no one had ever painted before any subject from this still little-known poet," but he was proved wrong, and happy for it. Each of them, along with Millais, would find in Keats, over the next two decades, a periodic source in the poet's narrative romances, in paintings such as *The Flight of*

Madeline and Porphyro During the Drunkness Attending the Revelry (1848), *Isabella* (1848–49), and *Isabella; or the Pot of Basil* (1866–68). They would find in the young Keats a matching youth of their own: a richness of material, a sensuous glamour, "a fuller Nature . . . a Revivalism, whether it be classicism or medievalism." They would find, as Millais does in *Lorenzo and Isabella* (1849)—probably the most interesting and best executed of the Keatsian illustrations—a narrative at once immersed in period detail and "glories" yet fluid in modern temper and anxiety.

No less than the artists attempting to "capture" the living Keats in a posthumous Keats, the Pre-Raphaelites had an agenda whose symbolism included both object and color, meaning and message. Holman Hunt's Royal Academy entry, on that fateful day he met Rossetti, was ignored—probably—because of its literary as opposed to grand historical or sublime landscape content. It also exhibited some passion—the passion of a nobody young painter interpreting a nobody young and long-dead poet. As if to make sure the painting had a context, the show's catalog copy quotes the *St. Agnes* stanza in full.

> *They glide, like phantoms, into the wide hall;*
> *Like phantoms, to the iron porch, they glide;*
> *Where lay the porter, in uneasy sprawl;*
> *With a huge empty flagon by his side.*
> *The wakeful blood hound rose, and shook his hide,*
> *But his sagacious eye an inmate owns;*
> *By one, and one, the bolts full easy slide:—*
> *The chains lie silent on the footworn stones;—*
> *The key turns, and the door upon its hinges groans.*

The picture now hangs in the Guildhall Art Gallery in London and is still a vivid drama of rich reds and browns. Holman Hunt painted it in the evenings by candlelight, appropriate for the sources of light within the scene—an operatic scene layered with perspective, the lovers in the foreground stage left, the revelry in the background stage right, the drunken porter practically spilling out of the frame in front. The St. Agnes story itself, which is a winter tale, is based on an ancient superstition that a young woman would see her future husband in a dream if she fasted on St. Agnes' Eve. The fiction has parallels in Boccaccio and French medieval romances, thus the likely reason for its particular historical setting. Keats wrote the poem in a little more than a week in January 1819, in season. Whatever he thought of it—and he clearly had an audience in mind in writing it—he placed it third in the order of his last book of poems, with two other narrative romances—*Lamia* and *Isabella*—leading off, followed by the spring odes, some light verse, and ending with "To Autumn," "Ode on Melancholy," and *Hyperion: A Fragment*. *Lamia, Isabella, The Eve of St. Agnes and Other Poems* becomes, in fact, the book's title. All of these poems were written in a matter of months in his last, truly, living year. Keats's agenda for *Eve of St. Agnes*, and for all his verse romances, was the same as Byron's and Sir Walter Scott's, whose verse narratives outsold novels, with thousands and thousands of copies in circulation. These late eighteenth-century carry-over forms made Byron wealthy and paid down Scott's enormous family debt. Keats was no lord and too poor to be much indebted. With the Pre-Raphaelites, poor Keats—an appellation that forever seems to follow him—becomes pretty Keats. In the most effective of the illustrations, Millais's *Lorenza and Isabella* (based on *Isabella; or the Pot of Basil*), the dramatic complexity, visual subtlety, and character insight combine to create a picture of real depth of field—there are at least a dozen people at the dinner table, including one standing—without violating the importance of the foreground action, the most famous detail of which is the foot-jabbing of the greyhound by one of Isabella's murderous brothers.

Yet for all its beauty and intelligence, the picture remains an illustration, an interpretation of an interpretation of how the brothers "could not in the self-same mansion dwell / Without some stir of heart, some malady." Keats again borrows from Boccaccio, adding his own romantic green gothicism, specifically through the agency of Isabella's secreting of her lover's head within a pot of basil. The edge of melodrama may belong to Keats, but so does the resonance of his gorgeous language, qualities that become exaggerated in the hands of his Pre-Raphaelite "discoverers"—in terms of which the evocative turns into the explicative, the lyrical into narrative, the imagination into intention. Rossetti, Holman Hunt, and Millais come to Keats nearly thirty years after his death; they see in certain of his poems a purpose of their own, which is to make public his most salable images—images that he himself, young and ambitious as he is, wishes to be sold. The Pre-Raphaelites, though, represent the most transparent part of this Keats, the side of his secondary writing that presents a drapery of poetry converted to a well-disguised didacticism.

They likely found Keats with the help of Richard Monckton Milnes, who in 1848, the first year of the illustrations, published the first muted biography, *The Life, and Literary Remains of John Keats.* Not surprisingly, the mixed result is something of a hodgepodge of personal anecdotes, letters, extensive borrowings from Brown's abortive Keatsian memoir, Milnes's own narrative and commentary, plus some 67 poems (of approximately, when the count was finally in, 160 poems). The biography was received with modest Victorian response, warm but with reservations about Keats's qualified masculinity ("A pale flower by some maiden cherished," according to Shelley) and aggressive sensuality—the very qualities, in the yet longer pictorial poems, that the Pre-Raphaelites thought so attractive. Milnes—later Lord Houghton—had been a part of the 1829 stellar group at Cambridge that had linked and celebrated Keats and Shelley both by reprinting, at no little expense, an edition of *Adonais*, the great pastoral elegy that promoted its own didactic, distorted portrait of Keats. Arthur Hallam and Alfred Tennyson were other star members of the group. (When Tennyson's first collection of poems appeared, the Tory *Quarterly Review* sarcastically noted that the young poet was "a new prodigy of genius, another and brighter star of the galaxy or *Milky Way* school of poetry, of which the lamented Keats was the harbinger.") The Milnes biography was reissued, with additional poems and materials, in 1856, as the reputation of Keats, if not his image, began to achieve greater attention and definition. Had Rossetti or Holman Hunt or Millais read it closely, they would have had a chance at "Another Version of Keats's *Hyperion*," the great follow-up piece of a poem that Keats was working on in his last creative months, the poem that came to be called "The Fall of Hyperion. A Dream." In this poem, Apollo replaces Saturn while Moneta, the goddess of memory and poetry, confronts the dreamer poet. The poem, composed "in a more naked and grecian Manner . . . the march of passion and endeavour . . . undeviating," was meant to mark the separation from the decorative romance narratives. Rossetti or Hunt or Millais might have recognized a different kind of Keatsian face—mother to son—in the ghostly, maternal, projected visage of Moneta, the face behind the face that Brown's Shanklin drawing hints at and Severn's deathbed portrait almost captures, the life mask turned to death mask. Writes Keats:

> *Then I saw a wan face,*
> *Not pined by human sorrows, but bright-blanched*
> *By an immortal sickness which kills not;*
> *It works a constant change, which happy death*
> *Can put no end to; deathwards progressing*
> *To no death was that visage . . .*

The robust illustrations of the Pre-Raphaelites reveal no concept of, let alone interest in, the Keats who conceived of this passage. The Pre-Raphaelites were looking for and at a different Keats—a Keats less naked, surely, less simply sculpted. Like a good many Victorians who, given the choice, would elevate beauty over truth, their implied if silent portrait of such a passage might well resemble the alleged 1818 rendering by the Lawrence School portraitist George Henry Harlow, who supposedly caught sight of Keats in a social setting—at Haydon's studio, perhaps, or Leigh Hunt's cottage—sketched him, and later transformed him into a painting. In a way the long speculation concerning the portrait's authenticity is beside the point. Whether Harlow in fact painted it or Keats posed for it is irrelevant, so why make the case in the first place? It looks like none of the seemingly numberless imitative Keats portraits. Sometime well after Keats's death, the Harlow painting shows up in the hands of a wealthy collector in Bristol (curiously, the site of much of Chatterton's fantasy writing). The collector goes broke and sells it to a Bristol art dealer, who in turn, in 1933, sells it to a dealer in Boston from whom a lady in Buffalo buys it, then bequeaths it to its present owner, Reverend Palfrey Perkins, back in Boston. All the while, the painting remains titled *The Poet Keats, Lawrence School*. Perkins has it assessed by Louis A. Holman, an art expert and friend of Amy Lowell, Keats's first American biographer, who declares that "possibly some good painter happened to meet Keats—liked his face, and asked him to sit. As it was not a commission, the artist took liberties—that is, refined the mouth and nostril to suit himself. Knowing all the portraits of Keats (in print form), and having studied this portrait daily for six months, I am convinced that *Keats sat for it*."

Why refine the mouth and nose if not to make of a thing the thing you want? If Harlow did indeed paint this portrait, he, too,

contrived an illustration of a face so aristocraticized and generi-
cally handsomed-up that its family resemblance is anonymous.
Keats the poet, even into the twentieth century, apparently needed
to look the part of the poet who wrote of nightingales and urns
and faery lands afar, romances and *Endymion*. How different
from the melancholy young man in the Rembrandt School por-
trait in the Dulwich Gallery who one day, unbidden, surprised the
good eyes of Cowden Clarke and Vincent Novello, two friends of
Keats, with the truth of his resemblance. And because it is done
live and quickly, and thus through hand-eye coordination only—
no intervening mind's-eye of the beholder—even Severn's early
(1817), much-imitated charcoal drawing of Keats in left profile
has a spark of the brooding fire that Haydon realized in the same
profile of Keats in *Christ's Entry*. Severn's drawing is rough and
callow; Haydon's painted portrait detail is brilliant. Haydon
makes Keats's the liveliest face in the picture. The white worm of
the tubercle bacillus had yet to become an intimate of his body,
a condition, like a cancer, that the Harlow portrait and Severn's
later self-serving version of the poet could not allow. Keats's
eighteen-year-old brother, Tom, would be dead of consumption
within a year, "pale and spectre-thin." John would spend months
trying to nurse him back to health, as he had nursed their mother
eight years before when she was also dying of consumption. By
the time, in 1819, that Brown makes his spontaneous study of
Keats's right side, the hectic look of injury will now seem part of
the subject's thoughtful face, the black-and-white and soft gray
pencil tones part of the paling of Keats's color and the accelera-
tion of age.

COLD PASTORAL

. . .

Thou, silent form, dost tease us out of thought
As doth eternity: Cold Pastoral!

1

SOMETIME AROUND FOUR IN THE AFTERNOON ON FRIDAY, FEB-
ruary 23, 1821, Severn, now part-time painter, full-time nurse,
lifted Keats once again from what seemed like drowning. The
mild Roman winter had turned early toward a Roman spring.
Flower vendors in greater numbers had started business in the
piazza, and if the windows had been opened even a little, you
could have easily heard their hawking above the street noise. But
the windows were closed. Keats had to be lifted up because the
coughing and "clay-like expectoration" were coming back—"in
large quantities," Severn later said. Yet because the night sweats
had also returned, Keats asked Severn not to stay too close.
"Don't breathe on me, it comes like ice."

Since the last heavy hemorrhaging, more than a month
ago, the death process had moved with new speed, "a ghastly
wasting away": first the coughing of "a fawn coloured mix-
ture" of blood and phlegm, then diarrhea, then laxity and
gripping of the bowels, then food—warm milk and pud-
ding—then the cycle starting over again, with the sweats last-
ing usually until dawn. The waste itself was mucus, nothing
solid, though in the struggle not to go under, the expectora-
tions seemed to thicken and boil in the throat. This is what
was happening now, and would happen off and on for another
six to seven hours. Between his bouts with suffocation, Keats
slept or drifted, only to awake in pain. Then that night, at
eleven o'clock, a year after the first hemorrhage and near suf-

focation, Keats let the mess of blood be swallowed and the pain go. "His eyes looked upon me with extreme sensibility but without pain—at 11 he died in my arms." Some fifty-eight years later, when Severn himself was dying in Rome, his last thoughts returned to this moment and to yet a new picture of Keats that he wanted to paint: "Keats lying calm in death, and a beautiful spirit bending over him." In the end, though, the deathbed drawing would, in the workings-out of time, have to suffice, with Severn as presiding artist-angel, who, in the middle of the night, with barely a candle to see by, would outdo himself in rendering the fatigue and darkness haunting the figure of Keats, whose exposed head and matted hair are saturated, as if having emerged from immersion.

Severn's biographer and chief apologist, William Sharp, concludes that "throughout life Severn was a strange mixture of childlike vanity, genuine humility, high aims and ambitious efforts, with accomplishment often far short." He adds that, at the same time, "strangely enough, he was conscious of less fear, of a self-possessed calm, whenever the peril of death was actually imminent." And although James Clark, Keats's Roman doctor, thought Severn "not the best suited for his companion"—too lightweight, too excitable, too—in Ruskin's fine phrase for Severn—"daintily sentimental"—Severn proved, in spite of his high-strung nature, to be a first-rate nurse if not a first-rate artist. In the four short months between leaving England, arriving in Italy, setting up house in Rome, and ministering to the daily graphic needs of a sick and dying man, Severn grew in the same role that Keats himself had filled in his service to his brother Tom just three years earlier.

Sharp suggests two seminal experiences behind Severn's relative calm in confronting death, perhaps the calm that permitted Severn the clarity to really see Keats on the night of the deathbed sketch. For example, when Severn was eight years old, he had "gone with a schoolmate named Cole to bathe in some water-filled gravel-pits, and in one of them his companion ventured beyond his depth and was drowned. There was no one near at the time, so the child had to watch his comrade perish, and then to make his way home, carrying the drowned boy's clothes, and break the news to Mrs. Cole."

The second experience, at age twenty-one, involves William Haslam, friend to both Keats and Severn, and the friend who talks the young obscure painter into accompanying the young obscure poet on the long voyage to Rome. "When Severn . . . and Haslam reached the [theater] doors an hour before the time of opening, the crowd was already large: ere long it became so great that the Haymarket was almost blocked by it. The entrance to the pit was through a small door and along a narrow passage. In the struggle which ensued upon the opening of the doors Severn was separated from his friend and soon afterwards stumbled and fell, with the result that he was speedily trampled into unconsciousness and, indeed, escaped death by little short of a miracle. At last, as the crowd thinned, some one noticed that an unfortunate was being done to death, if not already dead, and gave the alarm. The unconscious body ('thin as a skeleton almost, to start with, and now flattened out like a pancake') was uplifted and conveyed over the playgoers' heads to the front of the pit, where there was less risk of suffocation." Severn in those days was an inveterate theatergoer and was determined—short of death—not to miss the actress Sarah Siddons playing Queen Katherine in *Henry VIII*. Thus he "watched the performance in a dazed fashion till Mrs. Siddons appeared, when 'her impressive demeanour and magical dignity and pathos' so affected nerves already feverishly excited that he sat as one entranced and conscious of some new and vital influence in his life." These words referencing awe could be equally applied to Severn's attitude toward Keats, an attitude that both focuses and blurs Severn's vision of his friend over the years, making him sometimes a reliable, sometimes an unreliable narrator, which as a witness and memorist of Keats places him between his commitment as a nurse and his middling talent as an artist.

As is obvious in his classic deathbed portrait of Keats, Severn is most trustworthy on the spot, in the living moment. In a fragment of a letter never sent to Keats's publisher, John Taylor—dated the day before Christmas 1820—Severn writes that "Keats is much changed somewhat for the worse—at least his mind has much, very much—and this leaves his state much the same and quite as hopeless. Yet the blood has ceased to come; his digestion is better, and but for a cough he must be improving, that is, as respects his body. But the fatal prospect of consumption hangs before his mind's eye, and turns everything to despair and wretchedness. He will not hear a word about living—nay, I seem to lose his confidence by trying to give him this hope, for his knowledge of internal anatomy enables him to judge of every change accurately, and adds largely to his torture. He will not think his future prospects favourable. He says the continued stretch of his imagination has already killed him. He will not hear of his good friends in England, except for what they have done—and this is another load; but of their high hopes of him, his certain success, his experience, he will not hear a word. Then the want of some kind hope to feed his voracious imagination—" This has a ring of accuracy that Severn's later memoir prose never quite achieves; it rides the nerve of an intensity that cannot be resurrected, only imitated or reinvented. The insight that Keats's singular power of imagination—so gifted in health, so brilliant in dire anticipation ("When I have fears that I may cease to be")—has turned against him, in fact, "has already killed him," represents Severn writing and thinking at his best. You can hear in his words his sense of anxiety and compassion, fear and resignation, fantasy and failure. And Keats still has two more months in which to die even further, with Severn attending, commenting on, and, occasionally, painting.

Compare this acumen to Severn's variable memory—one example from the "Reminiscences," the other from his 1863 *Atlantic Monthly* article "On the Vicissitudes of Keats's Fame."

> *Poor Keats was ordered to Italy to save his life, threatened by misfortune and consumption. He was going alone, in a merchant-ship, to Naples, and the voyage was all arranged, and he was to sail next day. Haslam said to me, "Severn, why should you not go?" I answered, "Why should I not?" He then said, "How long would it take you to get ready?" "If I can have six hours," I said, "in that time I'll be ready." Straight I went to Sir Thomas Lawrence, who gave me a letter to Canova, and another to a German artist. On my way I went to my dear angel-mother, who was not taken by surprise, but approved, and undertook to get my trunk ready so that I might depart at daylight. During the evening and night I managed to settle all my affairs, and with a solitary £25, fortunately paid me for a miniature of a lady in a white satin bonnet and feathers, I returned to my father's house just after midnight, to take farewell of my dear family, from whom I had never till then been (definitely) separated.*

>   ---------

> *Haslam said to me, "As nothing can save Keats but going to Italy, why should you not try to go with him, for otherwise he must go alone, and we shall never hear anything of him if he dies." "Will you go?" I answered, "I'll go." "But you'll be*

long getting ready," he added; *"Keats is actually now prepar-*
ing. When would you be ready?" "In three or four days," I
replied, "I will set about it this very moment."

Besides the confusion concerning the amount of time that Severn
will need to prepare for a journey almost impossible to prepare
for, including forgetting his passport, he neglects to mention at
this juncture that "this determination of mine was almost a death-
blow to my poor dear father, who reasoned with me in every way
as to the rashness of the step, and pointed out that by thus taking
matters into my own hands I might even forfeit my chance of
gaining the Academy pension. But I had no ear to his arguments,
and as I had certainly the virtue of the donkey—obstinacy—in
the highest degree, so my plan went on preparing." This is a pat-
tern that will obtain until the end of Severn's life: on the one
hand, a talent for the moment; on the other, a talent for missing
its memory. Only in a letter, much later, does he own up to how
difficult it was to "separate" from his family. "My poor father, in
his abstraction, stood in the doorway, and when I attempted to
pass him he struck me down to the ground . . . This made a tragic
scene . . . this blow like the act of madness. My dear mother
interposed, as also my sister and friends, to protect me. Tom,
then nineteen years old and strong , held my father against the
door. . . ." Severn had a brother Tom as well, also nineteen but
of exceptional health.

2

ON THE DAY BEFORE KEATS'S DEATH AND THE DAY AFTER,
Severn writes to Haslam, then Brown, with essentially the same

message: "My spirits, my intellect, and my health are breaking down"; "I am broken down beyond my strength." From that gray morning when they boarded the *Maria Crowther*, on September 17, 1820, until now, February 23, 1821, Severn had been rarely, almost never, out of Keats's presence. "I can get no one to change with me—no one to relieve me," he lamented, and his lament had been close to becoming a self-elegy. From one of simple, early friendship begun in the autumn of 1816 to an absolute connection lasting these last six months, the relationship had become symbiotic, mutually close but not necessarily mutually beneficial. In spite of his apparent iron immunity to consumption, Severn had been incrementally worn down emotionally, physically, and in every other way he could think of. The final days, with their slow-wheel inevitability, were especially heavy.

At times during his last days he made me go see the place where he was to be buried, and he expressed pleasure at my description of the locality of the Pyramid of Caius Cestius, about the grass and the many flowers, particularly the innumerable violets, also about a flock of goats and sheep and a young shepherd—all these intensely interested him. Violets were his favourite flowers, and he loved to hear how they overspread the graves. He assured me "that he already seemed to feel the flowers growing over him." . . . From time to time he gave me all his directions as to what he wanted done after his death. It was in the same sad hour when he told me with greater agitation than he had shown on any other subject, to put the letter which had just come from Miss Brawne (which he was unable to bring himself to read, or even to open), with any other that should arrive too late to reach him in life, inside his winding-sheet on his heart—it was then, also, that he asked

*that I should see cut upon his gravestone as sole inscription,
not his name, but simply "Here lies one whose name was writ
in water."*

This eloquent excerpt, which Sharp calls "a memorable pas-
sage," is from yet another unpublished series of notes that Severn
filed under "Recollections." It may be uncharacteristic in flow
and focus, but it is suggestive of the author's hold on his mate-
rial granted enough intensity. Sharp's "biography" of Severn is
based on letters and several loose manuscripts—*Incidents from
My Life* (1858), *On the Adversities of Keats's Fame* (1861), *On
the Vicissitudes of Keats's Fame* (1863), *Adonais . . . with notes by
Joseph Severn* (1873), and *My Tedious Life* (1873)—all of which
amount to recollections as reminiscences. Except for *Vicissi-
tudes*, a rewritten version of *Adversities*, the thrust of Severn's
prose is journal-like, epistolary, and, depending on the state of
his memory at the time, episodic, inconsistent, sometimes sac-
charine. Late in life he even tried fiction—a novel and some sto-
ries. Like his painting, his prose is mediocre; like his memory,
his grip on the past is often tenuous. Keats, in all areas of his
life, becomes his redeeming subject, his inspirer. "I owe almost
everything to him, my best friends as well as my artistic prosper-
ity, my general happiness as well as my best inspirations." This
comment comes from the perspective of time and realization.
But for now an almost speechless Severn had to survive Keats's
death, its immediate aftermath, and the fallout of the stress of the
constancy of sickness and difficulty in dealing with a patient at
the edge. How many times, in his more lucid moments, had Keats
himself expressed his empathy for Severn—" 'What trouble and
Danger have you got into for me—now you must be firm for
it will not last long.' " Just being a witness was no less painful.
"Each day he would look up in the doctor's face to discover how

long he should live—he would say—'How long will this posthu-
mous life of mine last'—and that look was more than we could
ever bear—the extreme brightness of his eyes with his poor pal-
lid face—were not earthly."

It would take Severn weeks to come back to even a semblance
of himself. And in the days, the hours right after Keats's death,
Severn, too, had to be nursed. "The first thing Dr. Clark did when
he arrived too late to see Keats again in life was to feel my pulse,
to command me to keep perfectly quiet, and to order an English
nurse to take charge of the sick-room." It was a full weekend.
On Saturday afternoon, Gherardi, Canova's maskmaker, cast
molds of one of Keats's hands and feet and the skeletal face—
thin, wasted extremeties. On Sunday, Dr. Clark, with the help
of a friend, Dr. Luby, performed a limited autopsy, enough that
Clark could say that this was the worst case of consumption in
his experience. Keats's lungs were "completely destroyed," the
whole chamber of the thorax black. No one could imagine how
Keats had lasted this long. "O! I can feel the cold earth upon me,"
he had said, quietly, more than once. And in the coffin confines of
the sickroom/bedroom in which the autopsy had taken place, his
senses had not let him down. Proportionally, the room was exactly
like a grave. On Monday, February 26, in the predawn dark, a
funeral procession consisting of Clark; Luby; the English sculp-
tor Richard Westmacott; a Reverend Wolff, who was to preside;
William Ewing, an artist friend who actually had to help Severn
get dressed; and, of course, Severn himself wound its way south
the several miles to the so-called Protestant Cemetery, or the
Testaccio Cemetery or "Cimitero Acattolici," depending. There
were about the same number of mourners as there had been well-
wishers when Keats and Severn had departed from Gravesend
six months before. Severn was "deeply affected by this last clos-
ing scene, particularly as I was the only personal friend present

from among the little band of devoted friends whom the poet had left behind in England." By agreement, the ceremony lasted moments, because non-Catholics (*acattolici*) were not to be buried in sunlight, though by the time the minimally Christian formalities had been observed the sun was well risen.

Sheep and goats, daisies and violets—that was about as religious as Keats could abide. So to that extent he got his wish. He was laid to rest in what was referred to then as the Meadows of the Roman People—large, open fields partly framed by the ruins of the old Aurelian Wall and the Pyramid of Cestius, as far from the houses and churches of the faithful as possible and still be "in" Rome. The anti-Catholic cemetery—a small section of the greater grounds—was likely no less pagan than the pastures. Keats was the fifty-first entry in the Register of Burials: "John Keats, English Poet, Died the 24th February 1821, Buried the 25th ditto in the morning at 15 o'clock." The Romans had their own way of keeping time, ending the day at 6 p.m. Just a few feet away lay another lost soul, Shelley's young son William, who the year before had succumbed to malaria and whose body would be moved in two short years to join the ashes of his father. Also nearby was another Englishman, an Oxford graduate named Langton, who in 1738 became the first person buried in the cemetery. He was, like Keats, twenty-five when he died.

Green pastures and sheep in the meadows were just about the limit of the fulfillment of Keats's wishes for his "posthumous existence." His intended, ironic epitaph—an impulse of both anger and calculation, as if in challenge to the poetry gods— soon became the postmortem subject of discussion, division, and, finally, compromise among friends within the broken Keats Circle. Like much of his original writing, Keats probably synthesized "writ in water" from more than one source, primarily Beaumont and Fletcher's *Philaster*, Act V, Scene 3: "All your better deeds / Shall be in water writ." Lying those last days in the confinement of his narrow sickroom, staring up at the floral designs on the ceiling and listening to the alien street noise on the Spanish Steps and, in the middle of the night, the undersong of the Bernini fountain, he must have felt as far as possible from anything he knew and valued, certainly as far as possible from his sense of his own and his work's worth. He had feared, most of all, that he would leave nothing of importance behind, nothing worth remembering, for his friends. Yet "here lies one whose name was writ in water" does not mean that the unnamed name will always be so written. *Was* is the operative verb. And the fact that Keats did not want his name to appear on the tombstone adds only interest to the mystery of who might be buried so anonymously. The unnamed is, after all, written in stone, not water. If the epitaph resides somewhere between pathos and *tragicus*, it is also poetry. He feared he had failed, his body brought down by disease, his poems belittled by Tory critics. But he also knew something: Trust the writing.

3

IN THAT IMMEDIATE, VULNERABLE, SHADOWY TIME, THAT extremely emotional, difficult phase we sometimes call the aftermath—in the aftermath of his death, not unlike the fragility of any judgment, Keats's reputation, such as it was, seemed indeed to have been written in water, if not blood. "There were few Englishmen at Rome who knew Keats's works, and I could scarcely persuade any one to make the effort to read them, such was the prejudice against him as a poet . . . 'Here lies one whose name was writ in water, *and his works in milk and water*'—this

I was condemned to hear for years repeated, as though it had been a pasquinade." This social ridicule, Severn would find, would fade with time, particularly because the mocking words were written on air. Less ephemeral, however, were the words added to the belated tombstone by Brown, the five hundred lines created by Shelley in *Adonais* and the words and lines of derision and condescension penned by Byron, Hazlitt, and DeQuincey. Absent were the words of all the friends, at least a half dozen, who were going to write—while the fire was still fire—Keats's biography, who were going to but for one good reason or another never got to it. This aftermath lasted for years, then decades, and threatened to become indelible in 1845, when John Taylor, who had been not only Keats's publisher but his benefactor in the worst of times, sold the copyright to the poems and unpublished manuscripts for next to nothing, underscoring the fact that the poet's work was effectively out of print in England.

Keats had written, "But, when I am consuméd in the fire, / Give me new Phoenix wings to fly at my desire." His funeral was hardly history before Italian authorities were in his bedroom stripping the walls, confiscating personal property, and removing furniture, all to be piled in the piazza and burned. The Italians, unlike the English, believed in the communicability of consumption, even if they were not exactly sure of what it was and how it was caused. So right outside the windows from which Keats had thrown an inedible supper, his bed, chairs, and a few borrowed books were purged. Severn had managed to convince the landlady, Signora Angeletti, that Keats had never slept nor spent significant time in any of the other rooms, which saved a rented pianoforte as well as Severn's painting supplies. "Those brutal Italians have nearly done their monstrous business. They have burned the furniture—they have done their meetings—and I believe, at least hope, no more of these cursed cruelties will take place. They have racked me in my most painful moments . . ." No doubt, had Keats's body been among the rented paraphernalia, he, too, would have been purged, burned like paper and wood, like Shelley's body, on the beach at Viareggio. And had Keats written anything, letters or parts of a poem, in his posthumous Italian hours, they would have also likely gone up in flame. Yeats says that poetry is wasted breath. Perhaps. But some words, because of their timing and harmful self-serving associations, are noncombustible, words such as Brown's epitaph for Keats, Shelley's elegy for Keats, and the words of the many who wanted Keats to die as a weakling. These words were unburnable, and became essential to the lore that is the story of Keats's unique immortality. Like his writing, they would take on their own posterity.

With the rooms at 26 Piazza di Spagna no longer available to him—because of their connection to sickness and to their memory of Keats—Severn moved around the corner to 18 Via di San Isidoro, which meant that he was still very much a part of the English colony in Rome. In no time, through introductions by William Ewing and Ewing's friend Seymour Kirkup, who had both attended the funeral, Severn became a charmed member of the English community as well. "The death of Keats, although he was unknown, and my devoted friendship, had become a kind of passport to the English in Rome . . . a 'treasure-trove' to me as a young artist, invaluable, as it was my introduction to my future patrons . . ." Among the mix of his emotions, Severn felt insolated from what he knew and loved; Keats, after all, had been his life, as it were, for the last half year, among strangers in a strange place. In addition, Severn was anxious about his submission—*The Death of*

Alcibiades—to the Royal Academy for its traveling fellowship, money he desperately needed in the wake of all that had happened so far from home. Becoming accepted in the whirl of the Roman English social circle could not, financially or emotionally, compensate for a successful career as an artist, however much such acceptance might help. He was not even sure if his submitted painting—sent by boat from Rome to London—had survived the sea voyage. And true, on arrival it was misplaced for a while.

Spring had passed, and on good advice Severn decided to leave Rome and its evil summer air and spend the hot months in the hills. At the end of July, still 1821, he writes to Brown that with "the approach of the hot and dangerous weather I shall be obliged to go away, and that without placing a stone on poor Keats's grave. All his papers I have sent you, packed safely in a box of divers things . . . they will arrive in London about August or September. Mr. Taylor has written me of his intention to write some remembrance of our Keats."

This letter, along with the publication in June of *Adonais*, marks the beginning of the conflict and a falling out of friends that would obscure and delay a true picture or an accurate portrait of a poet unknown outside their small imperfect circle. John Taylor, for one, as Keats's publisher and owner of copyright, recognized that this moment, in the immediate aftermath of the death, was the time to begin to find the larger audience that Keats's work deserved. The fact that he failed on every count to turn his opinion into action would have a lot to do with surrendering his ties to Keats's poetry and reputation more than twenty-five years later. In his August answer to Severn's letter of the month before, Taylor writes: "I find by your letter to Mr. Haslam that you have designed a tomb in the form of a Grecian altar, with a lyre, &c. This is said to be executed, I think, by some English sculptor, but you want an inscription. I can conceive none better that our poor friend's melancholy sentiment, 'Here lies one whose name was writ in water.' It is very simple and affecting, and tells so much of the story that none need be told. Neither name nor date is requisite. These will be given in his life by his biographer. So, unless something else is determined on, let this line stand alone. I foresee that it will be as clear an indication to posterity as the plainest, everyday inscription that one may find in Westminster Abbey." Thus in Taylor's eyes, Keats was destined to be among the English poets in Westminster Abbey willy-nilly; the process of recognition required only the right start. And he understood, perfectly: The poetry in Keats's deathbed desire was to appear poignant and anonymous on his gravestone. In Taylor's mind, the implicit mystery of the singular inscription was the first step in building the biography and immortality of Keats. The idea of the broken-stringed lyre would be Severn's contribution, based, he claimed, on a conversation he had with the poet back in their waning days in Hampstead when Keats began to be aware of how ill he was. Keats, according to Severn, had requested that "a Greek lyre with four strings broken" be cut into his stone. Severn had obliged by making a sketch of the image in Brown's copy of *Endymion*.

Severn, however, did not send Keats's aftereffects to his publisher; he sent them to Brown, who felt that Taylor was a "mere bookseller" and "Neither comprehended" Keats nor "his poetry." Furthermore, when "I mentioned to you my fears about Mr. Taylor's memoir"—this from a late summer letter in the same time frame from Brown to Severn—"I omitted to make known the original cause of those fears. It was this. Immediately on receipt of your letter announcing poor Keats's death, almost in the same newspapers where there was notice of his death, even before Mrs. Brawne's family and myself had got our mourning, in those very newspapers was advertised 'speedily will be published, a biographical memoir of the late John Keats, &c.' and I, among others, was applied to by Reynolds to collect with all haste, papers, letters, and so on, to assist Mr. Taylor." Brown's proprietary passion regarding Keats doubtless has several sources, and would show itself again and again for the rest of his life. But for the nonce, Taylor—and those associated with Taylor, such as John Hamilton Reynolds, Keats's first poet friend and the young man who, remarkably enough, first introduced Brown to Keats—is the target. "This indecent bustle over (as it were) the newly covered grave of my dear friend shocked me excessively. I told Mr. Taylor it looked as if his friends had been collecting information about his life in expectation of his death. This, indeed, was the fact . . . I will not consent to be a party in a bookseller's job."

This was, indeed, the fact: Keats the poet, in his publisher's view, needed to be tended to immediately in order to place his work before a possible public and before just any memoir of his life, "the biography," could replace the poetry. Taylor had probably planned to republish poems and add new ones as the centerpiece of the life, assuming the cooperation of Brown, Severn, and George Keats. Taylor was hardly alone in his announced intention. Almost every friend or acquaintance within the Keats circle would sooner or later propose a Keatsian monograph, memoir, or biography—including Charles Cowden Clarke, Keats's great boyhood friend; Charles Dilke, Keats's sometime neighbor and supporter; Reynolds himself, in recognition of a colleague; Leigh Hunt, Keats's early mentor; Richard Woodhouse, correspondent and keeper of much valuable "Keatsiana"; George Keats, surviving brother and legal heir to Keats's papers; Charles Brown, intimate and adviser, who actually—eventually—got around to writing an abortive memoir; and Joseph Severn, whose various autobiography is the single record of Keats's last days. Yet before the life of Keats could be seriously considered and before the poetry reevaluated, Brown felt—and following the lead, so did Severn—that it was Keats's death that now needed tending, namely the question of his epitaph. The thought that Keats should lie under a line of such an annihilating, apparently despairing farewell was more than Brown could bear. And besides, there was no accounting, no blame assigned, no cause designated for the death of Keats. It was a silent stone. What bothered Severn was the anonymity on the face of what should have shone with identity. What bothered Brown was the blame. Brown, like Shelley, had an affection for conspiracy, which too often cast them both in the role of the didact. Although Brown's diagnosis—that Keats's "disease is of the mind"—emphasized a psychosomatic source, and Shelley's diagnosis—that "agitation . . . ended in the rupture of a blood-vessel in the lungs"—emphasized a more "medical" source, both agreed that "savage criticism . . . produced the most violent effect on his susceptible mind." Hence, he must not have been in his right mind when he told Severn what he wanted his tombstone to say, and not say. Otherwise it looked as if Lockhart and Croker, of *Blackwood's Edinburgh Magazine* and *Quarterly Review*, respectively, the most prominent attackers of Keats, had won a posthumous victory in addition to killing him outright. For their different political and personal reasons, neither Brown nor Shelley could let such a perceived victory stand.

Nevertheless, in the early fall of 1821, a full six months following Keats's funeral, Severn comments in a letter to Brown, "Why how singular that none of you can lament out his Epitaph. I agree with you that more should be written than the line he desired." Brown, though, "can do nothing for the epitaph to my own satisfaction." "Every minute," he responds, he is "expecting . . . a knock by Hunt at the door with an epitaph for Keats." He adds that he likes Severn's idea "of the lyre with broken strings." On the other hand, "Mr. Taylor sets his face against that, and against any words except what Keats himself desired to be put on his tombstone." Then Brown says a remarkable thing: "an epitaph must necessarily be considered as the act of the deceased's friends and not of the deceased himself," and, warming to this subject, that "in obedience to his will, I would have his own words engraved there, and *not* his name, letting the stranger read the cause of his friend's placing such words as 'Here lies one,' &c., somewhat in the following manner:—'This grave contains all that was mortal of a young English poet, who, on his death-bed, in bitter anguish at the neglect of his countrymen, desired these words to be engraven on his tomb-stone: HERE LIES ONE WHOSE NAME WAS WRIT IN WATER.'" So in the course of writing back to Severn, Brown invents, with much hesitation, a draft of an inscription that with some modification will become not only regretted but immortal. Brown concludes that he finds "it a difficult subject," this epitaph, and that if there is any objection he will withdraw. Severn, who has more than once excused himself as being "not a master of words to show what I feel or think," embraces Brown's suggestion, and sets about trying to raise funds for the actual headstone itself as well as the required sculpting of figures and lettering, a process that will take up to two years from the death date to complete. Meanwhile, in a January 21, 1823, letter to Brown, who has well since moved, along with Hunt, to Italy, Severn begins with the news that he has "just returned from the Funeral of poor Shelley," whose "ashes were not permitted to be placed in the Old Ground where his Child lay, so that we were driven to the alternative of the new place, and of disinterring the Bones of the Child and placing them together"—the "new place" being but a stone's throw from Keats's grave, "which is not yet done."

4

THE LONG-SUFFERING FOUR-FOOT MARBLE TOMBSTONE, THE top half of which is the relief of a four-stringed lyre, was finally set in the winter of 1823. It is supposed to resemble a Greek altar, rectilinear in dimension, cut at its height into an arc. The bottom half elaborates Brown's words a bit. In a combination script and bold caps:

This Grave
contains all that was Mortal
of a
YOUNG ENGLISH POET
Who
on his Death Bed
in the Bitterness of his Heart
at the Malicious Power of his Enemies
Desired
these Words to be engraven on his Tomb Stone
"Here lies One
Whose Name was writ in Water"
Feb 24th 1821

The fact that Keats's name is missing must have offered Brown a certain license to elevate his rhetoric to an implicit counterattack. The politics of the epitaph is just generic enough to cover the liberal sentiments of many. It is basically an anti-Tory epi-taph and almost totally obscures Keats's evocative intentions. Brown sensed from the beginning the difficulty of the task of who should have the last words and what they should be. He and Severn wrote back and forth continually on the subject, particu-larly after Brown had moved to Italy and was pushing Severn to finish the project. "If not too late pray reflect a little more on the inscription for our Keats. Remember his dying request that his *name* should *not* be on this tombstone, and that the words 'Here lies one whose name was writ in water' should be. I thought you liked my inscription, for you said so. All his friends, Hunt, Rich-ards, Dilke, and every one I showed it to, were greatly pleased with it. You seem to imagine it does not honour him enough, but, to our minds, it says more in praise than if his name were men-tioned." Keats's missing name was what bothered Severn most.

There is a great deal going on at this moment, at least from Severn's point of view. In addition to trying to raise Keats's stone, let alone decide on what should be on it, Severn has become involved in the monument business generally. "There is a mad chap come here, whose name is Trelawny. I do not know what to make of him . . . He comes as a friend of Shelley, great, glow-ing, and rich in romance. Of course I showed all my paint-pot politeness to him, to the very brim—assisted him to remove the ashes of Shelley to a spot where he himself (when this world has done with his body) will lie. He wished me to think, myself, and consult my friends about a monument to Shelley. The situation is beautiful, and one and all thought a little basso-relievo would be the best taste. I was telling him the subject I had proposed for Keats, and he was struck with the propriety of it for Shelley . . ." The subject proposed for Keats was a "little Monument . . . more worthy him than ours, to be placed (if it is thought better) in Hampstead Church," a notion dismissed by Brown because, in 1823, Keats's "fame is not sufficiently general . . . his name is unknown to the multitude. Therefore I think that proper to his name being somewhat more celebrated, a monument to his memory might even retard it, and might provoke ill-nature, and (shall I say?) ridicule. When I quitted England his words were still unsaleable." Severn's notion for the English monument is Severn standard issue for the sentimentality that will follow in the posthumous portraits: "a Basso-relievo of 'Our Keats sitting, habited in a simple Greek Costume—he has half strung his Lyre, when the Fates seize him. One arrests his arm, another cuts the thread, and the third pronounced his Fate.' "

Keats's fate. What a curious phrase. Severn's interim fate will be to remain in Rome for the next eighteen years, establishing himself as an artist, a leader in the English community, a husband and father, and, most of all, a friend of Keats. "Certainly I gained more from poor Keats, who is dead and gone, than from any other source." He will continue to press for a Keatsian monument, but by 1830, the venue, not surprisingly, will have changed. "Now I have thought a good deal of it, and am going to propose *that we erect a monument to his memory here in Rome* . . . I have a subject in my mind for the Basso Rilievo, which I think I once mentioned to you before"—the correspondent is, again, Brown. "It is Keats sitting with his half-strung lyre—the three Fates arrest him—one catches his arm—another cuts the thread—and the third pronounces his end. This would make a beautiful Basso Rilievo, and the gravestone is so unworthy him, and so absurd (as all people say), and as the spot is so beautiful, I hope you will agree to it." In seven years, Severn's description of his sculpture idea has remained doggedly identical, suggesting just how focused he could be when the need, in his mind, was imperative. Playing the role of Keats's nurse, as a much younger man, the need was no less focused. But he understands now, as will Brown, who later refers to the gravestone inscription as "a sort of profanation," that the words over Keats's head are a mistake, and that he and Brown are responsible. No wonder he is so committed to a monument alternative, stone against stone, so to speak. The sad part is that Severn's new idea is worse than the present one, the old idea, because it softens into dream light the honesty and simplicity called for. Early on, in the weeks and months right after the death, Severn was in the habit of making the trip out to the Pyramid of Cestius to spend time at the grave. "I liked the loneliness, as I had so much to commune with myself as regards the future. Among many visits I made to Keats's grave at Monte Testaccio was one of a very striking nature. In the twilight of the full moon I found a young Italian asleep, his head resting against the gravestone, his dog and his flock of sheep about him, with the full moon rising beyond the Pyramid of Caius Cestius. One long moonbeam stole past the Pyramid and illumined the outline of the young shepherd's face, and to my eye realized the story of Endymion." This is "a beautiful Basso Rilievo" in a different guise.

Fearing, perhaps, the fantasy—or fancy—of such a scene, Keats, from the start, tried to place perspective on *Endymion* by labeling it "a test of Invention." For him it was a "trial . . . of 4000 lines of one bare circumstance," to be filled with romance and poetry. It was also an assignment that Hunt had made for a competition between Keats and Shelley, a competition that Shelley won by two months with *The Revolt of Islam*, a long, long poem, which, unlike Keats's *Endymion*, is seldom paid attention to. Severn, in his invoking of the shepherd, is anticipating the romantic postures of illustration that the Pre-Raphaelites will invest in twenty-five years down the road. For him, however, the moment is neither fancy nor fiction; it is real, and no less real than his allegorizing projections of monuments for a beloved

Keats—hyped attempts at stays against Keats's oblivion. Luckily, Severn's hopes for marble and gilded monuments did not come to life, though, in seemingly no time, Shelley's "powerful rhyme" in some ninety hyped Spenserian stanzas did. In direct contradistinction to the hesitations and delays regarding the headstone and the decades-long squabbles over whom and what regarding the biography, Shelley's pastoral elegy for Keats—a warm pastoral, indeed—was written in three months in spring after the death and published in midsummer. You could say that Shelley began the poem almost upon hearing of Keats's passing, because it is probable that the news did not reach him until March and he began writing in April.

Adonais, as a monumental epitaph, is a tour de force, no doubt, comparable to Milton's *Lycidas*, which it is often placed beside. Its material antecedents go back to the Hellenic laments of Bion and Moschus; its formal and floral antecedents borrow from Spenser and Milton. It moves within a sequence of concentric circles, returning again and again to the speaker's imploration of a shared grief for a young poet lost, nipped in the bud, like Thomas Chatterton, to whom Keats had dedicated *Endymion*—thus another circle of connection. The "bud," the flower analogy, is only one of the ultimate errors the poem subscribes to and perpetuates. By the sixth stanza, Keats has become "Like a pale flower by some sad maiden cherished," a line that unintentionally paraphrases the "palely loitering" knight-at-arms whom *la belle sans merci* "cherishes." Or is it the youth who "grows pale, and spectre-thin, and dies" in "Ode to a Nightingale"? The point is that in lifting Keats to Adonais status, Shelley genericizes him as a "delicate and fragile . . . young flower . . . blighted in the bud," as he writes in his preface to the poem. In other moments, Keats lies "in dewy sleep" or turns into a "herd-abandoned deer struck by the hunter's dart." Or else he "is a portion of the loveliness / Which once he made more lovely," a "frail Form, / A phantom among men; companionless / As the last cloud of an expiring storm." Or "His head was bound with pansies overblown." And so forth. *Adonais*, intentionally or otherwise, makes of Keats a victim, the poet under pressure, pursued by Eumenides-like enemies, and finally done in. Inevitably, Keats, as Adonais and as persecuted figure in the poem, becomes a mask for Shelley himself, expatriate and isolated in Italy. The last fifteen or so stanzas—by far the best and most disciplined writing—seem in fact to absorb Keats into a larger Shelleyan subject, the mortality of poetry itself, the grave of which, as the Eternal City, is Rome. By the last stanza, the one most quoted, Shelley is predicating his own death, "Far from shore, far from the trembling throng . . ." where "I am borne darkly, fearfully afar." His spirit, he says, will join Adonais in "the abode where the Eternal are"—but a few feet away in Rome's Protestant Cemetery.

5

ABOUT A MONTH AFTER KEATS HAD TEA WITH MR. AND MRS. Gisborne, at Leigh Hunt's Mortimer Terrace address, Keats received, from Pisa, a letter from Shelley dated July 27, 1820. "I hear with great pain the dangerous accident that you have undergone, & Mrs. Gisborne who gives me the account of it, adds, that you continue to wear a consumptive appearance. This consumption is a disease particularly fond of people who write such good verses as you have done, and with the assistance of an English winter it can often indulge its selection . . . Mrs. Shelley unites with myself in urging the request, that you take up your residence with us.—You might come by sea to Leghorn, (France is not worth seeing, & the sea air is particularly good for weak lungs) which is within a few miles of us. You ought at all events to see Italy . . ." After complimenting Keats's "good verses," Shelley cannot help but play the critic in closing off his letter: "I have lately read your Endymion again . . . and ever with a new sense of the treasure of poetry it contains . . . though treasures poured forth with indistinct profusion—This, people in general will not endure, & that is the cause of the comparatively few copies which have been sold." On August 16, Keats answers that "If I do not take advantage of your invitation it will be prevented by a circumstance I have very much at heart to prophesy—There is no doubt that an English winter would put an end to me, and do so in a lingering hateful manner, therefore I must either voyage or journey to Italy as a soldier marches up to a battery." Rome, not Pisa, would be his destination. Before he quits his letter, however, Keats returns serve by commenting on Shelley's most recent poem *Cenci*—"as from yourself from Hunt." "There is only one part of it I am judge of; the Poetry, and dramatic effect, which by many spirits now a days is considered the mammon. A modern work it is said must have a purpose, which may be the God—an artist must serve Mammon—he must have 'self-concentration' selfishness perhaps. You I am sure will forgive me for sincerely remarking that you might curb your magnanimity and be more of an artist, and 'load every rift' of your subject with ore. The thought of such discipline must fall like cold chains upon you, who perhaps never sat with your wings furl'd for six Months together."

The inherent friendly rivalry between a poet whose father was a lord and a poet whose father started out as a stableman was respectful enough, and Shelley's Italy offer, for sure, was genuine, because he always had a houseful. But for Keats—about

whom Brown had said, "I succeeded in making him come often
to my house by never asking him to come oftener"—the Shelley
household promised to be too much like Hunt's had been that
last summer in England when Keats had nowhere else to go: fam-
ily chaos. Besides, in spite of the eternal linking of their names,
Keats was not all that fond of Shelley. Temperamentally, and in
almost every other way, they were poles apart.

That last summer, Keats's appearance went from seemingly
robust to consumptive pale in a matter of months, reinforcing
the fiction that the "malicious power of his enemies" had finally
overtaken him and worn him down to wasting. The rumor was
in the air, easy to believe, and too few of his friends disbelieved
it. But it is one thing to speak an opinion or note it in a diary; it is
another to publish it, which Shelley did, to incalculable effect—
once Keats was dead—in his Preface to *Adonais*. The final para-
graph reads like a petition.

*The circumstances of the closing scene of poor Keats's life were
not made known to me until the* Elegy *was ready for the press.
I am given to understand that the wound his sensitive spirit
had received from the criticism of* Endymion *was exasper-
ated by the bitter sense of unrequited benefits; the poor fel-
low seems to have been hooted from the stage of life no less
by those on whom he had wasted the promises of his genius
than those on whom he had lavished his fortune and his care.
He was accompanied to Rome and attended in his last ill-
ness by Mr. Severn, a young artist of the highest promise,
who, I have been informed, "almost risked his own life, and
sacrificed every prospect to unwearied attendance upon his
dying friend." Had I known these circumstances before the
completion of my poem, I should have been tempted to add my
feeble tribute of applause to the more solid recompense which*

the virtuous man finds in the recollection of his own motives.
Mr. Severn can dispense with a reward from "such stuff as
dreams are made of." His conduct is a golden augury of the
success of his future career—may the unextinguished Spirit of
his illustrious friend animate the creations of his pencil, and
plead against Oblivion for his name!

Shelley may be pleading against oblivion for Keats's name, but he is doing it in a rather left-handed way. Keats has been "hooted from the stage of life no less by those on whom he had wasted the promise of his genius than those on whom he had lavished his fortune and his care"—meaning what? By his enemies, of course, but by his friends as well? Who are those on whom he lavished his fortune and his care? And the word *promise* suggests a career closer to the potential of the boy-poet Chatterton than to the real achievement of a maturing Keats. By honorific association, Shelley also brings Severn and Brown into the *Adonais* picture: Severn, the companion, who *is* an artist of "promise" and who, as the years pass, will begin more and more to subscribe to the enemy theory, which will later be melded with the broken-heart or love theory involving Fanny Brawne ("His illness and death were pioneered by despair. He was hurried down a sea of troubles to death"); and Brown, who uses as an epigraph stanzas 42 and 43 from *Adonais* to launch his abortive *Life of Keats* and who opens his narrative with "These lines are from 'Adonais', an elegy by Shelley on the death of Keats. When 'Adonais' was sent to me from Italy, I recognized, in these lines, my own every day, involuntary inevitable reflections on the loss of my friend." In other words, Severn and Brown both accept and implicitly agree with Shelley's assumption that Keats was "hooted from the stage of life." The term *condescension* understates Shelley's misguided attitude here, though he may be less at fault, because he received his impressions second and third hand. Severn and Brown knew better, or should have. But, then, Keats's doctors themselves tended to be wrongheaded and ill-serving. Shelley's poem and its preface, because they have the powerful imprimatur of print and because they are the first public words on the scene, carried tremendous weight. One would have had to contradict them immediately in print. Furthermore, Shelley is Keats's perceived friend, and we are very clear who the enemy, regardless of its Tory anonymity, is. The enemy is every liberal's enemy in Regency England—the Tory press and, namely, John Gibson Lockhart and John Wilson Croker.

Interesting, too, that Shelley imagines Keats writing with a pencil rather than a pen.

In a March 1841 letter to Severn—twenty years after Keats's death—Brown makes the observation that "I am well aware that a poet's fame is more likely to be injured by the indiscrimate admiration of his friends than by his critics"—a belated but frank admission from the man who composed, as Keats's closest friend, the burdensome epitaph and who now is "convinced of the error." "If a dying friend, a good man, leaves strict orders for the wording of his epitaph, he should be obeyed . . . I have long repented of my fault, and must repeat to you what I said in Rome, 'I hope the government will permit the erasure of every word, with exception of those words to which he himself limited his epitaph.' " The Italians, of course, declined. In the eleventh canto of *Don Juan*, Byron picks up the theme from Shelley's and Brown's immortal words and plays with it.

LX
John Keats, who was killed off by one critique,
Just as he really promised something great,

If not intelligible, without Greek
Contrived to talk about the Gods of late,
Much as they might have been supposed to speak.
Poor fellow! His was an untoward fate;
'Tis strange the mind, that fiery particle,
Should let itself be snuffed out by an article.

Keats's mind, state of mind, health of mind again come up. Weak mind, weak character, too—*weak* here meaning effeminate, too sensitive, flower delicate. Or in Hazlitt's words—and Hazlitt was someone whom Keats admired: "A canker had blighted the tender bloom that o'spread a face in which youth and genius strove with beauty; the shaft was sped—venal, vulgar, venomous, that drove him from his country, with sickness and penury for companions, and followed him to his grave."

Before the end of the decade in which Keats dies, Leigh Hunt decides to anticipate his surviving peers and publish a memoir, a memory book, dedicated to *Lord Byron and Some of His Contemporaries.* Its centerpieces concern the three poets who have each died too young—Keats at twenty-five, Shelley at twenty-nine, Byron at thirty-six, all within three years of one another, and well before Coleridge and Wordsworth, their seniors. At 440 pages, the book is filled with portraits, impressions, and episodes from the lives, as Hunt recalls them, of all the Romantic anthology poets, plus two final sections on "Recollections of the Author's life" and "Visit to Italy." Hunt's memory is more coherent but no less self-serving than Severn's. He has Keats dying "having just completed his four-and-twentieth year," for example, and promotes several other biographical errors or half-truths, a few of which are unintentionally funny, such as his assertion that Keats's head—like Byron's and Shelley's—was "remarkably small in the skull . . . a puzzle for the phrenologist." Hunt's description of

Keats overall is no less give and take away. "He was under middle height; and his lower limbs were small in comparison with the upper, but neat and well-turned. His shoulders were broad for his size: he had a face, in which energy and sensibility remarkably mixed up, an eager power checked and made patient by ill-health . . . If there was any faulty expression it was in the mouth, which was not without something of the character of pugnacity. The face was rather long otherwise; the upper lip projected a little over the under . . . Mr. Keats was sensible of the disproportion above noticed, between his upper and lower extremeties; and he would look at his hand, which was faded, and swollen in the veins, and say it was the hand of a man of fifty."

In his eighteen-page section on Keats, Hunt is remembering in a jumble of chronology, confusing—as if his four years of friendship were all one time—the early, vital Keats, who wrote "Chapman's Homer," with the Keats of the summer of the meeting with the Gisbornes. Hunt's own lack of self-knowledge enters into the picture, too. In making the point, for instance, that *Endymion*'s "great fault" is not only its "will-fulness of rhymes" (what Keats would later call, in an act of self-criticism, "pouncing rhymes") but its "unpruned luxuriance," he seems to have forgotten the fact that these are Huntian faults, and are the originating complaints against cockney verse—and the florid Hunt in particular—by Tory critics. As poetic fallacies, over-luxuriance of imagery and feminine-ending forced rhymes were generally the stuff of Bluestocking as well as "cockney" verse. But to conservatives, it was all the same upstart, heart-on-the-sleeve, commoner sensibility. Certainly, twenty years into the future, when the Pre-Raphaelites discover Keats, the sensitivity/sensuality issue will be considered a Keatsian hallmark, but notably in works of romance narrative—such as *Eve of St. Agnes* and *Isabella*—and of a wholly different level of maturity from *Endymion*: this time, a "pruned" luxuriance. (Keats will spend most of 1819, the year of his best writing, trying to rid himself of Hunt's early influence, a "weak-sided" rhetoric. He will succeed beyond all expectation.) In confusing time frames and biographical fact, Hunt will also imply, through perhaps unconscious innuendo, that Keats's poetic sensitivity, too much in evidence in the beginning poet, is a handicap to Keats's growing character, which seems fragile enough without the attacks of illness and enemies. After all, Keats is not the only possible victim of Tory critics and consumption. By definition, "romanticism" in total is grist for Tory mills, whereas Hunt, Byron, and Shelley each feel at different times vulnerable to the wasting disease. Byron is reported to have once snidely said, looking into the mirror, "I look pale. I should like to die of a consumption." "Why?" asked a guest. "Because the ladies would all say, 'Look at that poor Byron, how interesting he looks in dying.' "

There is a moment at the close of Hunt's confused commentary on Keats that is emblematic of his sympathy turned sodden and, wittingly or otherwise, against his young friend. And because he is, at the time, seen as Keats's mentor and chief supporter, it is all the more damningly effective. As usual, Hunt's vagueness ("All this trouble was secretly aggravated by a very tender circumstance, which I can but allude to . . .") creates an opportunity for those who would take it.

Mr. Keats had felt that his disease was mortal for two or three years before he died. He had a constitutional tendency to consumption; a close attendance to the death-bed of a beloved brother, when he ought to have been nursing himself in bed, gave it a blow which he felt for months; and meanwhile the rascally critics came up, and roused an indignation in him, both against them and himself, which he could ill afford to endure. All this trouble was secretly aggravated by a very tender circumstance, which I can but allude to thus publicly, and which naturally subjected one of the warmest heart and imaginations that ever existed, to all the pangs, that doubt, succeeded by delight, and delight, succeeded by hopelessness in this world, could inflict. Seeing him once change countenance in a manner more alarming than usual, as he stood silently eyeing the country out of the window, I pressed him to let me know how he felt, in order that he might enable me to do what I could for him: upon which he said, that his feelings were almost more than he could bear, and that he feared for his senses. I proposed that we should take a coach, and ride about the country together, to vary, if possible, the immediate impression, which was sometimes all that was formidable, and would come to nothing. He acquiesced, and was restored to himself. It was nevertheless on the same day, sitting on the bench in Well Walk, at Hampstead, nearest the heath, that he told me, with unaccustomed tears in his eyes, that "his heart was breaking."

6

NO ONE, NOT EVEN BROWN AND SEVERN, KNEW, OR COULD know, Keats well enough to see the whole twenty-five-year picture, not even George, who emigrated to America before his brother became seriously ill, and was absent in the time of Keats's great creative period. There was carryover and interchange and introductions among all the friends of Keats's different "eras," whether childhood, school days, apprenticeship, medical studies, or "the living year" and its consequences. But there was no one who was a direct and complete witness to his growth, his many moves, his changing health. Tom, the slight, sweet youngest brother, had been closest to Keats emotionally. George had been the practical, almost "older" brother. When George had married and left England, Brown had become the surrogate brother; then Severn, ready or not, had had to play several roles, one of them being *like* a brother. Each of them saw Keats as he could, but not the whole Keats, such as a whole Keats could be seen in the immediate years after his death. Thus Hunt, who knew Keats best in that transitional time between giving up his planned medical profession and entering the unknown, uncertain future of poetry, had little Keatsian background to go on, only rumor and hearsay. So, as regards Keats's reticent past, Hunt must guess, extrapolate, fill in, and—in the fact of Fanny Brawne—allude to. The drift of Hunt's memory of his young friend has affection behind it, yet, like much of the warm feeling from many of Keats's peers, a quality of condescension, too. Hunt's characterization of Keats as, in effect, another Chatterton, as a greatly talented boy-poet greatly cut off, reinforces the precious image of him as a "bardling"—that is, a five-foot poet—whose precocity got ahead of the reality. Keats will, in some imagined future, be recognized, says Hunt, but as a genius of promise rather than a writer of achievement on the scale of, say, Byron and Shelley. "I venture to prophesy . . . that Mr. Keats will be known hereafter in English literature, emphatically, as *the Young Poet*." Add to this assessment Shelley's Adonais myth of the fragile, exquisite flower and Brown's epitaph of the no-name "Young English Poet" killed by "the Malicious Power of his Enemies" and you have a fairly strong argument for an aesthetic sensibility too sensitive for a trivializing Regency world, a world still caught between the eighteenth century and revolution. Byron, for one, forced by Hunt to read "Ode on a Grecian Urn" and "Ode to a Nightingale," pleads ignorance to Keats's "poetical concentrations." How could there be, Byron asks, "music unheard"? And what is the meaning of a beaker "full of the warm south"? "It was Lord Byron, at that time living in Italy, drinking its wine and basking in its sunshine, who asked me."

Lord Byron and Some of His Contemporaries, whatever its ultimate merit and motive for being—Hunt likely wrote it as a moneymaker—fills a void. Byron was the literary lion of the age, Shelley the outcast expatriate, Keats the great young poet who almost was. Each life suggested a compelling story worthy of a novel perhaps, and each of them had ended up dying dramatically in exotic, foreign lands. Byron and Shelley would soon enough find their apologists and testifiers. Keats would have, for the longest time, Hunt's "brothers in unity" and nothing else except the quarrels of his friends over who would best serve his immortal interests—interests that demanded cooperation and collaboration. Brown and Severn thought Taylor unqualified to write a memoir let alone an original biography. Taylor, Reynolds, and George thought Brown too self-serving. As Brown's later editors, Dorothy Hyde Bodurtha and Willard Bissell Pope, put it in 1937: "Within six months of his death, Keats's friends present a picture we should gladly efface from the records: the unhappy spectacle of heirs fighting over an estate—in this case, the manuscripts of the poems and letters and the right to make them public. The amazing quality of the performance is that Keats's friends put so high a value on papers which the literary world had deemed of no value. It was as though they were fighting for the best seats in an empty, dark theatre."

Whatever the value his friends placed on his papers, few of them had faith that in their lifetimes Keats's memory would be rightfully honored. Mostly they were concerned to get his character cleared up. Sensitivity is one thing, wilting flower another. "Leigh Hunt's account of him is worse than disappointing; I cannot bear it," writes Brown. "It seems as if Hunt was so impressed by his illness that he had utterly forgotten him in health." And again: "I hate Hunt's account of him, though every sentence, I verily believe, was intended to show his honour and fame; but what does that matter when he manages to make him a whining, puling boy?" These quotes are from letters that Brown wrote to Fanny Brawne and Charles Dilke in 1828 and 1829, respectively. As correct as such opinions may be, as judgments they pretty well represent Brown's sense that no one belonging to the broken Keats circle was up to the task of fully "knowing" his friend and thereby remembering him as both a man and a poet. No one except him, Brown, though Dilke, Reynolds, Taylor, and, of course, George Keats would forever entertain a contrary view—that the Keats they knew was their Keats, the real Keats, the whole Keats. Each of them would have to die, or be close to death, before his specific hold on memory and material would relax. George would die in 1841, Brown in 1842, Dilke in 1850, Reynolds in 1852, and Taylor, who had since surrendered his copyright to the poems in his and Hessey's possession, in 1864. (Not long after the Milnes biography appeared, Hessey wrote to Taylor that "I always regretted that you did not take Keats's Name & Fame in hand. You & Woodhouse knew more of him than any one, and you might have made a very interesting Book of his Memoirs.") Excepting the word-averse Severn, those who had lived within Keats's lifetime had seen him on a more or less daily basis, had argued with him and celebrated, worked with him and cared for him. These closest of his friends would have to disappear before a full and fair portrait of him could begin to be put together and set in print. Each of his friends would leave notes and fragmentary comments, letters and testimonies, details and memorabilia, but nothing—perhaps naturally enough—with narrative perspective, inclusive distance, or dot-connecting coherence.

Keats had written, in an early, prescient letter, that "A Man's Life of any worth is a continual allegory—and very few eyes can see the Mystery of his life—a life like the scriptures, figurative." It is the figurative part that defeated Brown when at long last he sat down and tried to draw from memory his *Life of John Keats*. It would take him from 1829 to 1836 just to get started. Once he did, what he produced some fifteen years after Keats's death was a lecture delivered at his local Literature, Science, and the Fine Arts club in Plymouth (The Plymouth Institution, December 29, 1836) and revised, in three drafts five years later, into a roughly fifty-page monograph. Initially, Brown's idea was to counter Hunt's limp-wristed impression of Keats and to supersede those he considered ignorant or inept as possible biographers. But year after year as he procrastinated making good on his promise to remember his friend, he began to alienate those whose help with information and copyright he needed, including his old school acquaintance Charles Dilke and Keats's brother George. Dilke at one point accuses Brown of trying to "capitalize" on Keats's death, to in effect cash in on the friendship. George, for a variety of reasons, is not ready to give over his rights to unpublished poems—poems that he and Brown over time have fair-copied. Even Severn, in 1834, in exasperation asks, "What are you doing about Keats's Life? *The time has come, and* I FEAR THE TIME MAY PASS." When Brown finally presents his summary life of Keats, quoting a few sample poems and passages, only one person in the Plymouth Athenaeum audience has the slightest knowledge of, let alone more than passing interest in, the work of John Keats, and that is Coleridge's second son, the Reverend Derwent Coleridge, Master of Helston School, Cornwall. Mostly, says Brown in a self-conscious letter to Hunt, the lecture had a "remarkable reception . . . less on his account as a poet than on account of its interest as a piece of biography, read by the friend of a young poet—no matter who it was. It . . . exalted me as his friend, a compliment which I had endeavoured to avoid, but possibly the endeavour had directly the opposite effect."

He has meant only, Brown promises Hunt, to write "at greater length than your's." Yet while Hunt's version of a "whining, puling Keats" reinforces—in fact underscores—the Adonais myth and the tombstone inscription, Brown's abortive biography warps the posthumous vision in the opposite way, but with a similar result. Rationalist, deliberative Brown cannot see the figurative, cannot accept "the Mystery," the larger implications of Keats's life. He does remember crucial encounters and episodes: their first meeting, on the Hampstead Road; the summer tour of the North Country; the composition of certain central poems, such as the nightingale ode and *The Eve of St. Agnes*; the first hemorrhage, in February 1820 at Wentworth Place; the emerging relationship with Fanny Brawne; the dinners, the plays, the collaboration on *Otho the Great*. Brown's memory is like his Shanklin drawing of Keats—straightforward and accurate. He knows what he knows, and in this spirit admits that he is guessing at Keats's birth date, which he claims to be October 29, 1796, only a year and a couple of days off. In spite of the intimacy of the drafts of his memoir, however, Brown cannot resist the Shelley impulse of turning Keats into a martyr.

After twenty years, with all the charity of which my nature is capable, my belief continues to be that he was destroyed by hirelings, under the imposing name of Reviewers. Consumption, it may be urged, was in the family; his father and his younger brother had both died of it; therefore his fate was inevitable. Perhaps it was so; perhaps not. The brother who died was very tall and narrow chested; our Keats was short, with well-proportioned limbs, and with a chest remarkably well-formed for strength. At the most, it comes to this: if an hereditary predisposition existed, that predisposition might not have been called into action, except by an outrageous denial of his now acknowledged claim to be ranked as a poet of England. Month after month, an accumulation of ridicule and scoffs against his character and person, did worse than tear food from the mouth of a starving wretch, for it tore honour from the poet's brow. Could he have been less sensitive, could he have been less independent, could he have truckled to his self-constituted judges, could he have flattered the taste of the public, and pandered to their will and pleasure—in fact, could he have ceased to be John Keats, he might have existed at this moment, happy as one of the inferior animals of the creation.

Keats's mother, of course, not his father, died of consumption. This is the penultimate paragraph of the last emendation of Brown's *Life of Keats*, and it signals the tone and thrust of the overall argument of the ragged text. It repeats, after nearly two decades, Brown's implacable epigraphical theme regarding "the Malicious Power" of Keats's "Enemies," reinforcing the perceived weakness of character that he means to be against. No accident, then, that the epigraph for the memoir comes from *Adonais*, lines 370 through 383, including the "loveliness . . . made more lovely" passage. Thus Brown, in effect, begins and ends his memory of his friend subscribing to the critics-killed-Keats apologia. But similar to his hesitation concerning the script for the headstone, Brown is reluctant to commit into public his opinion. "I knew this task was my duty . . . Therefore to compel me to my duty, I boldly put down my name at our Institution for a lecture, on 27th December, on 'The Life and Poems of John Keats.' Now that it is advertised, the card printed, the members looking forward to it, there is no retreating: it must be done."

A deeper reason for his hesitation is the difficulty, not just the dutifulness, of the task. In his absence, Keats has become for Brown a presiding presence. "As soon as I begin to be occupied with his poems, or with the *Life* . . . it forcibly seems to me, against all reason . . . that he is sitting by my side, his eyes seriously wandering from me to the papers by turns, and watching my doings. Call it nervousness if you will, but with this nervous impression I am unable to do justice to his fame." These two quotations are from letters that Brown writes to Milnes in conjunction with turning over all of the remaining poems and related material he has gathered and held on to all these years. Brown will send Milnes a copy of the memoir as well. In addition to Brown's fear of failing "to do justice" to Keats's fame, his nervousness might also be conjured as guilt—guilt mixed with lingering grief, guilt that after all this time still seems to burden his behavior toward George, Dilke, the *Blackwood's* and *Quarterly* critics, anyone in the line of fire of his anger, and self-anger. There may or may not be fair and honest justification for Brown's not being in Hampstead at the end of the summer in 1820, but like it or not, in those terrible, terminal days of quitting England, Keats was essentially alone, just as, in late spring of that year, he had been excused from the house that now bears his name by Brown's annual announced need to rent his half of Wentworth Place for the season. Brown had once remarked that Keats, more than most, could not bear too much solitude. And true enough, here was Keats, all these ghost years after, sitting at Brown's side, watching Brown's doings.

7

ON JULY 1, 1822, NOT QUITE EIGHTEEN MONTHS AFTER KEATS had been buried in the *acattolico*, or Protestant Cemetery, in Rome, Shelley set out by boat—his new two-masted vessel alternately known as *Ariel* or *Don Juan*—to sail to Pisa to meet Leigh Hunt, whom he had not seen in four years of exile. Shelley's new friend Edward Williams, with whom he and Mary, along with Williams's wife, Jane, were sharing Casa Magni on the Gulf of Spezia, went with him. The rest of the story is, more or less, history. Mary, who had a mind for foreboding, did not want her husband to make the water journey. "A vague expectation of evil shook me to agony, and I could scarcely bring myself to let them go." As Shelley himself had written at the close of *Adonais*, "The massy earth and sphered skies are riven! / I am borne darkly, fearfully, afar." Shelley, physically and emotionally, may have seemed a blithe spirit, but he was also a determined soul, stubborn, "driven." Most of his life was about running, moving, disappearing. So on that first day of July, he and Williams sailed south from the Bay of Lerici to the little port town of Leghorn, near Livorno, just outside Pisa, arriving well before nightfall. Hunt, Marianne, and their brood of children were set to occupy half of a large house, Casa Lanfranchi, that Byron had rented for the time being. Byron, however, no lover of domesticity or its children, was being more than rude to the Hunt family, particularly the mother, a woman who tended to be on the edge, always. Shelley's arrival, therefore, was not only welcomed but necessary to maintain even a modicum of civility. Byron, apparently, had expected Hunt to arrive alone. Shelley stayed on six days as a young uncle to the situation, promising Williams that by Sunday, July 7, they would return to their own families. Hunt later reported that they spent that last day together touring the streets and central part of Pisa, where the Duomo, the Leaning Tower, the Baptistry, and the Camp Santo all congregrate into a jewel. Shelley was still relunctant to leave his friend in such hostile circumstances, but Williams was insistent. As a parting gesture, Hunt placed in Shelley's hands his only copy of Keats's final volume, *Lamia, Isabella, the Eve of St. Agnes and Other Poems*—something, he said, to read on the boat ride back. "Keep it," he added, "till you give it me with your own hands." And with that, Williams and Shelley left for Leghorn, Livorno, and the Mediterranean.

For a month it had not rained, each day the heat building into clouds from which nothing fell but heaviness and humidity. With the air glaring white and the ground "hard-fired," sailing the waters offshore must have been inviting, which is what Shelley had been doing since his beautiful new boat had been delivered in May. He was not, frankly, much of a sailor, thus not much of a reader of weather. When he went out alone, he would invariably put in at one of several coves (and caves) close to home. He wrote most of *Triumph of Life*, his last and most mature work, in such settings. When he sailed any distance, Williams or others with experience would go out with him. That Monday morning, leaving Leghorn, the sultriness and breathlessness of the heat had turned at the coastline into mist, then blind fog. The storm, which everyone hoped for, was finally showing up, or would be soon, a fact that the impatient Williams ignored and the impetuous Shelley could not take seriously. The possible rain and rough seas were less of a worry, it would turn out, than the sea fog. Once the *Ariel* was well into it, it became the chief concern of those who knew better, such as Captain Roberts, who had built Shelley's boat, and Trelawny, Byron's "biographer" and as much of a pirate as he (Byron) was poet, both of whom were left in Leghorn after the farewells. At about fifteen or more miles out, and after a few hours in the Gulf of Spezia in high seas and deep fog, Shelley's boat went under, either because of an encounter with another boat or by its own mishandling. Although the actual storm lasted less than half an hour, far at sea it lasted long enough. Williams's body came ashore at the mouth of the Serchio River; the body of Charles Vivan—a young man who had hitched a ride—washed onto the sand at Massa, twenty miles north. Shelley's body floated for ten days before beaching at Viareggio.

> Viareggio, 18 July, 1822. *Your excellency, It is my duty to inform you that this morning the rough seas threw up a corpse which had been partly consumed, which, after due inspection by the Tribunal in the interests of Public Health, has been buried on the shore, covered with quick-lime in compliance with the Marine sanitary regulations.*
>
> *We have no information regarding same, but it is thought likely to be one of the young Englishmen who are reported to have drowned on the passage they undertook as far back as July 8th, in a small brig-shaped launch which left Leghorn for the Gulf of Spezia, the sea hav-*

ing thrown up the other body on the Tuscan shore. Your
Excellency's etc.

G. P. Frediani

P. S. A circumstance which confirms my idea that this
must be one of the said Englishmen, is that an English
book was discovered in the pocket of the double-breasted
tweed jacket which he was wearing.

This is the official letter from the governor of Viareggio to the Secretary for Home and Foreign Affairs. Williams's body, it was decided, would be borne back to England for burial, Shelley's to Rome and the Protestant Cemetery, where his son William lay next to Keats. "*Adonais,*" Mary Shelley would lament, "is not Keats's elegy, it is his very own." First, however, and for any number of healthful, useful, and symbolic reasons, it was decided that the bodies should be exhumed from their quicklime graves and burned on their respective beaches. Williams was turned to ash on August 15 on the coast of Tuscany, Shelley the day after at Viareggio on pyres of pine, frankincense, wine, oil, honey, and salt. The ashes were placed in small oak boxes lined with black velvet and labeled with brass plates with their names in Latin, including age, country, and cause of death. At Viareggio it was all men who witnessed the burning of the funeral pyre: Byron, Trelawny, a Captain Shenley, and, of course, Hunt, who brought with him enough guards (dragoons and soldiers) to keep at a distance the growing crowd of sightseers. When the original fuel was inadequate to the task, some of the guards gathered debris of driftwood and splintered spars and planks from other shipwrecks. Shelley's body, in particular, so ravaged by its travels, seemed resistant to reduction, especially his great heart, which Trelawny finally retrieved and later gave to Mary, who lived for thirty more years, though the heart had long since become dust and leaves.

The *acattolico* graves of Keats, Shelley, and some of those closest required a certain reconfiguration in the years ahead, each time necessitating dealing with Roman bureaucratic authority. Severn, who had, in the year following Keats's death, already begun to establish himself as an artist and presence in English-speaking Roman society, helped a good deal with funereal negotiations. The Protestant Cemetery, not long ago a sheep's meadow and a people's picnic pasture, was becoming a Poet's Cemetery, but not without trial and error. On January 23, 1823, six months after Shelley's body washed ashore, his ashes were laid to rest in the new, enclosed portion of the ground still officially referred to as the Meadows of the Roman People, some distance from where Keats and Shelley's son William lay. Two months later, when Trelawny—ever inventive, always looking ahead—arrived to see just where his friend was buried, he wrote to Mary that "the ashes of my noble Shelley" were "mingled in a heap with five or six common vagabonds." Within a month, with Severn's considerable help, Trelawny found a more suitable spot set off and up against the old Aurelian wall. Severn, naturally, cannot avoid mentioning his idea for a monument to Keats, which Trelawny asserts would be perfect for Shelley as well. Nothing, however, comes of either idea. Instead, as with Keats's headstone, a compromise is reached, though in Shelley's case with profoundly more understatement. Hunt's Latin phrase COR CORDIUM would cap the stone, with a Trelawny-chosen quotation from *The Tempest*—Shelley's favorite Shakespeare—to underwrite: "Nothing of him doth fade / But doth suffer a sea change / Into something rich and strange."

Well into the future, in 1881, Trelawny's own sea-changed body will, in fact, lie next to Shelley's, in the same year that

Severn's aged body will be placed next to Keats's, after negotiations that Severn can no longer be a part of. Severn had died in late summer of 1879, almost sixty years—a lifetime in those days—from the death of Keats. His final diary entry had read, "I begin to feel the loneliness of having lived too long," a remarkable epitaph in itself. Shelley's son William would have to be moved and brought to a belated rest just north and west of Keats and the ashes of his father.

Death became a means of redressing imbalances and rectifying tragically severed connections; death, and this island of green space with its assortment of ilex and stone pine and palm trees and a sharply scaled pyramid, like a church steeple or pagan sign, would become oddly exemplary. But for the longest while the high grass would have to be maintained by sheep and the traffic of picnickers, some friend or caring soul would replace the grave flowers that were forever disappearing.

The question of epitaphs, like the flowers, had a life of its own. Shelley had the advantage of a straightforward, quick, and mythic death, a death by water that he had beautifully predicted. Keats, on the other hand, suffered a confused death by increments, whose cause no one, least of all the doctors, could or would be clear about. Keats himself, in his anonymous grave, seemed in life no less sure of what killed him, though some days more than others he seemed to get it right: a disease of the lungs, not the heart and mind. When Severn's body was removed from its original grave to its juxtaposition to Keats, the temptation to name this long-dead partner was overwhelming. The script, therefore, under Severn's name reads, "Devoted friend and death-bed companion of JOHN KEATS." And because in death, in hindsight, such symmetries are possible, the broken lyre on Keats's stone is paralleled by a palette with all its brushes intact.

THIS MORTAL BODY

. . .

Yet can I gulp a bumper to thy name,—
O smile among the shades, for this is fame!

1

ON JUNE 22, 1818, TWO YEARS TO THE DAY BEFORE HE SAT
in Hunt's living room having his one and only tea with the
Gisbornes, Keats and his brother George and his brother's
bride, Georgiana, along with Charles Brown, boarded the
Prince Saxe Cobourg Liverpool coach, bound west-northwest
through "Stony-Stratford, Lichfield, and the Potteries." It was
a Monday morning, and they left just before noon, expecting
to arrive in the port of Liverpool thirty-two hours later. They
all probably rode on the top of the coach, for the view and the
reduction in expense. In all likelihood, the boot of the coach was
top-heavy, too, because George and Georgiana carried with
them their worldly possessions—as much, at least, as could be
sensibly borne across the Atlantic to the interior of America.
George was dressed like any early eighteenth-century English
gentleman: high-collared waistcoat, breeches, stockings, smart
shoes. Georgiana wore a high-waisted muslin gown and either
a coal-scuttle bonnet or a country straw hat tied under the chin
with ribbons. George had just turned twenty-one; Georgiana
was between seventeen and nineteen, depending on the con-
jecture of her birth date. Neither one had the bearing, let alone
the appearance, of an emigrant. Brown, on the other hand, the
inveterate traveler, was flushed out in a tartan suit, a plaid over
the shoulder and a white hat for his bald head, plus an oilskin
packed for the rain—a regular "Red Cross Knight," according
to Keats. Keats himself, no less noticeable, wore a fur hat, a

well-weathered jacket, and a plaid. He and Brown were taking a different kind of journey altogether from the newly married couple. Theirs was to be a full-summer walking tour, first of the English Lake District, then north into the Highlands, eventually topping off in John O'Groats, the northernmost point in Scotland, before starting south and home along the North Sea coast.

Tom Keats, in the summer of 1818, was somewhat conspicuous by his absence. The summer before, Tom and George had spent a happy yet expensive time in Paris while John had lodged in Oxford trying to get his first test at a major poem— *Endymion*—off the ground. Restlessness was part of all three brothers' dailiness. They were always planning trips, always on the move, whether in town or out of town. Restlessness was one of the results of their orphaning.

Fanny Keats, kept like a captive princess within their guardian Abbey's household, must have felt the need to get out and about keenly. By the fall of 1817, however, when the brothers had returned to Hampstead and Well Walk from their various journeys, it was clear that something, perhaps serious, was wrong with Tom. He was already, in fact, spitting blood. Though taller than his older brothers, Tom was also considerably thinner—bird chested, delicate featured, more like a Shelley than a Keats. John, the oldest and the shortest, was robust and broad shouldered, like their father. George was a type in between, medium in height, medium and temperate in every other way. But the bird-like Tom looked frail, always had. It was as if, in the diminuendo of male birth, there had been a falling off in the birthing of the Keats brothers, with John the healthiest and Edward, the fourth Keats son, dying in childhood. Tom was third in line. Tom's relative health at this moment is crucial because George and John have come of age and in no time so will Tom. Their intimacy with and dependency on one another is beginning to come to closure. George has plans, John has plans; Tom, for some while, seems to have involuntarily set for himself a career as a patient.

More travel seems to be Tom's only plan. The irony cannot be lost that one of the trips that he and John have in mind is spending the winter in Italy when John returns from his "Scottish tour," with the hopes that a softer climate will make the difference and reverse Tom's "English" illness. Although, in two short years it will be John, not his brother, as the patient contemplating Italy, for now Tom is resting at their Well Walk address, being attended by friends and Mrs. Bentley, their benevolent landlady. Tom has been, certainly in John's eyes, the heart center of the triad of the brothers. On one of their most companionable evenings, when they were still living in Cheapside, it is Tom whom Keats celebrates in one of his most tender sonnets, "To My Brothers."

Small, busy flames play through the fresh-laid coals,
And their faint cracklings o'er our silence creep
Like whispers of the household gods that keep
A gentle empire o'er fraternal souls.
And while, for rhymes, I search around the poles,
Your eyes are fixed, as in poetic sleep,
Upon the lore so voluble and deep,
That aye at fall of night our care condoles.
This is your birthday Tom, and I rejoice
That thus it passes smoothly, quietly.
Many such eves of gently whispering noise
May we together pass, and calmly try
What are this world's true joys—ere the great voice,
From its fair face, shall bid our spirits fly.

The great voice, fair faced or otherwise, has been audible within Tom's hearing for longer than either of his brothers has been willing to admit. This poem marks Tom's seventeenth birthday; it also pretty closely marks the beginning of the burden that his health will represent to George and John, who will for the next year or so alternately serve as companion and nurse. Each of the brothers will suffer the weight and guilt of the experience.

John, in particular, with his medical training and his boyhood nursing of his mother, is well aware of the symptoms of consumption, blood-spitting being the first. This is what might be termed, in the young lives of the three Keats brothers in late spring and early summer of 1818, a crossing moment, a moment when certain decisions cannot be reversed, cannot be quite yet understood—"we are in a Mist," writes Keats to Reynolds in May from Teignmouth—and cannot be controlled or known for their possible unintended consequences. George, who for so long has brother-sat Tom while John has moved about trying to complete *Endymion*, has decided to strike out on his own: get married and seek opportunity in the New World, especially because, except for companioning his young brother, he has not been gainfully employed for more than a year. ("You know," Keats writes to Bailey, "my Brother George has been out of employ for some time. It has weighed very much upon him, and driven him to scheme and turn things over in his Mind.")

With the completion of his trial by poem, Keats's first attempt at an epic, he will now be expected to take over more or less full-time care and concern for Tom. Yet Keats has his own intentions and hopes for the summer, primary among them "a pedestrian tour through the north of England and Scotland as far as John o Groats." He has high, ambitious reasons for such a journey, which will "make a sort of Prologue to the Life I intend to pursue—that is to write, to study and to see all Europe at the lowest expence. I will clamber through the Clouds and exist." As for Tom, the last thing he wants to be is a burden, and he, no less than his brothers, closes at least one eye on his true condition, a pattern that will repeat itself when Keats takes on similar symptoms. Just within a few short days in March, for example, Tom's plight goes from "Tom saying how much better he had got" (March 13) to "Poor Tom—who could have imagined such a change" (March 18) to "Tom has been much worse: but is now getting better" (March 21). Throughout the spring and into the summer, the wish for health will obscure the fact of it.

Teignmouth, on the coast of Devon, had been the hoped-for winter retreat from the bone-chilling cold of London, with George and John taking turns caring for Tom. Instead it had been storm wind and horizontal rain almost constantly, which meant—now that John was there in close quarters with his brother, in rooms practically sealed off—an unhealthy proximity, a pattern that would be repeated in fall in Hampstead once John returned from his northern walks. At fourteen, Keats had already played physician to their mother, whose wasted consumptive body surely rose in his imagination here with the pale, withering Tom, who by this time had begun to hemorrhage. And it takes no imagination to connect Tom to their mother and her several relatives who have died of consumption, and to link that lineage to oneself. Within days of Tom's first violent convulsion of blood, Keats tries to joke away his obvious depression in a telling comment to Bailey, complaining, of all things, about the wet weather. "When a poor devil is drowning, it is said he comes thrice to the surface, ere he makes his final sink if however, even at the third rise, he can manage to catch hold of a piece of weed or rock, he stands a fair chance,—as I hope I do now, of being saved." (Hemorrhaging, as Keats will discover, is a lot like drowning.) But as Tom's health stabilizes in the weeks ahead they both feel it is time to return to London, to George, and to the future—a future in which George is soon to join a world of independent responsibilities.

The beginning of the trip from Teignmouth back to London goes well enough; "My Brother has borne his Journey thus far remarkably well," so Keats writes to friends from Honiton. But outside of Bridport, in Dorset, in what will become Hardy country, Tom has another hemorrhage. Many days later, in a long thank-you note to "Miss Mary Ann Jeffrey/Teignmouth/ Devonshire," thanking her for "kind solicitude," Tom writes from Well Walk that "the rest of the journey pass'd off pretty well after we left Bridport in Dorsetshire—I was very ill there and lost much blood—we travell'd a hundred miles in the last two days—I found myself much better at the end of the journey than when I left Tartarey alias Teignmouth—the Doctor was surprised to see me looking so well, as were all my Friends— they insisted that my illness was all mistaken Fancy and on this presumption excited me to laughing and merriment which has deranged me a little—however it appears that confinement and low spirits have been my chief enemies and I promise myself a gradual recovery—."

2

AT THE CLOSE OF THE JEFFREY LETTER, TOM ALLUDES TO HIS much mulled over project of going to Italy—"most likely to the town of Paiva"—where he looks forward to acquiring "a stock of knowledge and strength which will better enable me to bustle through the world—I am persuaded this is the best way of killing time." If John gets back soon enough from his summer "in the Clouds," all the better. They can once again travel together. For the time being, though, "I shall be here alone and I hope well—John will have set out on his Northern Expedition George on his Western . . . Johns will take four months at the end of that time he expects to have achieved two thousand miles mostly on Foot—George embarks for America." From that June 22 moment when George and John leave Tom very much alone in order to start their separate, disparate journeys, the three brothers will never be together again. At the port of Liverpool, George, with his bride Georgiana, will sail into a whole new and unchartable life, far into the rough interior of a new world. John, with his new resolve to put the apprenticeship of *Endymion* behind him and with his new friend Brown as a tour guide, will test himself in more ways than he can imagine in the next, demanding two—not four—months. Tom, of course, will not get to Italy; he will not get anywhere and will be waiting for John in Well Walk once the halved Northern tour is over. It may be true of all families of multiple brothers or sisters that siblings of the same sex form a kind of singularity and that one brother or one sister stands out or represents the whole, particularly when they come in threes. With, say, the Brontë sisters, of the three one dominates and takes on qualities of the other two, becomes, in fact, a resolution of the other two—Charlotte, the eldest, combines the lyricism of Emily and the darkness of Anne. So, too, *Jane Eyre*, *Wuthering Heights*, and *The Tenant of Wildfell Hall* are aspects of one consciousness. George and Tom were not writers, but they were intimates of the work of their elder brother; they were in their turn muse and matter in the work.

Until he left for America, George kept Keats's poems or copied them or both, serving often as John's agent and social facilitator—indeed, introducing Keats to what became, in history, much of the Keats Circle, including Joseph Severn, Charles Dilke, and William Haslam. "George has ever been more than a brother to me, he has been my greatest friend," Keats says in 1818, and a year later, well after George has emigrated, "George always stood between me and any dealings in the world." To the extent that Keats has any practical sense, any job-seeking or money-managing awareness, George represents that grounded part of his character. Tom, on the other hand, "who understood John's character perfectly" and who also worshipfully kept copies of his brother's early poems, represents something of the soul of Keats. It is no exaggeration to suggest that Tom's long illness and the long-suffering of their mother's illness and death that it reinacts, along with Tom's and the mother's emotional vulnerability, even innocence, go to the core of Keats. Tom, especially, in many ways, as a vital yet paling presence, anticipates Keats's maturing sympathetic contract with the world; he becomes the living correlative for Keats's forgiving emotion. And when Tom does finally give in to the consumption that has reduced him to a ghost, just days following his nineteenth birthday—December 1, 1818—he becomes that central quality of imagination we call inspiration, a grief figure that again and again needs to be addressed, reinvoked, reconciled—not simply as a knight-at-arms or a youth grown "pale, and spectre-thin" but as an enlarging emblem, a motivating measure, a rich resource of loss to which—to paraphrase Wordsworth—the poet repairs as to a fountain. Whatever Tom's literal death meant to Keats—and with George "lost" in the middle of America and Fanny Keats virtually locked away, it meant everything—Tom becomes for Keats a fountain of an elemental fraternal emotion. "I Have two

Brothers one is driven by the 'burden of Society' to America the other, with an exquisite love of our parents and even for early Misfortunes has grown into a affection 'passing the Love of Women'—I have been ill-temper'd with them, I have vex'd them—but the thought of them has always stifled the impression that any woman might otherwise have made upon me—I have a Sister too and may not follow them, either to America or to the Grave—Life must be undergone, and I certainly derive a consolation from the thought of writing one or two more Poems before it ceases."

These words, written a little more than a week before George is to set sail, certainly imply Keats's state of mind, a melancholy mixture of fatalism, ambition, and profound affection—that "temper that if I were under Water I would scarcely kick to come to the surface." But they also reveal how necessary family, in one form or another, is to Keats. George's imminent "disappearance"—the thought of it as much as the fact of it—has placed Keats into one of his deepest depressions. Tom's vexing illness and ultimate death will then shift the emotional scale beyond the warp and woof of "despair and energy," as Keats has once characterized it, to something more transforming. Beginning with the winter of 1819 and the escapist *Eve of St. Agnes* through the great spring and autumnal odes of the rest of the evolving year, Keats will discover his full creative life, the so-called "living year." Tom, in death, will turn into a source, a figure at once ambiguous, exclusionary, and sometimes conspiratorial, a collaborator whose existential example will both inspire and confirm to Keats that he too may die from what has killed his brother. Worse, with Tom's death at the transition between autumn and winter, Keats will sense that he has in fact begun to die—is, in little pieces, dying. Yes, "Life must be undergone, and I certainly derive consolation from the

thought of writing one or two more Poems before it ceases"—
this in a letter to Bailey days before the trip to America and the
journey north begin.

3

SO WITH THE HOPEFUL TOM MORE OR LESS ENSCONCED AT
Well Walk in Hampstead, George and John and John's new
sister-in-law and the intrepid Charles Brown ride on the out-
side of the Liverpool coach through Redbourn, then "over the
Chiltern hills and across the Ouse at Stony-Stratford, through
Northamptonshire and Warwickshire in the brief summer night,
and into the quiet cathedral city of Coventry at dawn; along the
borders of Shropshire as the sun swung high and down into the
plains of Cheshire with the mountains of Wales showing blue
toward the west; then across the Mersy and into Liverpool at last
in the early evening"—as Aileen Ward, one of Keats's fine biog-
raphers, imagines the trip, which was a full waking day and almost
half of another. Keats and Brown are set to start their walking
tour early the next morning; George and Georgiana are not sure
when the tide and ship's schedule will mesh. And because there
is no point in not letting the newlyweds sleep in, all good-byes
are said on the night they arrive in Liverpool, with the expecta-
tion that John, and perhaps Tom, will join the American Keatses
within a year or so and become citizens of the New World. Keats
has joked a month ago that once he is sure of George's com-
mitment to emigration, he looks forward to becoming America's
first great poet.

As luck would have it, Keats's tour of the North of the Mother
Country in the old world begins with a coach ride and ends with

a boat ride. The ground is too uninteresting between Liverpool and Lancaster to waste leather walking, thus Lancaster, forty miles north, is to be his and Brown's intended true starting place. They might as well have skipped Lancaster, too, with its spinning mills ("That most disgusting of all noises") and poverty and parliamentary election politics at full bore. (Wordsworth, Keats will soon find out, is campaigning for the Tory incumbent, Lord Lowther, against the Liberal Henry Brougham, who has defended Hunt at his infamous trial. "Wordsworth versus Brougham!! Sad—sad—sad—.") They are out of there before dawn the next day, and henceforth truly on foot.

Several and various themes dominate Keats's and Brown's well-documented Northern tour—documented by Keats through a series of a dozen letters and by Brown through a partly published journal. For Brown, the major theme is a return to Scottish roots that he has not experienced before—"return," that is, to a sense of ancestry, to sources that indeed mark his character, mark his thrift, his puritanical purchase on justice and injustice, his plainspoken practicality, his strict business acumen, his selective generosity, his aggressive maleness, his narrowness, his bawdy humor, his survival skills. The Northern tour for him is a confirmation of a conjured heritage, a familial past that supersedes his difficult younger years. It will be a physical challenge and an exotic adventure for sure, but it will also be a personal experience: "We were not bound on a journey of discovery into the busy haunts of men." For Keats, the walking tour is meant not only "to make a sort of Prologue to the Life I intend to pursue" but to announce a life as a practicing poet as opposed to a practicing physician. This is what might be called a voluntary theme, a theme by choice. However, other major themes, although involuntary, quickly begin to define Keats's and Brown's journey. The weather, for instance: weather that proves daunting, often enervating, especially in the form of relentless rain; weather of every description and degree and often including a steady chill wind. The weather has a direct and ultimate effect on Keats's health, which becomes the dominant involuntary theme. There is also the leitmotif of the odd assortment of people they encounter, which could be considered a theme of circular descent, à la Dante, were it not for the fact that a good portion of the time they are climbing, "through the Clouds," up Skiddaw, the cliffs of Staffa, and Ben Nevis. Inevitably, there is the theme of the undulant, terra incognita of the landscape itself—sometimes domestic, sometimes rustic, sometimes wild, but always strange, "views . . . that make one forget the divisions of life."

The original plan was essentially to circumnavigate the northern tier—frontier, really—of the British Isles, a plan that would come to include a brief crossing to northern Ireland. On the whole, though, the trip became for Keats a mixed long walk from Lancaster to Inverness along a bleak, sometimes beautiful path through the Lake District and the Cumberland mountains, the Borders (with a side trip to Donaghadee and Belfast), up into the western loch country of Scotland, then over to the Isle of Mull and the Inner Hebrides, then up the Great Glen and the southeastern shore of Loch Ness, and finally Inverness itself. The trek—discounting the distraction of Ireland—was some four hundred foot miles, miles that do not fully account for the ascensions of and climb-downs from a variety of mountains. They average ten miles a day, and on a good day—when the rain is either in recess or softened into a "Scotch mist"—twice that distance. Some days they rest or are stymied. " 'Weather permitting,' unless of the bad and excessive kind, was not of much force in our agreement. But, on the morning of our departure, ready to start at four, a heavy rain detained us till seven. The interim was occupied with Milton, and I particularly preached patience out of

Samson Agonistes. When the rain subsided into a Scotch mist, we chose to consider it as appropriate and complimentary"—this from the beginning of Brown's journal. Well into the trip, he is less complimentary: "During the night there had fallen much rain; many fleas in the beds; and in the morning, clouds and drizzling rain prevented us from ascending Helvellyn." One commentator speaks of "the sheer wetness of the walking tour" and makes a point of "the irony of the inscription Keats composed for his own tombstone in Rome three years later: 'Here lies one whose name was writ in water.' " They had planned to cover two thousand difficult miles, including the distance from London.

The complex of issues facing Keats at this moment, this summer of 1818, still almost a year before the great spring odes, is crucial. Tom is dying, in the hands of friends; Keats's undercurrent of guilt about leaving his brother is manifest in the number and length of letters written to Tom (seven of the twelve) in sometimes antithetical circumstances. Keats himself has begun his tour in far less than perfect shape. Two weeks before starting out, he writes Severn that "The Doctor says I mustn't go out" and to Bailey that "I am not certain whether I shall be able to go on my Journey on account of my Brother Tom and a little indisposition of my own"—both prophetic admissions. Another prophecy, related to weather and health, is his complaint to Reynolds, from Teignmouth two *months* before, that "We are here still enveloped in clouds—I lay awake last night—listening to the Rain with a sense of being drown'd and rotted like a grain of wheat." Yet a controlling issue is Keats's sense of mission regarding this prologue to the life he intends, however long or brief that life may be. "I find cavalier days are gone by," he writes his publisher, Taylor. "I know nothing I have read nothing and I mean to follow Solomon's directions of 'get Wisdom—get understanding,' " by which he means to seek out experience itself, particularly the experience of the sublime—that surpassing visual and spiritual sense, for instance, that landscape and the natural world, at their most awe-inspiring, give to the viewer. "There is no such thing as time and space, which by the way came forcibly upon me on seeing for the first hour the Lake and Mountains of Winander—I cannot describe them—they surpass my expectation—beautiful water—shores and islands green to the marge—mountains all round up to the clouds"—this from his first journal-letter to Tom barely twenty-four hours north of Lancaster.

A few days later, July 1, landscape as a fact, if not as a sublimity, will have temporarily degenerated to little more than scenery. It is the nobility and "the glory of Patriotism" in the guise of Scottish dancers—"as fine a row of boys and girls as you ever saw"—that will for now supersede the countryside. The preference for people over the picturesque is not new for Keats, but here in this passage in Ireby ("the oldest market town in Cumberland"), in which "The difference between our country danes and these scotch figures, is about the same as leisurely stirring a cup o'Tea & heating up a batter pudding," his love of true community is revalued. "This is what," he says in his second letter to Tom, "I like better than scenery." But most of the people whom he and Brown encounter are far from being fresh country dancers. Many are either wandering veterans of King George's various wars, men such as Wordsworth's leech gatherer, unemployed, marginalized, surviving; or simple, poor tenant farmers who live with their families in dirt-floor cottages or "very small and low" huts. Sometimes, as one contemporary travel writer puts it, the housing is so temporary that it "must very soon fall down," consisting "of four stakes of birch, forked at the top, driven into the ground; on these they lay four other birch poles, and then form a gable at each end by putting up more birch sticks, and crossing them sufficiently to support the clods with which they plaster this skeleton of a hut all over, except a small hole in the side for a window, a small door to creep in and out at, and a hole in the roof ... The covering of these huts is turf cut about five or six inches thick and put on as soon as taken from the moor. ...." Ireland, Keats comes to believe in just the briefest of visits, is even worse on the human poverty scale. The Scots are at least relatively clean and orderly. "The barefoot Girls look very much in keeping—I mean with the Scenery about them—Brown praises their cleanliness and appearance of comfort—the neatness of their cottages &c It may be—they are very squat among trees and ferns and heaths and broom, on levels slopes and heights—They are very pleasant because they are primitive—but I wish they were as snug as those up the Devonshire vallies."

In addition to old soldiers, farmers, shepherds, and barefoot girls, they will run across any number of characters, from "an old toper, Richard Radshaw, drunk as a sponge," once prominent and well off but then his good wife died, to the "Traveller" who claims to have seen Edmund Kean on stage in a Shakespeare play though he cannot remember which, plus numerous landladies and guides. In Ireland, the encounters with "poor dirty creatures" will set in Keats's mind the low standard, including a site between Portpatrick and Belfast of such grotesquerie that Keats is both repulsed and fascinated. He records it as if he were rendering a landscape or a portrait. He writes to Tom in his fifth letter: "On our return from Bellfast we met a Sadan—the Duchess of Dunghill—It is no laughing matter tho—Imagine the worst dog kennel you ever saw placed upon the two poles from a mouldy fencing—In such a wretched thing sat a squalid old Woman squat like an ape half starved from scarcity of Buiscuit in its passage from Madagascar to the cape,—with a pipe in her mouth and looking out with a round-eyed skinny lidded, inanity—with a sort of horizontal idiotic movement of her head—squat and lean she sat and puff'd out the smoke while two ragged tattered Girls carried her along—What a thing would be the history of her Life and sensations."

4

AND SENSATIONS. THE SENSES, THE SENSUAL, THE FEELING life, the emotive imagination that will become the trademark and hallmark of the personality of Keats's best work will come to stand in direct contrast to his most self-consciously ambitious work, which is to write with what he imagines to be philosophic impact and import. But Keats's intellectual ambitions will ultimately be absorbed, because his empathic, undeviating emotional intelligence is essential to his artistic temperament. Cowden Clarke remarks that a young Keats's response to a detail from Spenser's *Faerie Queene* was to hoist "himself up, and looked burly and dominant, as he said, 'what an image that is—*sea-shouldering whales!*' " And another time, Clarke remembers, "when we were reading the 'Cymbeline' aloud, I saw his eyes fill with tears, and his voice faltered when he came to the departure of Posthumous, and Imogen saying she would have watched him—

> *'Till the diminution*
> *Of space had pointed him sharp as my needle;*
> *Nay follow'd him till he had* melted from
> The smallness of a gnat to air*; and then*
> *Have turn'd mine eye and wept.'"*

Years later, Keats would tease Woodhouse with the extravagance that he could enter the life of a billiard ball as it rolled over the tabletop, with "a sense of delight from its own roundness, smoothness, volubility, & the rapidity of its motion."

Speaking through the correlatives of the senses and identifying with the correct colors and shadings of emotion, finding *that* language will become second nature to Keats. But after the sleepy dusks and odorous shades of *Endymion*, after the grotesque luxuries of Isabella combing the hair, kissing the face, planting the corpse of her dead lover's severed head into a grand pot of basil as if it were an urn, after the floral influence of Hunt and the high-minded hyperbole of Haydon, after "The stretched metre of an antique song" that *Endymion* and *Isabella* represent, Keats is looking to treat his subjects "in a more naked and Grecian Manner." Of all the great poetic hopes implicit in the intended transformative length and depth of the Northern tour, the powerful effects of the landscape and its people and the rich testing experience of travel are preeminent. The Duchess of Dunghill represents a kind of gothic landscape, just as the mountains and lakes, waterfalls and sun-streaking clouds are valuable only to the extent that they can be identified with, not as personifiers but as collaborators of thought and feeling and awe. The impulse is Wordsworthian; the practice, in the mode of the objective lyric, will become Keatsian. And though both approaches to nature interrogate and celebrate the human, for the poet there is always the core question of style, of form, of reach, of numinous emotional power. When Keats writes Haydon—who is still a mentor in January 1818—that "in Endymion I think you may have many bits of the deep and sentimental cast—the nature of *Hyperion* will lead me to treat it in a more naked and Grecian Manner—and the march of passion and endeavour will be undeviating," he is already understanding that something remarkable must change in his art. *How* it will change is something else again. The beauties and luxuries of the Hunt era in his poems must turn into writ-

ing that is harder, truer, larger, what he is consistently referring
to as "more philosophic." In Keats's mind the greater lyric he is
looking for, as an accommodation to the size of his ambition—an
ambition to compete with Wordsworth, Milton, even Dante—is
not lyric at all but a new notion of epic, which his first references
to *Hyperion* suggest. The *march* of passion and the *undeviating*
"endeavour" speak to length, scope, totality. *Hyperion*, by far his
most ambitious conception of a poem to date, is part of his plan
well before he has any clear program of how to achieve it, how
to start, how to set himself up to write it. He is intuiting that
the bower enclosures of his early poems, right up through the
embowering in *Endymion*—which he has really just completed in
the winter of 1817—must open or at least enlarge to include the
complexity, the simultaneous light and dark, of an imaginative
world capable of "negative capability."

Much of his important thinking—thinking well beyond the
skills and substance of the early poems—is replete in the letters,
in which the discussion and debate—really with himself—has
been going on a year or more before the commitment to trav-
eling, walking through the north, is ever sealed. The letters to
Reynolds, to Bailey, to his publisher Taylor, even to his brothers
in this period between the fall of 1817 through the spring of 1818
create close to a narrative of his transformation as a meditator,
then maker of poetry. Many of his most famous utterances on the
shape and spirit of his mission appear in advance of its execution
as poetry—not as theory so much as a thoughtful working-out,
a workshop of ideas put to practical use as well as a valuing of
the past, particularly the aspects of those past poets useful to his
project. In November 1817 he writes to Bailey that he is "Certain
of nothing but the holiness of the Heart's affection and the truth
of Imagination—What the imagination seizes as Beauty must be
truth." In December he writes to George and Tom that "several

things dovetailed in my mind, & at once it struck me, what quality went to form a Man of Achievement especially in Literature & which Shakespeare possessed so enormously—I mean *Negative Capability*, that is when a man is capable of being in uncertainties, Mysteries, doubts, without any irritable reaching after fact & reason." In February 1818 he writes to Reynolds that "We hate poetry that has a palpable design upon us—and if we do not agree, seems to put its hand in its breeches pocket. Poetry should be great & unobtrusive, a thing which enters one's soul, and does not startle it or amaze it with itself but with its subject. — How beautiful are the retired flowers! how would they lose their beauty were they to throng into the highway crying out, 'admire me I am a violet! dote upon me I am a primrose!' " In May, to Reynolds again, "I will put down a simile of human life as far as I now perceive it . . . I compare human life to a large Mansion of Many Apartments, two of which I can only describe, the doors to the rest being as yet shut upon me—The first step into we call the infant or thoughtless Chamber, in which we remain as long as we do not think—We remain there a long while, and not withstanding the doors of the second Chamber remain wide open, show a bright appearance, we care not to hasten to it; but are at length imperceptibly impelled by the awakening of the thinking principle—within us—we no sooner get into the second Chamber, which I shall call the Chamber of Maiden-Thought, than we become intoxicated with the light and the atmosphere."

Gradually, Keats continues, this chamber of maiden thought becomes darkened "and at the same time on all sides of it many doors are set open—but all dark—all leading to dark passages— We see not the ballance of good and evil." He concludes—and includes Reynolds—"We are in a Mist—we are now in that state—We feel the 'burden of the Mystery.' " The growth of mind over this relatively short period anticipates the growth in the quality of the poetry, though it does not guarantee it. A year before, in the fall of 1816, Keats apologizes to Severn that he will not be able to meet for a Saturday afternoon walk through some ambient countryside, "especially because I particularly want to look into some beautiful Scenery—for poetical purposes." This is at least a light year from the philosophical passage of letters that will soon follow and the decision to take on the Northern walking tour, with all its sublime scenic promise for Keats's post-*Endymion* poetry. In his brightest moments, Keats was always looking for a new era in his existence, whether it was meeting Hunt or Haydon or Wordsworth or encountering intimate or great landscapes or confronting the awesome Elgin Marbles or falling in love. *Endymion* had been "a test of Invention"; *Hyperion*, as thought up and thought about, would be on a whole different stylistic and conceptual scale altogether. Keats sees the walking tour as the literal first step in achieving his ambition, an ambition directed toward the writing of an epic poem, or a poem on an epic stage, worthy of the English poets—of Spenser, Milton, and Wordsworth, whose *Prelude*, the last true English attempt at a new epic vision, he will never know about. "Why endeavour after a long Poem? ... Do not the Lovers of Poetry like to have a little Region to wander in where they may pick and choose, and in which the images are so numerous that many are forgotten and found new in a second Reading: which may be food for a Week's stroll in the Summer." This certainly describes the method in *Endymion*, an exercise of "4000 Lines of one bare circumstance" filled with set pieces of poetry, and filled out episodically. *Hyperion*, however, will need a different, inherently compelling method, a means transparent to the energy, sweep, and story of its subject. It will need a language purged of every excess but power. It will need an organic yet commanding raison d'être.

"Did our great Poets ever write short Pieces?" This youth-

ful and largely rhetorical question begs the question of length
that has preoccupied Keats from the beginning of his commit-
ment to poetry, the result being that until the spring of 1819, his
breakthrough spring, he tends to write exclusively what might be
termed "spot" sonnets—that is, sonnets in and of the moment—
or protracted verse narratives, rhyming in couplets, thought out
in couplets, saved from their closed-in eighteenth-century dat-
edness by their continuing enjambments—and, of course, by
their whole feeling life. "I stood Tip-Toe . . ." and "Sleep and
Poetry" are the obvious hopeful examples. *Endymion* stretches
almost past endurance the beautifications of these two earlier
poems, and though it keeps the couplet intact, the result is to
much greater, more complicated, accumulating effect. ("And, as
he passed, each lifted up its head, / As doth a flower at Apollo's
touch. / Death felt it to his inwards—'twas too much: / Death
fell a-weeping in his charnel-house. / The Latmian persevered
along, and thus / All were re-animated.") *Hyperion* will chose
Milton as its model and speak in martial blank verse, a profound
adjustment for Keats, once he has configured what he wants to
say and how to structure—really, how to begin—what is for
him a more demanding and searching form. "The Polar Star of
Poetry," an epic structure of undulant lyric intensity, a construct
of the mind about the mind divided, a sustained archetypal act of
the negatively capable imagination.

5

FIRST, THOUGH, THE TRIAL AND ERROR OF EYE-LEVEL EXPE-
rience. If *Hyperion* becomes, in part, Keats's response to his
inward Northern journey, the letters to Tom and a few favored

others are the record, however elevated, of the visible, physical tour, which is for Keats no less an expectant traveling to a new world than George's crossing to America. "Here beginneth my journal, this Thursday, the 25th of June, Anno Domini 1818," Keats self-mockingly writes to Tom. In the course of the twelve letters—which in the main amount to a running account of their place-to-place daily excursions and his and Brown's commerce with the local population—Keats consistently touches on the bad food ("we dined yesterday on dirty bacon dirtier eggs and dirtiest Potatoes with a slice of Salmon"), the weather ("We are detained this morning by the rain"), and his health ("I shall be prudent and more careful of my health than I have been"). He also, curiously, brings up the more serious matter of his mortality, or immortality— more than once and in different disguises. In his second journal letter, to George and Georgiana, he closes with the cryptic comment that "We will before many Years are over have written many folio volumes which as a Matter of self-defence to one whom you understand intends to be immortal in the best points and let all his Sins and peccadillos die away." In his sixth letter, to Reynolds, at the end of a commentary on what comes out as "Family values"—praising Reynolds's soon-to-be wedding, celebrating George's choice of a mate, anticipating "my little Nephews in America"—he concludes that "Things like these, and they are real, have made me resolve to have a care of my health." And in the ninth letter, to Bailey, in a reference to his young sister, "She is very much prisoned from me—I am afraid it will be some time before I can take her to many places I wish—I trust we shall see you ere long in Cumberland—at least I hope I shall before my visit to America more than once I intend to pass a whole year with George if I live to the completion of the three next."

The three years next add up to something over a thousand days. If you count the date of the letter to Bailey, July 18, 1818, Keats has almost exactly 945 days to live. You need not get into misty areas of numerology, psychic phenomenon, or the palmistry of fate to be aware that Keats is intuiting a fatalism well supported by the evidence of his family, particularly on his mother's side, where consumption has been a common source of death. Indeed it is common in the culture, just as the pale, suffering artist, coughing into a white handkerchief, is a cultural cliché. After all, Keats has written, mere months before, his highly rhetorical Shakespearean sonnet "When I have fears that I may cease to be." Is that not a prediction, or at least a preoccupation? Well, yes, in a Romantic poet sort of way; but when you hear the poem out, it becomes much more interested in love than in death, appealing more to carpe diem than *mortis causa* ("And when I feel, fair creature of an hour! / That I shall never look upon thee more . . ."). This reference in the letter to Bailey, however, is different. It is written straight out in prose and it is located within the context of Keats's family, not his art. It is addressed to someone directly. And it is different in tone and impulse from the "morbidity of temperament" often assigned to Keats—his "blue devils," his sudden changes of mood, his ups and downs evident in many of his letters, where in a moment he can go from self-mockery and brilliant wit to self-analysis to depression or indolence. The letters from the Northern tour are only just less ambivalent in state of mind, and thoroughly muted in those to Tom. Yet nowhere in the travel letters, or in their actual travels, does Keats's combination of concerns come into greater focus than in his and Brown's stopover visits to the burial place and birthplace of Robert Burns—the Scots national poet—in Dumfries and Alloway, respectively, at the beginning and in the middle of July.

Wordsworth had been a disappointment. He had been an absent monument, and worse was the reason for his absence—his apparent conversion to the Tory cause, demonstrated firsthand in his canvassing for the Viscount Lowther. Thanks to Tory support, he had been able to give up poverty in the process of his political support. Burns, on the other hand, who died of drink at thirty-six, the year after Keats's birth, had stayed true to his birthright liberal principles, whether by poverty, passion, or poetry. As Keats writes to Tom, in the third letter, "You will see by this sonnet that I am at Dumfries . . . Burns' tomb is in the Churchyard corner, not very much to my taste, though on a scale, large enough to show they wanted to honor him—Mrs. Burns lives in this place, most likely we shall see her tomorrow—This Sonnet I have written in a strange mood, half asleep." Throughout the travel letters Keats supplements his journal prose with poems—some serious, some comic, some parodies of the locals, some plain bad; this was a habit in much of his correspondence his whole writing life. As a practice it seemed to remove a certain pressure to compose. If he could fold a poem in among a conversation, it might enter the world sidelong, like an afterthought or an extracurricular activity. Even the odes seem to have been sketched on scraps of paper before being organized and fair-copied. The sonnet he offers Tom just pops up in some news about hearing from Georgiana, a letter forwarded from Liverpool. Keats likes the poem enough to pass it on even though it is reminiscent of praise sonnets to Hunt and Haydon and others he has admired from an earlier era in his development.

The Town, the churchyard, & the setting sun,
The Clouds, the trees, the rounded hills all seem
Though beautiful, Cold—strange—as in a dream,
I dreamed long ago, now new begun . . .

There follow a few weak lines, then an abrupt insight: "All is cold Beauty; pain is never done." Then a closing apology: "I have oft honoured thee. Great shadow; hide / Thy face, I sin against thy native skies." Except for a possible feeling of humility, it is not clear why Keats feels the need for an apology to Burns, even rhetorically. Perhaps the effects of his first experience with scotch have already started ("half asleep")—instead of the next day, as he claims. "There are plenty of wretched Cottages, where smoke has no outlet but by the door—We have now begun upon whiskey, called here *whuskey* very smart stuff it is—Mixed like our liquors with sugar & water tis called toddy, very pretty drink, & much praised by Burns."

Of course, there is no reason to question Keats's letter inclusion of his sonnet "On visiting the Tomb of Burns"; it is in part his homage to a figure he admires, in addition to being a compositional habit. It is as well an attempt to make a meaningful moment memorable. A week later he writes to Tom that "These kirkmen have done Scotland harm—they have banished puns and laughing and kissing (except in cases where the very danger and crime must make it very fine and gustful. I shall make a full stop at kissing for after that there should be a better paren*t*thesis: and go on to remind you of the fate of Burns. Poor unfortunate fellow—his disposition was southern—how sad it is when a luxurious imagination is obliged in self defence to deaden its delicacy in vulgarity, and riot in things attainable that it may not have leisure to go mad after things which are not." This remarkable statement—unusual in its discourse from Keats's normal tone with Tom—suggests one poet's further empathy with another poet, then pushes toward a deeper identification. It is as if Keats were talking about himself, about a southern luxurious imagination in conflict with hard northern reality, and about the longing created by the impasse. The tomb sonnet for Burns is—whatever else it is—nonthreatening; its posture is familiar, celebratory: "Cold beauty" even anticipates "Cold Pastoral" in the urn ode, both funereal oxymorons. Then, two weeks after the visit to Burns's grave, Keats and Brown arrive in Alloway, outside of Ayr, where Burns was born. In the letter to Reynolds, Keats seems to be writing en route: "I am approaching Burns's Cottage very fast—We have made continual enquiries from the times we saw his Tomb at Dumfries—his name of course is known all about—his great reputation among the plodding people is 'that he wrote a good MONY sensible things'—One of the pleasantest means of annulling self is approaching such a shrine as the Cottage of Burns—we need not think of his misery—that is all gone—bad luck to it."

Keats's spirit seems high: He and Brown are "talking on different and indifferent things, when on a sudden we turned a corner upon the immediate county of Aire—the Sight was as rich as possible—I had no Conception that the native place of Burns was so beautiful—the Idea I had was more desolate, his rigs of Barley seemed always to me but a few strips of Green on a cold hill—O prejudices! it was rich as Devon." Keats's investment in what he is seeing as he warms to the sight feels profoundly more personal than the reports from the Lake District. "I endeavour'd to drink in the Prospect, that I might spin it out to you"—he is still writing to Reynolds—"as the silkworm makes silk from the Mulbery leaves."

Besides all the Beauty, there were the Mountains of
Annan Isle, black and huge over the Sea—We came
down upon every thing suddenly—there were in our way,
the "bonny Doon," with the Brig that Tam O'Shanter
cross'd—Kirk Alloway, Burns's Cottage and then the
Brigs of Ayr—First we stood upon the Bridge across

the Doon; surrounded by every Phantasy of Green in
tree, Meadow, and Hill,—the Stream of the Doon, as a
Farmer told us, is covered with trees from head to foot—
you know those beautiful heaths so fresh against the
weather of a summers evening—there was one stretching
along behind the trees.

Then Keats's high spirits get the better of him.

I wish I knew always the humour my friends would be in
at opening a letter of mine, to suit it to them as nearly
as possible I could always find an egg shell for Melan-
choly—and as for Merriment a Witty humour will turn
any thing to Account—my head is sometimes in such a
whirl in considering the million likings and antipathies
of our Moments—that I can get into no settled strain in
my Letters—My Wig! Burns and sentimentality coming
across you and frank Floodgate in the office—O scenery
that thou shouldst be crush'd between two Puns—

One of the puns is allusive, the other private: "I can suck mel-
ancholy out of a song, as a weasel sucks eggs" (*As You Like It*,
II.v.12–14). Frank Fladgate Sr. had taken Reynolds on as a "pupil"
in his law office, along with Frank Fladgate Jr. Keats's head in a
whirl is just where his head is at this moment, with or without the
toddies. "We went to the Cottage and took some Whiskey—I
wrote a sonnet for the mere sake of writing some lines under the
roof—they are so bad I cannot transcribe them." The sonnet at
the grave site invokes the same eulogic idea: a moment's monu-
ment to honor a memory. But apparently Keats has a better opin-
ion of the first than of this second, birthplace, sonnet. Once inside
the birth cottage, his mood has shifted radically. "The Man at the

Cottage was a great Bore with his Anecdotes—I hate the rascal—his Life consists of fuz, fuzzy, fuzziest—He drinks glasses five for the Quarter and twelve for the hour,—he is a mahogany faced Jackass who knew Burns—He ought to be kicked for having spoken to him." You could chalk up this abrupt change in mood to many sources, not the least the whiskey (Keats's small body had low tolerance). But four days later he is still bringing the birth-cottage incident up, this time to Tom. "Then we proceeded to the Cottage he was born in . . . We drank some Toddy to Burns's Memory with an old Man who knew Burns—damn him—and damn his Anecdotes—he was a great bore—it was impossible for a Southren to understand about 5 words in a hundred—There was something good in his description of Burns's melancholy the last time he saw him. I was determined to write a sonnet in the Cottage—I did—but it is so bad I cannot venture it here—." And the next day, in Keats's letter to Bailey, he mentions the cottage visit and the failed sonnet again: "I had determined to write a Sonnet in the Cottage. I did but lauk it was so wretched I destroyed it."

Later, in his aborted biography of Keats, Brown notes that the turning of Burns's birthplace into what amounts to a whiskey shop had a considerable effect "towards the annihilation of Keats's poetic power." Brown, however, as was his tendency with many of Keats's poems, saved the much-referred-to birthplace sonnet anyway—entitled prophetically with its first line, "This mortal body of a thousand days." Indeed, speaking of mortal bodies, there is a goodly list of Keats's poetry savers, fair-copiers, and poem keepers. At different times George, Tom, Brown, Woodhouse, even Charles Dilke and Cowden Clarke, among others, preserved the poetry, recognizing the need and the importance for the future.

Keats, though, had something of a quixotic attitude toward

the maintenance of his poems, his shorter poems in particular. This is not to suggest that he was in any way indifferent to their value as potentially published works, but rather that for a mind in a whirl of "considering the million likings and antipathies of our Moments," anything more than the fluidity of composition was beyond his immediate concentration, if not concern. Brown, in the biography, recalls that "In the spring of 1819 a nightingale had built her nest in my house. Keats felt a tranquil and continual joy in her song; and one morning he took a chair from the breakfast-table to the grass plot under a plum-tree, where he sat for two or three hours. When he came into the house, I perceived he had some scraps of paper in his hand, and these he was quietly thrusting behind the books. On inquiry, I found those scraps, four or five in number, containing his poetic feeling on the song of our nightingale. The writing was not well legible; and it was difficult to arrange the stanzas on so many scraps. With his assistance, I succeeded." You have to wonder what "Ode to a Nightingale" might have become without Keats's ordering assistance, let alone his rendering of murky individual stanzas on scraps.

6

SCRAPS AND THROWAWAYS AND PARTS OF LETTERS: KEATS DID usually get around to fair-copying his own lyric poems, though not always. He had ambition's eye regarding his perception of the lyric, the shorter form. He believed in it insofar as it went. It was not long enough or big enough or, sometimes—in the case of his occasional sonnets—important enough to think of beyond the therapy or comedy of the moment. This is not to say that he was a disinterested sonnet and/or lyric writer; he is among the finest makers of sonnets in the language, whereas the great odes depend in their stanzaic intelligence on an editing and variation of the English, Italian, and Spenserian sonnet forms and the Spenserian stanza. It is to say when Keats writes to George, two months after returning from the Northern tour and after the first, and most damaging, of the *Endymion* reviews had appeared, that the bad notices are "a mere matter of the moment—I think I shall be among the English Poets after my death," he is expressing faith; it is to say that Keats believed not only that the epic, or long, long poem, was the means to immortality but that he believed he had the gift and endurance to create one, perhaps more than one. All he needed was time. *Endymion*, as he had said all along, was a young man's practice, an apprenticeship, not unlike those years he had spent preparing for and studying at Guy's Hospital. Short pieces might be the jewel in the symbolist's eye—the world in small for the sonneteer—but at this point they were not, in Keats's mind, capable of the scale of the sublime as he imagined necessary for posterity. Yet his first breakthrough poem, after some thirty poems of mostly sonnets, epistles, and occasional flatteries, was a grand sonnet entitled "On First Looking into Chapman's Homer," a gesture of no small visionary sweep within small compass, a poem drawn from a book among other books, with a mistake in it. That was more than a year ago. Since then he had published his first collection of poems, plus *Endymion*. Most of the poems, by title, were sonnets, short pieces.

The "Chapman's Homer" sonnet proposes a landscape of the mind, a summary of poetic allusions from reading "in the realms of gold." None of the "goodly states and kingdoms," however, compare to the revelation, the "pure serene," of "deep-browed Homer" as translated by Elizabethan George Chapman, especially when read "out loud and bold."

Then felt I like some watcher of the skies
When a new planet swims into his ken;
Or like stout Cortez when with eagle eyes
He stared at the Pacific—and all his men
Looked at each other with a wild surmise—
Silent, upon a peak in Darien.

It is probably unfair, in terms of apples and oranges, to place states and kingdoms against the skies and the discovery of a whole new ocean. The sheer geography reduced in size and focused here is amazing, and in its way puts the size and scale of the sonnet form to the test. And it is ironic that the source of the epiphanic vision is Homer himself, epic poet. Keats gets so lost in the excitement of his vision that he confuses Cortez, conqueror of the Quetzalcoatl cultures, with Vasco Núñez de Balboa, who actually discovered the Pacific. Regardless, after this October 1817 sonnet, Keats's first of an objectifying authority, he really does begin to travel in green and golden realms as he starts to work out—in his letters and the best of the poems—a sense of his aesthetic "principles" as well as a commitment to the call of forms transcendent of a page or two. At the core, this developing idea of his mission is his chief motive for the Northern tour—to find sources and the scale for great poetry, large poetry, poetry with philosophic backbone, mythic proportion. Thus far in his life he has been limited to fine pastoral scenes within the radius or a coach ride of London, landscapes he has grown up with: fields ready for harvest, cathedral elms parted by country lanes, heath, heather, and moor. Or he has pored his eyes into books, paintings, and sculpture. The North Country—beginning with the Lake District and the Lowlands and climaxing in the Inner Hebrides, the Highlands, and Ben Nevis—is his first experience with the wild, the free-ranging, and the otherworldly.

Good or bad, sonnets are a natural form for Keats, a kind of note-taking of a heightened moment, whether the occasion is located in society or in nature. Because he is writing under difficult circumstances, the poetry parts of his letters from the North must needs be entertainment (ballads, parodies) or short serious poems (sonnets). Of the many examples of his various moods, the poem "To Ailsa Rock" is, he says to Tom, "the only Sonnet of any worth I have of late written."

It is July 10, and Keats and Brown are making their way up the western coast of Scotland hoping to arrive in Ayr, and at Burns's birthplace, the next day. It is, of course, raining, not too heavily but nonetheless a slow soak. Everything is shades and intensities of green. "After two or three Miles of this we turned suddenly into a magnificent glen finely wooded in Parts—seven Miles long—with a Mountain Stream winding down the Midst . . . At the end we had a gradual ascent and got among the tops of Mountains whence In a little time I descried in the Sea Ailsa Rock 940 feet hight—it was 15 Miles distant and seemed close upon us—The effect of ailsa with the peculiar perspective of the Sea in connection with the ground we stood on, and the misty rain falling gave me a complete Idea of a deluge—Ailsa struck me very suddenly—" This was the degree of visual experience that Keats had begun to realize in Wordsworth country two weeks before, and now the ante had risen. The sonnet itself is like a real-life parallel to the bookish Chapman sonnet with—this time—Keats in the role of explorer, discoverer.

> Hearken, thou craggy ocean pyramid!
> Give answer by thy voice, the sea-fowls' screams!
> When were thy shoulders mantled in hug streams?
> When from the sun was thy broad forehead hid?

The poem continues with four more lines of rhetorical questions—an interrogative mode in many of his lyrics—and answers them with "Thou answer'st not; for thou art dead asleep. / Thy life is but two dead eternities—The last in air, the former in the deep, / First with the whales, last with the eagle-skies." Sonnets are not only natural to Keats, they can be—as he would conclude later—fairly easy to write—fun, in fact, regardless of the subject. What is interesting here is the value he places on this sonnet compared with, say, the more personal, revealing, and certainly intimate sonnet "On Visiting the Tomb of Burns," written a few days before the "complete Idea" of Ailsa. (Keats, remember, will also speak most highly of "Ode to Psyche" in the mix of the spring odes of 1819.) Something about the elevation of thought and language, the idea, appeals to Keats. "Ailsa Rock" is more public as a performance, safer, distant. It is, indeed, about distance, perspective—temporal as well as spatial—the sublime writ small. The day after this recommended sonnet is the day he and Brown spend much of the afternoon with the "mahogany faced old Jackass" who runs the whiskey shop that is, in the Scots national memory, Burns's birthplace, the jackass who, to Keats, is an insult to Burns's integrity and to the grave-site memorial and who is "the flat dog" who "made me write a flat sonnet." That is on July 11, roughly 950 days before the end.

"This mortal body of a thousand days" is considered by Keats so bad, so mortal in itself that he must destroy it—an act so unusual in his career that you would have to go back to his earliest days as a fledgling poet, when some of his verse *was* bad, to find a similar purging. The question arises, why would he value even the least of his list of spontaneous lyrics and sonnets and parodies on this walking trip and so expressly devalue the sonnet he writes in Burns's birth cottage—a poem he intends as a more appropriate homage than even the tomb sonnet, written days before, at the actual grave, a sonnet that practically genuflects its humility ("Great shadow, hide / Thy face! I sin against thy native skies")? Could the old whiskey seller be that much of a distraction? "His gab," says Keats to Reynolds, "hindered my sublimity." On the other hand, Keats seems to be blaming Burns, too, when he continues, in the Reynolds letter, toward the sad conclusion that Burns's "Misery is a dead weight upon the nimbleness of one's quill—I tried to forget it—to drink Toddy without any Care—to write a merry Sonnet—it wont do—he talked with Bitches—he drank with Blackguards, he was miserable—We can see horribly clear in the works of such a man his whole life, as if we were God's spies." Horrible clarity does not sort well with trying "to write a merry Sonnet," for sure. And being a spy capable of reading the hidden life between the lines of anyone's work is itself a mixed blessing, because invariably the work reads you. The July 11 sonnet, composed in minutes within the confines of the *spiritus mundi* of Burns's birthplace, while outside lies the Tam o'Shanter, intimate Burns countryside and beyond that, south and north, the majestic Ailsa Craig and the mountains of the island of Arran ("a grand Sea view terminated by the black Mountains of the isle of Annan. As soon as I saw them so nearly I said to myself 'How is it they did not beckon Burns to some grand attempt at Epic?' "): This July 11 sonnet is almost painful in its nakedness and directness.

> *This mortal body of a thousand days*
> *Now fills, O Burns, a space in thine own room,*
> *Where thou didst dream alone on budded bays,*
> *Happy and thoughtless of thy day of doom!*
> *My pulse is warm with thine own barley-bree,*

My head is light with pledging a great soul,
My eyes are wandering, and I cannot see,
    Fancy is dead and drunken at its goal:
Yet can I stamp my foot upon the floor,
    Yet can I ope thy window-sash to find
The meadow thou hast tramped o'er and o'er
    Yet can I think of thee till thought is blind,
Yet can I gulp a bumper to thy name—
O smile among the shades, for this is fame!

Whatever its confessional exposure—and Keats would have, first of all, rejected that direct an exposure—the rather didactic impulse of this sonnet is against a basic poetic principle of Keats, that poetry must not have a palpable design on the reader. The poem is not only obvious, it is angry; it is a bit "drunken at its goal." It is clearly aggressive, with a muscling attitude unusual in Keats. Its rhetorical stance, in keeping, is no less out front, assertive line by line. Although its rhyme scheme is English (three quatrains and a closing couplet), its argument is Italian (octave, sestet): The first eight lines define a state of being, the follow-up six pledge what "can be"—thus, also, what is. The hyperbolic tone, however, is more than simply barley-bree rhetoric. It is a way, emotionally, to fill the figurative room of the sonnet form and the literal room of Burns's space. The poem must have scared Keats because of its unmitigation, because of its apparently untransformed identification with the misery, the narrowness, the limitation of Burns's perceived life. The stamping on the floor, the opening of the window are vain attempts to break out of the claustrophobia; even thinking becomes blind, and the best I can do is to do what you did: gulp a bumper. Keats toasts Burns, but with the knowledge that this is what fame comes to—a smile among the shades, a name written in water. It comes to having your birthplace turned into a whiskey shop, as if to honor the cliché—the popular image of Burns—rather than his lyric words in their right order. Part of Keats's fear, here in this sonnet as well as in the travel letters, is that fame is not only ephemeral but founded in the least of things: flaws, popularity, inaccuracies, various memory.

As for immortality, it seems mortal too. Keats has just fifty days less than a thousand left. The figurative thousand—where does that come from? So far he has written a few excellent sonnets and many "weak-sided" ones, including, in his opinion, "This mortal body of a thousand days." In fact, it is so weak, or so revealing, that he is compelled to destroy it. *Endymion*, his apprentice try at an epic, is in hindsight a mortal exercise. Tom is ill, seriously ill, and Keats knows it; Keats may or may not ever see George again. His sister is virtually locked away. He understands the lineage of health—or ill health—that he has inherited. He has written nothing, before or here in the middle of the summer of 1818, in the middle of nowhere, that would even suggest immortality let alone earn it. And what is fame anyway if Burns is the template and this cottage, this "whuskey" space, is a testament to his memory and that outsized mausoleum in Dumfries, the grave of his poems? What is fame but a silent toast from an admirer who should perhaps have stayed silent? Ward, in her marvelous psychoanalytic narrative of Keats's life, states that the irony of "This mortal body of a thousand days" is summed up in the last line, "but the terror is in the first . . . Keats found himself staring at the prospect of his own death, less than three years ahead. The thought he meant never to express had slipped out, and as soon as he regained his balance he tried to expunge it." If Ward is speaking in terms of Keats's anxieties, and anxieties only, she may be correct. But why a thousand? Is it just a poetic number? If so, how could it be so close to the actual time line? Even Keats's medical knowledge does not account for the accuracy, especially because he was the most robust of the three brothers and Tom the most delicate. George, after all, lived into his forties. John Keats living into his forties, imagine that. Of course, then you would have to imagine Keats employed or making a living from his writing, his fame. You would have to imagine Keats owning property, voting Whig, or emigrating to America to become the first great American poet, famous or otherwise.

Another question arises. Keats knows his family's medical history in his bones; and for some time he has been painfully aware of Tom's marginal condition, an awareness reinforced by the fact of the sequence of travel letters, primarily to Tom. He may even have felt that, for the time being anyway, there was nothing more, medically, required for Tom, so why not take Brown's offer of companionship on a great walk. Tom himself seems to have encouraged both brothers in the fiction of his "doing better." This may not relieve the guilt, but it does change the scene and somewhat adjust the burden. Yet Keats, too, has been nagged by symptoms—colds, a certain indolence, and, specifically, an on-again, off-again sore throat. He has complained of a serious sore throat for no little while well before the trip north. Indeed, he has almost backed out on making the journey at the last minute for just that reason. Nevertheless, here he is, in the middle of one of the worst cold-catching climates on Earth, when nearly a whole year before he has "not been well enough to stand the chance of a Wet night." After the encounter with the ghosts of Burns, he and Brown head farther up the western coast of Scotland, to the Isle of Mull and environs, then, a week later, inland up through the Great Glen to make the climb of Ben Nevis, the highest point in Britain (4,400 feet). In the tenth letter, to Tom, Keats notes that "We set out, crossed two ferries, one to the isle of Kerrera of little distance, the other from Kererra to Mull 9

Miles across—we did it in forty minutes with a fine Breeze—The road through the Island, or rather the track is the most dreary you can think of—between dreary Mountains—over bog and rock and river with our Breeches tucked up and our Stockings in hand—" It is one thing to ride on the outside of the coach, the night coach or a coach in rain; it is another thing to walk over bog and rock and through mountain cold river water in your bare feet. And it is a third, even worse thing, to take to bed all that cold and dampness in "a shepherd's Hut" in "little compartments with the rafters and turf thatch blackened with smoke—the earth floor full of Hills and Dales."

The lodgings, the food (all oatcakes and watered whiskey), the chilblain climate of coastal Scotland and the inner islands must feel like punishment. Dr. Johnson thought so, humbled on his Shetland pony, when, along with Boswell, he tried to traverse the same territory. These elements certainly stand in contrast to the lake country where Keats and Brown began their journey: the Ambleside Waterfalls, for instance, near "Wynandermere," where "the weather is capital for views," and the "morning beautiful—the walk easy among the hills." The Falls themselves Keats spends a page on, as if to follow the stages of their tumbling. "What astonishes me more than any thing is the tone, the coloring, the slate, the stone, the moss, the rock-weed," he writes in his first enthusiastic letter to Tom, praising "the intellect, the countenance of such places." He goes on:

> *The space, the magnitude of mountains and waterfalls are well imagined before one sees them; but this countenance or intellectual tone must surpass every imagination and defy any remembrance. I shall learn poetry here and shall henceforth write more than ever, for the abstract endeavor of being able to add a mite to that mass of*

beauty which is harvested from these grand materials,
by the finest spirits, and put into existence for the relish
of one's fellows. I cannot think with Hazlitt that these
scenes make a man appear little. I never forgot my stature
so completely—I live in the eye; and my imagination,
surpassed, is at rest.

There is a quality of the intimate sublime in this reaction; there is also innocence, the hype of new experience turned into extravagance, with a seasoning of high-mindedness and literariness. Weeks later, having "surpassed" the poverties of the Lowlands and eastern Ireland, the Presbyterian graveyard and birthplace of Burns, a calendar of "characters," the soaking rains, the twenty and more miles a day of walking, the same clothes, the same food, the same gray hostels and cottages—overnights they could afford—after weeks of this, Keats has become wiser about the great wild country he is seeing but no less alive to it. And he understands he has paid a price. "I should not have consented to myself these four Months tramping in the highlands," he writes on July 22 to Bailey, "but that I thought it would give me more experience, rub off more Prejudice, use me to more hardship, identify finer scenes load me with grander Mountains, and strengthen my reach in Poetry, than would stopping at home among Books even though I should reach Homer." More—of course—like four weeks than four months.

And if, in his sonnet responding to Chapman's translation, he had reached Homer, he had not by any stretch even begun to achieve the reach of Homer, the epic. That does not mean he would not die trying. Ambition seemed to be surpassing the "prudent and more careful" concern of health. The Northern excursion had been meant, in great part, as a curative to the safe indulgences of *Endymion*—as a firsthand access to finer scenes, grander mountains, realer places. Yet in the same letter in which he reiterates his artistic ambition, the letter in which he destroys the "body of a thousand days" sonnet and offers Bailey its antidote: an extended fourteener in couplets, also preoccupied with "mortal days" and dying "of fame unshorn," in the same letter he underscores his prescience of a mortal timetable: "I intend to pass a whole year with George if I live to the completion of the next three": a timetable that he almost meets exactly.

He and Brown cross from Oban to Mull by ferry on July 22, then find themselves on "a most wretched walk of 37 miles across the Island," more tired, more wet and chilled with every mile. From Mull they will boat to Iona and from there to Staffa and to one of Keats's ultimate destinations, Fingal's Cave. In spite of his cold and sore throat, Keats's spirits are high. In his next to last letter to Tom (July 26), he runs a stream of descriptive detail as to the sights he is seeing, most of them ancient kirk artifacts and ruins ("But I will first mention Icolmkill . . . Who would expect to find the ruins of a fine Cathedral Church, of Cloisters, Colleges, Monasteries and Nunneries in so remote an Island?") or "magnificent Woods" and "many tombs of Highland Chieftans," culminating in a boat passage around and careful mooring at Staffa.

> *I am puzzled how to give you an Idea of Staffa . . . One may compare the surface of the Islands to a roof—this roof is supported by grand pillars of basalt standing together as thick as honey combs. The finest thing is Fingal's Cave—it is entirely a hollowing out of Basalt Pillars. Suppose now the Giants who rebelled against Jove had taken a whole Mass of black Columns and bound them together like bunches of matches—and then with immense Axes had made a cavern in the body of*

these columns—of course the roof and floor must be
composed of the broken ends of the Columns—such is
Fingal's Cave except that the Sea has done the work of
excavations and is continually dashing there—so that we
walk along the sides of the cave on the pillars which are
left as if for convenient Stairs—

"The Cave," concludes Keats, "far surpasses the finest
Cathedrall" for "solemnity and grandeur." He has found what he
imagines he has been looking for—a sense of the sublime beyond
"mere Scenes," in a natural setting worthy of awe, and alive with
visual drama. The visit to these inner islands off the Scottish coast
and the port town of Oban mark the actual beginning of Keats's
transformation from the *Endymion* poet to the *Hyperion* poet,
with the one in print and available to criticism and the other in
mind and still to be realized. The cloistered, lush bower, exposed
to Apollonian sunlight, becomes, in various later versions, "Like
natural sculpture in cathedral cavern," just as "the Druid tem-
ple" near Keswich, early in the trip, becomes, once Keats's vision
is clear of its penchant for foliage, "like a dismal cirque / Of
Druid stones, upon a forlorn moor, / When the chill rain begins
at shut of eve." More than anything it is the scale of Fingal's Cave
that impresses Keats. The "roof is arched somewhat gothic wise
and the length of some of the entire side pillars is 50 feet—About
the island you might seat an army of Men each on a pillar—The
length of the Cave is 120 feet and from its extremity the view
into the sea through the large Arch at the entrance—the colour
of the columns is a sort of black with a lurking gloom of purple
therin—" Interiors, intimate or grand, will play an important
part in Keats's imaginative life henceforth. As for his literal life,
by the time he and Brown make their way back to the mainland,
he is reacknowledging his "slight sore throat and think it best to

stay a day or two at Oban. Then we shall proceed to Fort William and Inverness."

Brown's report, in his *Life of Keats*, elaborates a bit: "For some time he had been annoyed by a slight inflammation in the throat, occasioned by rainy days, fatigue, privation, and, I am afraid, in one instance, by damp sheets. It was prudently resolved, with the assistance of medical advice, that if, when we reached Inverness, he should not be much better, he should part from me, and proceed from the port of Cromarty to London by sea." The notable adjective, in both their references, is "slight," an understatement of hope in the face of fact. Keats's sore throat had been around for months, well before the tour. "Slight" is both stiff upper lip and dangerous denial, and denial will become, as it has for Tom, the hallmark of diagnosis, whether it relates to Keats's inflammation, depression, or consumption. Keats, in his comment to Tom, mentions both Fort William, which is at the south end of the Great Glen, and Inverness, which is at the north end, a distance of seventy or so walking miles. Brown mentions Inverness only, implying an assumption about their stay in Fort William, an assumption of crucial consequences. Fort William is at the base of Ben Nevis, the cruelest, most perilous, most deceptive of mountains, because it seems small by alpine standards but is a killer to the careless, still claiming lives every year. It is to height what Fingal's Cave is to depth. In not alluding to either Fort William or Ben Nevis, Brown leaves the implication that, in spite of Keats's long-standing sore throat and the tour's punishment to his overall stamina, climbing the mountain, regardless of health considerations, is a foregone conclusion, with Keats himself equally complicit and in denial. Keats begins his last letter to Tom (August 6) with a mixed signal: "We have made but poor progress Lately, chiefly from bad weather for my throat is in a fair way of getting quite well, so I have had nothing of conse-

quence to tell you till yesterday when we went up Ben Nevis, the
highest Mountain in Great Britain—On that account I will never
ascend another in this empire—Skiddaw is no thing to it either in
height or difficulty."

From a distance, Ben Nevis resembles a massive shoulder
or a whale head, a sperm whale's head, though it is a thousand
feet higher than Greylock, the Massachusetts mountain that, in
snow, inspired Melville's *Moby-Dick*. Snow covers parts of Nevis
all year. Its superstructure of volcanic rock gives it an ancient
appearance; because of its actual old age, schist, shale, and great
loose gravel form a good deal of its surface, making traction to
the unwary tricky. At its summit, eight hundred feet short of a
straight-up mile, lies a hundred acres of stony void whose north-
east face is a sheer drop. There are several drops, in fact, within
its mass. "These Chasms," remarks Keats, "are 1500 feet in depth
and are the most tremendous places I have ever seen." Ignoring
the question of his health, Keats realizes that Nevis, perhaps even
more than Fingal's Cave, is the surpassing presence, the natu-
ral greatness that he has been in search of this whole journey.
"We set out about five in the morning with a Guide in the Tartan
and Cap and soon arrived at the foot of the first ascent which we
immediately began upon—after much fag and tug and a rest and
a glass of whisky apiece we gained the top of the first rise and saw
then a tremendous chap above us which the guide said was still far
from the top." Most of this final letter to Tom is the memory of
the ascent. "After the first Rise our way lay along a heath valley
in which there was a Loch—after about a Mile in this Valley we
began upon the next ascent more formidable by far than the last
and kept mounting with short intervals of rest until we got above
all vegetation, among nothing but loose Stones which lasted to
the very top." There were three more miles of this stony climb-
ing, vertical and narrow. "Before we got halfway up we passed

large patches of snow and near the top is a chasm some hundred feet deep completely gutted with it—Talking of chasms they are the finest wonder of the whole—they appear great rents in the very heart of the mountain though they are not, being at the side of it, but other huge crags arising round it give the appearance to Nevis of a shattered heart or Core in itself."

7

"I LIVE IN THE EYE," KEATS HAD WRITTEN HIS YOUNGEST brother at the start of the tour, "and my imagination, surpassed, is at rest." This largely rhetorical, wishful observation—here, atop the highest place he would ever be, and the most dangerous yet awe inspiring—is now turning out to be true in ways that Keats could not have imagined. "The whole immense head of the Mountain is composed of large loose stones—thousands of acres." Well, perhaps not thousands, but it must seem that way. "You are on a stony plain which of course makes you forget you are on any but low ground—the horizon or rather edges of this plain being about 4000 feet above the Sea hide all the Country immediately beneath you, so that the next object you see all round next to the edges of the flat top are the Summits of Mountains of some distance off—as you move about on all sides you see more or less of the near neighbour country according as the Mountain you stand upon is in different parts steep or rounded—but the most new thing of all is the sudden leap of the eye from the extremity of what appears a plain into so vast a distance." This last comment about the sudden leap of the eye into so vast a distance: the epic setting granting epic vision: this is, for Keats, surpassing. Typical of his sense of himself, and his sense of humor,

Keats will not let his visionary "cloud-veil" view of things stand ("After a little time the Mist cleared away but still there were large Clouds about attracted by old Ben to a certain distance so as to form as it appeared large dome curtains which kept sailing about, opening and shutting at intervals . . ."); he must deflate the moment and give Tom a bit of entertainment. "On . . . one part of the top there is a handsome pile of stones done pointedly by some soldiers of artillery. I climed onto them and so got a little higher than old Ben himself." "Mister John Keats five feet hight."

Brown does not find this explorer's pose all that humorous. "When on the summit of this mountain, we were enveloped in a cloud, and, waiting till it was slowly wafted away, he sat on the stones, a few feet away from the edge of that fearful precipice, fifteen hundred feet perpendicular from the valley below, and wrote this sonnet." Perhaps Keats is remembering his "stout Cortez with eagle eyes," but with a touch of irony, since the Ben Nevis sonnet is composed "blind in Mist" ("Upon the top of Nevis, blind in mist! / I look into the chasms . . ."). Keats ends his August 6 last letter to Tom by reversing his opening optimism about his health. "My Sore throat is not quiet well and I intend stopping here a few days," here being Inverness. Thus, having put himself at risk by making the difficult walk up the most difficult of British mountains, and making the difficult walk back down, he compounds the risk by walking in Scots weather the four days north to the dark capital of the Highlands. Inverness becomes the end of Keats's Northern tour—six hundred miles, he claims, of walking; four hundred miles by coach. By coach is how he will get from the northern tip of Loch Ness to Beauly to Dingwall to Cromarty, from which he will sail, on *The George*, on August 8 back to London, a coast-hugging voyage of ten days—a third of the time it will take him to sail to Italy two years later. Luckily, not only is he able to rest heading home but is allowed better food—beef, for one thing, which cheers his health. Rest and an improved diet, however, do not cheer his appearance. He arrives in London on August 18, takes the Hampstead coach to Pond Street, and walks down its long, windy hill to East Heath Road up to John Street and Wentworth Place—Brown's and Dilke's shared residence. It is twilight by this time, and only Mrs. Dilke, Maria, is at home; Keats had hoped to surprise the Dilkes before moving on up to Well Walk and Tom. It is light enough that, even standing in the doorway, Keats looks "as brown and shabby as you can imagine, scarcely any shoes left, his jacket all torn at the back, a fur cap, a great plaid, and his knapsack." Once he has settled into a chair and made a joke ("Bless thee, Bottom, bless thee, thou art translated"), Maria Dilke realizes that Keats has not received her husband's letter sent two weeks before to Inverness. Tom's precarious condition, in mountain-climbing nomenclature, has become precipitous. He is dying. Keats makes his quick good-bye and leaves immediately; thus there is no time for him to meet the Dilkes' summer neighbors, a Mrs. Brawne and her three children, who have rented Brown's half of the house until October. Mrs. Dilke has doubtless recommended Keats as an odd but interesting young man, close in age to at least one of the Brawne family—hence Mrs. Dilke's shock at seeing him so bedraggled from his journeys.

If we can recall Severn's deathbed portrait drawing of Keats, we have a sense of what Tom must have looked like to his poet-physician brother, especially because the last-stage symptoms of tubercular consumption are universal and must have been familiar to Keats from all his years of medical training. Tom by now has been coughing blood consistently—that is, phlegm flecked with blood. "Softened tubercular matter was now passing into his bronchial tubes . . . the cavities in the upper lobes of his lungs became ulcerated, so the lower portion gradually became tubercular too."

It is clear to Keats that the time of pretense and false hope has passed; Tom is terminal, and until the end, with George now gone, Keats will have to assume completely the role of nurse, even doctor—roles, ironically, he has trained for, in a knowledge he knows too well, better than he may have wished. Poetry, in addition to his sense of his own health, will have to be placed in some parallel circumstance, *beside* the part of being his brother's keeper. At some point, surely, Keats will find a balance between all the parts he must begin to play, a balance that will permit him to nurse-sit Tom and at the same time put to some use some of his summer's sublime visual experience, which is to say writing while on death watch. Perhaps if Tom lingers, a few of their friends will give Keats a break so he can join in on the occasional social function. Perhaps the threat of Tom's dying can be attenuated, postponed, particularly if we can assume a daily normalcy. Such balances do, in the autumn of 1818, work out. Keats begins, at Tom's bedside, the early drafts of *Hyperion*; he manages to get to see friends intermittently; he takes walks on the Heath; he even meets at last his once and future neighbor Fanny Brawne. September, October, November.

The fundamental fact, however, of this transitional period, this beginning, this first autumn of his so-called living year, is his confinement with Tom, which invokes the original muse figure in his imagination, his mother. Yet not so much, perhaps, the precise family figure as the configuration itself of dying, the familial, personal face of death. Keats, as a body and a temperament, favored his father, who was killed in a riding accident when Keats was eight; Tom, delicate Tom, resembled his mother Frances, whose passionate, vulnerable nature led her to make, after her husband's death, a series of bad decisions that caused not only a five-year separation from her children but a complete exhaustion of her financial, emotional, and physical resources. When Frances Keats returned to the fold—that is, her mother's house, in which her children now were being raised—her son John was fourteen and she, like Tom, was well on her way to dying of what Keats would call "the family disease." It says everything about the Keats we will come to know that he will appoint himself his mother's dedicated nurse and accept in himself a profound need to heal. Haydon, of all sources, would report in his diary years later that "during her last illness, his devoted attachment interested all. He sat up whole nights in a great chair, would suffer nobody to give her medicine but himself, and even cooked her food; he did all, & read novels in her intervals of ease." The juxtaposition of such a scene with the ongoing scene of his care for Tom is inescapable: the physician and the poet employing equal healing powers. Going on ten years apart, these archetypal tableaux reveal the writer and his muse bent within the same circle of contemplation, the act of suffering, then the art of suffering: the "wan face / Not pined by human sorrows, but bright-blanched / By an immortal sickness" become youth grown "pale, and spectre-thin," "which happy death / Can put no end to." In the future, in a lost instant, Keats would say he had "had no mother," meaning no one, at the crucial hour, meeting that role. For too many years she had been absent, drifting, alien. And then she was back, but briefly, and dying, and Keats himself would play the mother, the mortal witness. In Tom he could not help but see their mother's wan face, and perhaps the ghost of his own, the face of the future. There is no more absent yet charged void than the room of the dying; everything feels poured and emptied out in a moment. The air, the light, the darker shadings, the sounds and odors, the shapes of the enclosure all trap the impulse of the isolation. The intensity as well as the silences are inseparable from the imagination.

When Keats's mother died in March 1810 and he returned to Enfield, to school, one of his classmates reports that he gave way "to such impassioned and prolonged grief (hiding himself under the master's desk) as awakened the liveliest pity and sympathy in all who saw him"—under the desk, as if to return to the womb source of life in order to start over. When Tom died on the morning of December 1, 1818, the first thing Keats did was to post a letter to their sister, Fanny, that had been written the night before—"I have scarce any hopes of him"—that could not yet speak directly of his death. He then walked down High Street to a left on John Street and to Wentworth Place, where Brown—now well returned from having completed the Northern tour—was still asleep. Brown awoke to find Keats, like a sentinel, standing at the bedside. Brown knew why. Curiously, it was to Richard Woodhouse, Keats's publisher's lawyer and Keats's mainstay literary friend, that Brown wrote the announcement.

1 DECEMBER 1818

—*Woodhouse, Esq.*

HAMPSTEAD

TUESDAY 1ST DEC

Sir,
Mr Keats requests me to inform you his brother Thomas
died this morning at 8 o'Clock & without pain—Mr
Keats is pretty well & desires to be remembered to you—

I am, Sir,
Your obed hum Serv
Cha Brown

Haslam, the brothers' longtime mutual friend, was asked to write George in America. "Pretty well" pretty well understates the emotional isolation that Keats must have seemed to be in that morning. Brown, to his credit, grasped the state of things immediately and suggested to Keats that there was space for him right here, in his half of Wentworth Place. Unspoken in the offer was the evolving role of Brown as surrogate brother and the next-door Dilkes as surrogate family, though they both would be replaced in time by the somewhat itinerant Brawnes, who would, it turns out, be the first family to live in both halves of what would become known, in the twentieth century, as the Keats House, on Keats Grove, formerly John Street.

A Dreaming Thing

. . .

Who alive can say,
"Thou art no Poet—mayst not tell thy dreams"?

1

ON SEPTEMBER 21 AND 22, 1819, FROM HIS LODGINGS IN THE medieval town of Winchester, Keats writes four letters to four of his friends: one to his colleague-poet John Hamilton Reynolds; a second to his literary benefactor, Richard Woodhouse; a third to his former neighbor Charles Dilke; and a fourth to his housemate and sometime traveling companion, Charles Brown, who has been with Keats for much of the summer but has now gone off to Ireland and left the young poet in Winchester in a state of serene "solitarinesse"—a happy solitary state ("I am surprised myself at the pleasure I live alone in"), which for the social animal in Keats never lasts too long. A major theme running through all these letters is Keats's assertion that he must put behind him his "idle minded, vicious way of life" and "no longer live upon hopes"—meaning inheritance and money from poetry—"and take up abode in a cheap lodging in Town"—meaning Westminster—"and get employment in some of our elegant Periodical Works." He adds in his letter to Woodhouse that "I shall carry my plan into execution speedily." He asks Dilke, who has recently moved into central London to be near his son in school, to find him "any place tolerably comfitable." He announces to Reynolds that he has "given up Hyperion—there were too many Miltonic inversions in it . . . I wish to give myself up to other sensations." And he confesses to his confidant and collaborator Brown that "It is quite time I should set myself doing something . . . I had got into the habit of mind of looking towards you as a help in all difficulties."

The motivation for "the plan I purpose pursuing" is, inevitably, financial. He and Brown have for some time been "in fear of the Winchester jail" for various debt, a hard fact of life soon to be temporarily relieved by money gifts, small advances, and repayments of loans. (When an even younger Keats was somewhat flush and expecting more from his inheritance, he indulged the bad habit of lending money, especially to friends such as the unreliable Haydon.) And it is not only his own economic reality and prospect that Keats is facing: Since the spring every word from George has had a particular note of worry regarding money and the challenges of frontier life in America, culminating in the receipt on September 10 of a letter in which George pleads near bankruptcy. He and Georgiana have traveled across Pennsylvania to Pittsburgh, having coached south from New York to Philadelphia, then down the Ohio River to Cincinnati, and from there to Henderson, Kentucky, where they have met and for a while moved in with John James Audubon. Audubon, who at this point in his life is given more to schemes than dreams, has persuaded George to invest in a trading boat that promises a quick return on the dollar in its traffic up and down the Ohio and Mississippi. Problem is, the boat is still in Cincinnati lying in the mud on the bottom of the Ohio. Audubon himself is nearly broke and seems to have suffered equally from this bogus investment, a mitigating circumstance that helps save him from debtor's prison. (Audubon eventually bankrupts six partners, two of them relatives.) In the meantime, George will be rescued, ironically, by one of Audubon's brothers-in-law, William Bakewell, who, to further the irony, will be much of the reason that George will ultimately and really go bankrupt. The stress of this becomes a contributing factor in the consumption that kills him on Christmas Eve 1841 at age forty-four.

The obituary on Christmas Day in the Louisville *Daily Journal* reads:

> *Died,*
>
> *Yesterday, the 24th inst., Mr. GEORGE KEATS, a native of England, but for many years past a resident of this city, in the 44th year of his age.*
>
> *Mr. Keats was a younger brother of John Keats, the distinguished British poet, and possessed much of the genius, and all of the philosophy, benevolence, and enlarged philanthropy, of the lamented bard. The suavity of his manners and the charm of his conversation endeared him to all who knew him, and his enterprises and public spirit rendered him an inestimable member of society. There is not a man in our community whose death would be more deeply and universally mourned. When such a one passes away from among us, every heart feels a mysterious chill, as if touched by the awful shadow of the tomb.*
>
> *The friends and acquaintances of the deceased are invited to attend his funeral, from his late residence on Walnut street, to-day, at half past 2, P.M.*

For now, however, George's older brother John is feeling financial and other pressure from all sides ("things won't leave me alone"). Keats has already interrupted his Winchester idyll and made an abrupt weekend trip to London to try to raise funds for George; he has apparently failed. He has also tried to promote the possibility to Hessey (Taylor, Hessey's partner, and closest to Keats, is out of town) of bringing out a third collection of poems or even single issuings of *The Eve of St. Agnes* and *Lamia*—whose first draft he has just finished—as if, like Byron, he might turn a profit in a day. But no sale. Hessey reminds Keats that the firm is already a hundred pounds in arrears from *Endymion* and cannot afford the rush or the risk of a new Keats volume at the moment. "Otiosusperoccupatus" is one of Keats's pet phrases for the state he is in, and "mist" is one of his favored metaphors when he is least negatively capable: "To night I am all in a mist; I scarcely know what's what—But you knowing my unsteady and vagarish disposition, will guess that all this turmoil will be settled by morning." This is in the letter to Reynolds—after he has returned from London on September 15—to Winchester, "a fine place."

Keats's weekend in London has left him feeling alienated, which is his mood when he begins the fifth major letter of this seminal moment at the end of his writing career, a ten-day (September 17–27) meditation to George on just about everything on his mind not directly addressed in the letters to friends. "I had been so long in retirement that London appeared a very odd place I could not make out I had so many acquaintance, and it was a whole day before I could feel among Men—I had another strange sensation there was not one house I felt any pleasure to call at . . . I was out and everybody was out. I walk'd about the Streets as in a strange land." This is the kind of small confession one makes to one's brother, and perhaps the most interesting word in it is "retirement." George has sailed to America for employment and to find a home. John, who has yet to choose employment, is still in search of a home. "Retirement" is a homebody word, and Winchester has filled this need admirably. Indeed, running parallel in all the letters of this September interlude is the pivotal division in Keats's emotions between this settled, creative "retirement" in Winchester and the unsettling anxiety about his "profession," because poetry, as such, is poverty. On the one hand, as he writes to George, "I take a walk every day for an hour before dinner and this is generally my walk—I go out at the back gate across one street, into the Cathedral yard, which is always interesting; then I pass under the trees along a paved path, pass the beautiful front of the Cathedral, turn left under a stone door way—then I am on the other side of the building—which leaving behind I pass on through two college-like squares . . . garnished with grass and shaded with trees . . . I pass through one of the old gates and there you are in one College-Street through which I pass and at the end thereof crossing some meadows and at last a country alley of gardens I arrive . . . at the foundation of Saint Cross, which is a very interesting old place, both for its tower and alms-square . . . Then I pass across St. Cross meadows till you come to the most beautifully clear river— now this is only one mile of my walk."

On the other hand, in what seems like only moments before this walking account, Keats has commented on "the inveterate obstinacy of our affairs"—meaning the potential Chancery suit against a further Keats inheritance—and now speaks directly to George's financial plight: "On receiving your last I immediately took a place in the same night's coach for London—Mr. Abbey behaved extremely well to me, appointed Monday evening at 7 to meet me and observed that he should drink tea at that hour. I gave him the inclosed note and showed him the last leaf of yours to me. He really appeared anxious about it; promised he would forward your money as quickly as possible—I think I mention'd that Walton is dead—He will apply to Mr. Gliddon the partner; endeavour to get rid of Mrs. Jennings' claim and be expeditious . . . We are certainly in a very low estate: I say we, for I am in such a situation that were it not for the assistance of Brown & Taylor, I must be as badly off as a Man can be. I could not raise any sum by the promise of any Poem—no, not by the mortgage of my intellect." Abbey, the Keats's guardian, will, of course, as always be neither expeditious nor forthcoming. When Keats continues his journal letter several days later, he is so flustered that he confuses time: "Let the next year be managed by you as well as possible, the next month I mean for I trust you will soon receive Abbey's remittance." By the end of the letter, which has run on now for more than a week, he seems willing to accept as truth Abbey's invention of the threat of a lawsuit: "To be certain I will here state that it is in consequence of Mrs Jennings threatening a Chancery suit that you have been kept from the receipt of monies and myself deprived of any help from Abbey."

Winchester, from the middle of August until the first days in October, has been a respite, a temporary retreat from things. Yet at the same time "things," the outside world of obligation and connection, will not leave Keats alone. Money, if central, is only part of it. The problem of a "profession," of work, is another. He has, within only weeks, proposed careers as a journalist, a ship's surgeon on an Indiaman, or, acting in the profession he has trained for, an apothecary ("In no period of my life have I acted with any self will, but in throwing up the apothecary profession"). At one mad moment during his weekend visit to London, Abbey has recommended that Keats become a hatter ("I do believe if I could be a hatter I might be one"). Health is another concern ("I have got rid of my haunting sore throat—and conduct myself in a manner not to catch another"), ranging from nerves and the nagging sore throat that has "haunted" him, it seems now, off and on for well over a year to intimations of mortality ("They say men near death however mad they may have been, come to their senses . . ."). The consequences of the Northern tour and nursing Tom are, after a year of dormancy, coming home. His relationship with Fanny Brawne, who represents much hope in his life, is equally vexed: "Knowing well that my life must be passed in fatigue and trouble, I have been endeavouring to wean myself from you: for to myself alone what can be much of a misery?" And only days after these words to Fanny, Keats writes to his brother that "A Man in love I do think cuts the sorriest figure in the world." As for his own writing, on the same page of his September 22 letter to his friend Dilke in which he states that "I am fit for nothing but literature," he qualifies that "I have no trust whatever on Poetry—I don't wonder at it—the marvel is to me how people read so much of it."

There are even moments when "I am all in a Mess here— embowell'd in Winchester," when the fact is that Winchester "is the pleasantest Town I was ever in, and has the most recommendations of any." In addition to the fine air of the town-and-country daily walks, there is the setting itself, quintessentially English. "The whole town is beautifully wooded—From the Hill at the eastern extremity you see a prospect of Streets, and old Buildings mixed up with Trees—Then There are the most beautiful streams about I ever saw—full of Trout—There is the Foundation of St Croix about half a mile in the fields . . . We have a Collegiate School, a roman catholic School; a chapel ditto and a Nunnery! And what improves it all is, the fashionable inhabitants have all gone to Southampton." And the walks are not confined to daylight. "I should like a bit of fire to night," he writes to Woodhouse, "one likes a bit of fire—How glorious the Blacksmiths' shops look now—I stood to night before one till I was verry near listing for one. yes, I should like a bit of fire—at a distance about 4 feet 'not quite hob nob'—as wordsworth says."

2

THESE LETTERS AT THE END OF SUMMER AND BEGINNING OF autumn of 1819 are written more or less simultaneously, with the ten-day letter to George taking precedence. In the middle of his letter to Reynolds and a discussion of his new poems, Keats breaks mood to announce that "I must take a walk: for I am writing so long a letter to George; and have been employed at it all morning. You will ask, have I heard from George. I am sorry to say not the best news—I hope for better—" And to Woodhouse he breaks in to say that "I am still writing to Reynolds as well as yourself—As I say to George I am writing *to* you but *at* your Wife—" And balancing letters is not his only distraction. He interrupts his request to Dilke regarding help in finding living quarters in Westminster to comment that "this moment I was writing with one hand, and with the other holding to my Mouth a Nectarine—good god how fine—It went down soft pulpy, slushy, oozy, all its delicious embonpoint melted down my throat like a large beatified Strawberry." These interruptions in relief punctuate the back-and-forth, up-and-down tone throughout the mix of confession, commentary, and concern that marks this period, ending in the signing off in the letter to George with "Your affectionate and anxious Brother."

In this last anxious yet creative summer that is coming to a close, a sense of an ending is everywhere—in the letters, in the season, and, in hints and subtle hues, Keats's short, full life. Closure of one kind or another, complete with the various plans of a new beginning, is part of the complexity of Keats's concentration right now. "From the time you left me," he says to George, "our friends say I have altered completely—am not the same person—perhaps in this letter I am for in a letter one takes up one's existence from the last time we met—I dare say you have altered also—every man does—Our bodies every seven years are completely fresh-material'd—seven years ago it was not this hand that clench'd itself against Hammond—We are like the relict garments of a Saint: the same and not the same: for the careful Monks patch it and patch it: till there's not a thread of the original garment left, and still they show it for St Anthony's shirt."

Keats may well be a different person from the young, absorbed poet who spent evening after evening at the Hunts or days on end with Haydon; and of course he has been "altered" by Tom's death, George's departure, and an awareness of his own vulnerability. Experience, for Keats, is never lost, only compounded or enriched. This intensity obviously carries over to and informs the complexity, even variety, of the poetry. In the stretch of the last, this "living," year, he has written almost all of his best work, beginning with the first version of *Hyperion* (right after his return from the Northern tour), while just within the small space of the summer now passing he has produced the three best examples of the forms—after the sonnet—that have most preoccupied him: *Lamia*, a beautifully focused narrative romance; *The Fall of Hyperion. A Dream*, the transformative rewrite of the original epic fragment; and "To Autumn," his final ode and the perfection of the odal structure discovered the previous spring—indeed, "Where are the songs of Spring?"

"To Autumn," in particular, becomes the resonant model of Keats's own negative capability, especially when placed against the five hundred lines of *The Fall of Hyperion*, the first-person recasting of a mythic vision that interrogates both the mission and "capability" of the poet's role—the real poet versus the dreamer ("The poet and the dreamer are distinct . . ."). *The Fall* is a summer piece carried over from July, then given up; "To Autumn" is an end-of-summer weekend poem brought nearly instantly into full being. Keats abandons the one and completes the other on essentially the same day, September 21, as one season of 1819 turns into the "season of mists."

It is as if, only a few days after coming back to Winchester from the stress of his short, strained London visit, and just two days before he yields to the complicated yet necessary letters to his friends, Keats enters a calm, clarifying space, a space of momentary stillness free of "uncertainties, Mysteries, doubts," in which—as he writes to Reynolds—he suddenly realizes "How beautiful the season is now—How fine the air. A temperate sharpness about it. Really, without joking, chaste weather—Dian skies—I never liked stubble fields so much as now—Aye better than the chilly green of the spring. Somehow a stubble plain looks warm—in the same way that some pictures look warm—this struck me so much in my sunday's walk that I composed upon it." The mist in which he scarcely knows "what's what" now becomes, in "To Autumn," the transparency through which his harvest vision is achieved, a sublimation rich in "mellow fruitfulness" and "ripeness to the core" poised with "the stubble plains" of "the soft-dying day," stratified in the poem's three eleven-line stanzas in such a way as to plot the daylight hours into morning, afternoon, and evening; and decline their tones into recognition, celebration, and exhaustion; and explore their emotion as story, song, and elegy; and organize their work into the flowering of the field, the cutting and storing of the grain, and the careful venting of the void of the aftermath, which is the emptying out of the cornucopia.

This is the draft of the poem, after some revision, that Keats sent on Wednesday, September 22, to Woodhouse ("some I was going to give Reynolds"):

Season of Mists and mellow fruitfulness,
Close bosom friend of the maturing sun;
Conspiring with him how to load and bless
The vines with fruit that round the thatch eves run;
To bend with apples the moss'd cottage trees,
And fill all fruit with ripeness to the core;
To swell the gourd, and plump the hazle-shells
With a white kernel; to set budding more,
And still more later flowers for the bees
Untill they think wa[r]m days will never cease
For summer has o'er brimm'd ther clammy Cells.

Who hath not seen thee oft, amid thy stores?
Sometimes, whoever seeks abroad may find
Thee sitting careless on a granary floor,
Thy hair soft-lifted by the winmowing wind;
Or on a half reap'd furrow sound asleep,
Dased with the fume of poppies, while thy hook
Spares the next swath and all its twined flowers;
And sometimes like a gleaner thou dost keep
Stready thy laden head across a brook;
Or by a Cyder press, with patient look,
Thou watchest the last oozings hour by hours—

> *Where are the songs of spring? Aye, Where are they?*
> *Think not of them, thou hast thy music too.*
> *While barred clouds bloom the soft-dying day*
> *And touch the stubble plains with rosy hue:*
> *Then in a wailful quire the small gnats mourn*
> *Among the river sallows, borne aloft*
> *Or sinking as the light wind lives and dies;*
> *And full grown Lambs loud bleat from hilly bourne:*
> *Hedge crickets sing, and now with treble soft*
> *The Red breast whistles from a garden Croft*
> *And gather'd Swallows twitter in the Skies—*

Aside from spelling errors and punctuation adjustments, there are few final changes in this version of the poem, though they are significant. "White kernel," for instance, becomes the richer "sweet kernel"; "Dased" becomes the more tonally attuned, accurate, and softer "Drowsed"; and "gather'd" becomes the active, present-progressive "gathering" in the crucial last image. The revised and only surviving fair copy of the poem, with errors corrected and rewritten touches added, ends up in George's hands in America after John's death; George then gives it as a gift, in 1839, to a Miss Barker (late Mrs. Ward) of Louisville, who passes it on to her granddaughter in 1896, who bequeaths it, in 1925, to Amy Lowell of Brookline and Boston, and hence to the Houghton Library in Cambridge. Like the September letters, "To Autumn" was fair-copied on paper immediately available to Keats, paper he might well have brought back with him from his abrupt September 10 weekend in London, in this case wove paper watermarked "C Wilmott 1818," which means that the manuscript paper, now "immortal," was already at least a year old when Keats used it, making it, at this moment, about 180 years old, under glass. The paper's size is a little less than the standard 8½ by 11 and, appropriately enough, has taken on the oak-brown aspect of an autumn leaf. We can be thankful that poetry, notably great poetry, lives in the air as well as, ad infinitum, on the reprintable pages of the future.

Can a lyric poem of thirty-three lines achieve the awe and spaciousness of the sublime? "To Autumn" is a tone poem for sure, a twilit symbolist masterpiece realized independently—it seems—of its implied author, as if it were an object, self-created, within the harvest terms of itself. The subtlety of the poem's inherent voice makes it seem, further, that as a maker Keats has disappeared into the text, absorbed by it in the act of seeing it—seeing, interpreting, transforming the landscape now so familiar to him on his almost daily walks. It is also a painting in the sense that its visual, imagistic information is theatrically blocked out so as to be simultaneous yet sequential as the eye moves from foreground to middle ground to background—from "thatch eves" and "cottage trees" to "granary floor" and "brook" to "barred clouds" and "stubble plains" and "gathering swallows . . . in the skies." It is this specific Sunday's view of a last-summer-day's-beginning-of-autumn-day's transition, season to season, and at once this vision of eternal autumn, its mists, its fullnesses, its gatherings, its drowsiness, and its warmths that sets it apart. It is the full cup emptied, filled, then unfilled. The tone, therefore, is residually spiritual, elevated beyond the "autumnal" emotion; the feeling is one of surpassing exhaustion—"ripeness to the core," "o'er-brimmed," "last oozings hours by hours"—the pluralizing of our responses; the vision, ultimately, is of "the soft-dying day," the wind living then dying, "the wailful choir" of it all—vegetable, animal, human—singing while listening. Each of the great Keatsian odes suspends in lyric tragedy—none more purely and resonantly than "To Autumn," whose visionary size transcends its local space.

3

ON THE HEELS OF THE DRAFT OF "TO AUTUMN" THAT HE encloses in his letter to Woodhouse, Keats includes excerpts from *The Fall of Hyperion*, which, on this same summer-ending day as he has written to Reynolds, he "has given up" (". . . too many Miltonic inversions . . ."). It is as if he proposes to distract or entertain Woodhouse with his "Temple of Saturn" descriptions and his blank-verse "fine" sounds now that the poem fragment has lost his interest. He even adds some lines—"a sort of induction"—as an afterthought.

> *Fanatics have their dreams wherewith they weave*
> *A Paradise for a Sect; the savage too*
> *From forth the loftiest fashion of his sleep*
> *Guesses at Heaven: pity these have not*
> *Trac'd upon vellum, or wild Indian leaf*
> *The shadows of melodious utterance:*
> *But bare of laurel they live, dream, and die,*
> *For Poesy alone can tell her dreams,*
> *With the fine spell of words alone can save*
> *Imagination from the sable charm*
> *And dumb enchantment—*

Dreams and dreaming of all kinds have been central to the character of Keats's poems from the start. The "fine spell of words," as imagination's rescue from mere "sable charm / And dumb enchantment," has been a major tension in his choices of poetic genres, which is why he says he thinks of the charming and enchanting *Eve of St. Agnes* as a diversion and the earlier "smoke-able" and too simple *Isabella; or the Pot of Basil* as "a weak-sided Poem with an amusing sober-sadness about it." *Lamia* ("There is no objection of this kind to Lamia . . ."), the best and last of the romance narratives, ranks higher in his mind but is still, for Keats, on a level one ambition notch lower than the attempts at *Hyperion*, though he believes "there is that sort of fire in it which will take hold of people in some way—give them either pleasant or unpleasant sensations"; in other words, *Lamia* is a poem that might sell. But in terms of artistic, among-the-English-poets ambition, *Lamia* remains, like his other romances, a poem conceived as dreaming.

Which is a fair irony, because *The Fall of Hyperion* is co-titled *A Dream*.

For Keats the idea, let alone the image, of dreaming ("Do I wake or sleep?") is multilayered and hierarchical and goes back to his first fledgling efforts at poems ("Can death be sleep, when life is but a dream . . .") and his first serious tries at a sustained, if luxurious, lyric meditation ("Sleep and Poetry") and his first—and only complete—try at a romantic epic (*Endymion*), which is "full of sweet dreams." Dreaming, as a topical and thematic constant, seems to want to evolve into a perceived alternate state of deeper consciousness—as it does, in different ways, in Coleridge and Shelley—as well as an alternate state of mind in which the imagination—as opposed to "fancy"—can best make new synesthetic connections and visual discoveries. Dreaming, therefore, may begin in Keats's early poems as a poetic device and cliché, but it quickly—or at least by the time he returns from the North to nurse Tom—develops into the highest of mythic and metaphoric platforms on which to build. It becomes synonymous with the imagination, culminating in the spring odes, "To Autumn," and *The Fall*, another term for autumn. Yet dreaming, however graduated, cannot quite free itself of all its superficial attachments to "imaginings" and "soft floatings" or its symbolist associations with a poetry, like the great odes, that may be too beautifully self-referenced and self-contained, which is why, in the climactic inquisitor scene in *The Fall*, the roles of the dreamer and the poet are separated by the muse-goddess Moneta as "distinct."

Regardless of the notion of Keats as a quick study and quixotic personality, he is nothing if not about continuity in his poetry—stunning growth within a singular and ongoing context of concerns, themes, and commitments. Nightingales, bowers, flora, sleep, the heart, "pale immortal death," "A thing of beauty," "The end and aim of Poesy," and "The journey homeward to habitual self" help to detail the short but expansive narrative that is the story of Keats's years as a poet. Even the struggles of his gods—Endymion, Apollo, Hyperion—are defined by the same potential "knowledge enormous" of suffering and loss and the passage to transformation they promise. Endymion makes his first appearance in "I Stood Tip-toe"; Apollo makes his in both an ode and in Keats's youngish but underrated "Sleep and Poetry." The figure of Hyperion frames Keats's crowning creative last year, but as early as November 1817 and less than halfway through the writing of *Endymion*, he poses in a letter to his pastoral friend Benjamin Bailey that "I am running my head into a Subject which I am certain I could not do justice to under five years study and 3 vols octavo—" But he does not have five years or the sustained space of three volumes. Two months later he writes to Haydon that "in Endymion I think you may have many bits of deep and sentimental cast—the nature of *Hyperion* will lead me to treat it in a more naked and Grecian Manner—and the march of passion and endeavour will be undeviating—and one great contrast between them will be—that the Hero of the written tale being mortal is led on, like Buonaparte, by circumstances; whereas Apollo in Hyperion being a fore-seeing God will shape his actions like one." And by April, in the published preface to *Endymion*, Keats ends its apologizing by hoping that "I have not in too late a day touched the beautiful mythology of Greece, and dulled its brightness: for I wish to try once more, before I bid it farewell."

The "deep and sentimental cast" of *Endymion* offers one version of Keatsian dreaming; *Hyperion*, in both its incarnations, offers another version altogether—sculpted into a shaped blank verse, evoked in vast and ruined exteriors and sealed Piranesian interiors, and spoken through the voices of loss and longing. Although the points of view in each incarnation—omniscient speaker in the original, first-person speaker in the second version—are opposed, in each try at *Hyperion* the strongest passages are "more naked and Grecian" in manner whether or not too much of the writing echoes the "Miltonic inversions" that Keats claims have caused him to let *The Fall* trail off into ellipses. Where, however, is the line between style and substance? The Huntian excesses of *Endymion* not only enhance but substantiate its dreaming; the disciplining of style in the two *Hyperion*s, regardless of the Miltonic lapses, lifts its language to moments of the sublime. The "naked and Grecian" Elgin Marbles, which Haydon introduces Keats to at the British Museum, become no less a model for shaping the lines and delineating Keats's epic dream than do the writing samples of Thomas Chatterton, "the purest writer in the English language" and the writer whom Keats most "associates with autumn." A good part of Keats's growth as a poet is his questioning of the dreamer's role and the quality of the "fine writing" demanded by the art. Here at the end of his writing career, the language of dreaming has become truly the language of the experience. From the start, Keats's lyric and epic dreams have been inseparable from his poetic project—the "eternal law," the truth "That first in beauty should be first in might." Finding a language for this project has defined its ongoing process. "To Autumn," as Walter Jackson Bate points out, is "transparent before its subject." The most commanding passages in *The Fall* are equally one-on-one with the language of the experience—particularly important now because the experience of who is speaking and narrating and "experiencing" the poem in the second *Hyperion* is so other from the original. As *Hyperion* the *Fragment* becomes *Hyperion* the *Dream*, the emphasis moves from monuments of exteriors and dialogues of gods to the intimate architecture of the interior space of a single mind in articulate conflict with itself—from a model such as Milton to something closer to the gothic intensity of Dante. If "To Autumn," in this last phase, perfects the formal impulse of the spring odes, *The Fall of Hyperion. A Dream* turns the "failed epic" of *Hyperion. A Fragment* into something closer to an extended, modernist lyric.

4

THE PLACE IN HIS POETRY THAT KEATS HAS COME TO, IN HIS final days as a writer, is a practice of form in which the eye and the ear are indistinguishable—as they are, for example, in "To Autumn." Indeed, the synesthetic eye, the painter's eye, in this great ode acts as might a first-person pronoun, the entity to whom the poem is happening; but because the eye is essentially a lens—a sentient, capacious yet focusing lens—it affects a certain neutrality, an "objectivity." The profound shift in point of view in *The Fall*—from apparent objectivity in the first version to apparent subjectivity in the second—changes completely the announced entity to whom the poem is happening, and changes the story, too. Keats's dream-speakers, regardless of "point of view," make shibboleths of the distinctions between objective and subjective voices. It is the degree of distance of the speaker that makes the difference. "To Autumn" may be written in the third person, but it feels intimate, warm, softly spoken. *The Fall*, as a drama on an operatic soundstage, feels intense but far, as if the first-person speaker-narrator were somehow separate from the action and actor that he is, as if he were a narrator observed.

Tom's death may or may not be the major reason that Keats gave up on the first *Hyperion*. He says that style ("Miltonic inversions") stopped the second version after some five hundred lines. You have to think that point of view, the casting of the speaker, had something to do with both abandonments. By Book III—and the fragmentary last—of the first *Hyperion*, "Apollo is once more the golden theme!" His "dialogic" encounter with the "lonely Goddess" Mnemosyne takes over the poem, as does the crisis of his conversion from mortal to immortal, as he dies "into life" and begins to comprehend and identify with suffering.

> *Mute thou remainest—mute! yet can I read*
> *A wondrous lesson in thy silent face:*
> *Knowledge enormous makes a God of me.*
> *Names, deeds, grey legends, dire events, rebellions,*
> *Majesties, sovran voices, agonies,*
> *Creations and destroyings, all at once*
> *Pour into the wide hollows of my brain,*
> *And deify me, as if some blithe wine*
> *Or bright elixir peerless I had drunk,*
> *And so become immortal.*

Apollo, dreamer-poet and healer, and the revolutionary replacement for Hyperion the sun god, also, in a way, takes over the second version of *Hyperion* but in the guise of Keats himself, whose first-person struggle in the course of the poem addresses the question and function of true poetry and the true poet. The speaker wakes, after a "full draught" that "is the parent of my theme," from one kind of dream into another, an inebriation not unlike the transition that the dreamer in "Ode to a Nightingale" makes ("as though of hemlock I had drunk . . . O for a draught of vintage . . ."). He looks around and sees "the carved sides / Of an old sanctuary with roof august, / Builded so high, it seemed that filmed clouds / Might spread beneath, as o'er the stars of heaven." Then "far off" he sees a Saturnian old "Image, huge of feature as a cloud, / At level of whose feet an altar slept." Leading to the altar are steps, Dantean steps, that the speaker is commanded to ascend, or "die on that marble where thou art." To say the least, the climb is difficult if not lifesaving. Thus far his dialogue is with a "veiled shadow," whose answer to the question "What am I that should so be saved . . . ?" is "Thou has felt / What 'tis to die and live again before / Thy fated hour . . . Thou has dated on / Thy doom." The speaker, though, wants more answers from this mysterious but powerful affiliate of the now-vanquished old Saturn.

> *"High Prophetess," said I, "purge off,*
> *Benign, if so it pleases thee, my mind's film."*
> *"None can usurp this height," returned the shade,*
> *But those to whom the miseries of the world*
> *Are misery, and will not let them rest.*
> *All else who find a haven in the world,*
> *Where they may thoughtless sleep away their days,*
> *If by chance into this fane they come,*
> *Rot on the pavement where thou rotted'st half."*

It turns out that the prophetess, Moneta, is a progeny of Mnemosyne, and playing a similar, if very vocal, role. She accuses the speaker of being merely a dreaming thing: "What benefit canst thou do, or all thy tribe, / To the great world?" she asks. "Art thou not of the dreamer tribe?"

The poet and the dreamer are distinct,
Diverse, sheer opposite, antopodes.
The one pours out a balm upon the world,
The other vexes it.

In defense, the speaker has already asserted that "sure not all / Those melodies sung into the world's ear / Are useless: sure a poet is a sage, / A humanist, physician to all men." An Apollo, in other words. This part of the debate between Keats's stand-in and Moneta, lines 187–210 (Canto I), in which the aesthetic/philosophic argument comes down to the value of the poet to the world, especially the lyric poet ("melodies sung"), is the part that Woodhouse later claims to be the lines that "Keats seems to have intended to erase." If Woodhouse is correct, then Keats, at the end of his career, seems still in doubt as to his mission, let alone the means—epic, lyric, dramatic—to meet that mission. And he appears to be in doubt about his doubt, if he would erase its debate. The combining roles of poet and physician would seem to be exactly what Keats has prepared for, but at this moment these roles remain, for him, separate, even irreconcilable, at least as a practical matter. Yet if poetry "makes nothing happen" and if we despise any poetry "that has designs" upon us, then what are we left with? If poetry is dreaming, what makes it real? No wonder, according to Brown, Keats writes the spring odes on scraps of paper and is apparently unsure, regarding the nightingale ode, as to the order of the stanzas. No wonder, if Keats is a mere dreamer, that in his last collection, including *Lamia*, the odes are interspersed with lighter poems and pressed among romance narratives. Or is Keats, then, a Regency poet? Or a Huntian cockney after all? Or is this "tribal" argument—whether or not he meant for us to hear it—of a higher order than ambition or intention? In revising *Hyperion*, Keats not only changed point of view, he discovered his "characters"—figures rooted in memory, not mythology. He closes the passage that Woodhouse claims he "seems" to have wanted to erase by appealing to the very god he means to emulate by personalizing and attacking the issue and the perceived enemy:

> *Apollo! faded, far-flown Apollo!*
> *Where is thy mighty misty pestilence to creep*
> *Into the dwellings, through the door crannies,*
> *Of all mock lyrists, large self-worshippers*
> *And careless hectorers in proud bad verse.*
> *Though I breathe death with them it will be life*
> *To see them sprawl before me into graves.*

Keats is saying to Moneta that if mock lyrists represent what she calls "dreamers" and if he is such a dreamer, together they deserve their fate, so long as Keats can see "them sprawl before me into graves." "Before" is a rich ambiguity here because, as an adverb, it can refer at once to place and time—time, above all, being the qualifier now. Mock lyrists are obviously not the English poets whom Keats wishes to be among—no more than careless hectorers (his critics?) and large self-worshippers (Byron?) make up the tribal membership he would join. This is a painful, revealing moment, and its vulnerability leads to a recognition scene no less "autobiographical" in its impact. Keats understands that by arguing the point he is transcending its impact. And he understands that by arguing the point he is transcending its judgment, that by climbing the stairs he has passed a test, and that by "half" dying he is more than half alive now. In the depth and focus of his confrontation with Moneta, he has arrived at the "altar" of awareness. "Majestic shadow, tell me where I am . . . / What Image this, whose face I cannot see?"

Perhaps no moment in Keats speaks so directly as the moment when "sad Moneta," sole priestess of Saturn's desolation, whose "globed brain" still swoons with scenes "vivid . . . with an electral changing misery"—perhaps no moment so parallels Apollo's dying into life at the sight of and insight into Mnemosyne's "silent face" at the end of the fragment of the first *Hyperion* than the recognition scene in *The Fall* in which Moneta shows her face to the speaker, who by now has earned her "goodwill." He has listened and he has learned; her "immortal's sphered words / Could to a mother's soften."

> *But yet I had a terror of her robes,*
> *And chiefly of the veils, that from her brow*
> *Hung pale, and curtained her in mysteries*
> *That made my heart too small to hold its blood.*
> *This saw that Goddess, and with sacred hand*
> *Parted the veils. Then saw I a wan face,*
> *Not pined by human sorrow, but bright-blanched*
> *By an immortal sickness which kills not;*
> *It works a constant change, which happy death*
> *Can put no end to; deathwards progressing*
> *To no death was that visage; it had passed*
> *The lily and the snow.*

Like Apollo, the speaker's capacity to witness and comprehend is rewarded: "Whereon there grew / A power within me of enormous ken / To see as a God sees, and take the depth / Of things as nimbly as the outward eye / Can size and shape pervade." To see as a god sees, to see the goddess and the muse figure behind the goddess, the deathless face, past the lily and the snow, of the mother, to hear, in immortal sphered words her voice: here is Keats in his last writing addressing his sources—his mother, Tom, and his own "immortal sickness." To recognize the wan, tubercular face is the dreaming made real, memory made alive. It may be weakness on Keats's part to wish the same "mighty misty pestilence" that creeps "Into the dwellings, through the door crannies," on those he abhors, but he knows whereof he speaks. And to see as a god sees, in capacity and negative capability, is to see past the face, beyond the lily and the snow, into the mind, the brain itself, with its "electral changing misery," its "wide hollows," its "branched thoughts, new grown with pleasant pain," and its "wreathed" trellises. To see as a poet, a true dreamer, is to see as a healer and a knower.

5

MORE THAN THREE DECADES AFTER THE FACT, HENRY STEPHENS —one of Keats's roommates during his student days at Guy's Hospital and a poet himself (though a fan of Pope's, whom Keats despised) and the friend, during the summer of 1818, who had dinner with George, Georgiana, Brown, and Keats en route on their separate journeys to America and Scotland—writes to Monckton Milnes that his medical school memory of the young poet is still vivid: "In a room, he was always at the window, peering into space, so that the window-seat was spoken of by his comrades as Keats's place . . . In the lecture room he seemed to sit apart and to be absorbed in something else, as if the subject suggested thoughts to him which were not practically connected with it. He was often in the subject and out of it, in a dreamy way." Keats himself confirms this observation in a comment he makes to Cowden Clarke. "The other day during a lecture, there came a sunbeam into the room, and with a whole troop of creatures floating in the ray: and I was off with them to Oberon and fairy-land."

Stephens adds that Keats's passion "for Poetry was soon manifested. He attended lectures and went through the usual routine, but he had no desire to excel in that pursuit . . . He never attached much consequence to his own studies in medicine, and indeed looked upon the medical career as the career by which to live in a workaday world, without being certain that he could keep up the strain of it. He nevertheless had a consciousness of his own power, and even his own greatness, though it might not be recognized." Two key phrases here stand out: "medical career" and "workaday world," realities that to a young poet such as Keats, who would soon join the company of Hunt, Haydon, Shelley, and the independent Brown, seemed antithetical to the world and society that he wished to be in. He could see the struggles and compromises that friends were forced into, friends such as Reynolds—who would become a second-rate lawyer—and Severn—who would become a second-rate artist—and Rice—who would lose his health, it appeared, working long hours, day in and day out, in his father's law office. Their young artistic ambition and the need to make a living came to be at odds. Whether we think of Keats as working class or emerging middle class, he knew better than anyone, once he realized the limitations of his inheritance, that he would also have to join the workaday world. That is the crux of his letters' messages during this summer-to-fall period of 1819 when he writes his last great poetry in the same moment he is planning, or at least saying so, a viable financial future. His philosophic and graphic interrogation—in *The Fall*—of the role of the poet in a functional, vital, and thoughtful world is about beauty, of course, but it is pointedly about the truth of the place of the healer, the poet-physician. A medical career is a far cry from the poet as Apollo. Meanwhile, life interrupts, in its desultory way, Keats's requirement to come to a practical decision, because once he leaves Winchester in October, he has less than a year left in England, and less than half of that in Italy.

Stephens continues his commentary to Milnes, who is piecing together the inchoate bits of many memories of Keats some thirty years on by saying that "Poetry was to his mind the zenith of all his Aspirations: the only thing worth the attention of superior minds: so he thought: all other pursuits were mean and tame . . . The greatest men in the world were the poets and to rank among them was the chief object of his ambition. It may readily be imagined that this feeling was accompanied with a good deal of pride and conceit, and that amongst mere medical students he would walk and talk as one of the Gods might be supposed to do when mingling with mortals. This pride had exposed him, as may be readily imagined, to occasional ridicule, and some mortification." Stephens is remembering, "as may be readily imagined," with a touch of vanity and jealousy, perhaps less on the poetry side than on the medical side, because, although the twenty-year-old Keats may have been a dreamer at some of the lectures, he proves to be more than an able student on exams and during demonstrations, and within a month of his admission to Guy's is appointed to the prestigious position of dresser.

Keats's career as a "medical student" begins in the summer of 1811, after having been withdrawn, at fifteen, from the

Enfield School. His well-documented years as an apprentice to the apothecary-surgeon Thomas Hammond amount to an undergraduate education with a major in apothecary medicine and last about the same length of time, a little more than four years. He enters studies at Guy's Hospital in the fall of 1815, well enough prepared that he is the first member of his class to be appointed to a dressership. The fact that he registered at Guy's Counting House for a full year's study suggests strongly that he was aiming for more than the six-month requirement for an apothecary's license; he was looking to become a surgeon. (The step up in order to become a physician required the upper-class experience of university study, an opportunity unavailable to Keats's station.) A surgeon, in those days, was comparable to being what we now call a general practitioner. At this moment Keats is keenly aware that, regardless of his part of the inheritance from his grandparents—at least that part he knows about—he will need to earn a living, have a profession. On an apparently just-in-case basis, in July 1816, less than a year into his hospital medical studies, he takes and passes the exam for his "Certificate to Practice as an Apothecary." The page in the Register of Apothecaries' Hall reads:

189 Mr. *John Keats of full age*—
CANDIDATE
for a CANDIDATE to practice as an
APOTHECARY in *the Country.*

An APPRENTICE to
Mr. *Thomas Hammond of Edmonton*
APOTHECARRY FOR 5 years

Testimonial from Mr. *Thomas Hammond*—

LECTURES

2 *COURSES on ANATOMY and PHYSIOLOGY*

2-*THEORY and PRACTICE OF MEDICINE*

2-*CHEMISTRY*

1-*MATERIA MEDICA*

HOSPITAL ATTENDANCE

6 MONTHS at *Guy's and St. Thomas's*—

as

MONTHS at

168 Examined by *Mr. Brande & approved.*

Keats's somewhat double role as student and dresser con-
tinues for roughly another nine months following his certifica-
tion, until March 1817, almost to the day that his first collection,
Poems, is published. He has, since the fall of 1814, with the com-
position of his first known poem, "Imitation of Spenser" ("Now
morning from her orient chamber came, / And her first footsteps
touched a verdant hill . . ."), begun to play a third role, that of
a lyric poet. Poet-lawyer Wallace Stevens says "I was of three
minds." For Keats, his third mind was primary and predominate.
When he leaves his medical studies in order to pursue his pas-
sion, he will have written some forty-six poems, the majority of
which—including two extended lyrics ("I Stood Tip-toe" and
"Sleep and Poetry")—will appear in the first book, a book that
Shelley, among others, advises him not to put into print. This
simultaneity of potential careers—poetry and medicine—never
really abates; the figure of Apollo—poet and healer—becomes
Keats's true sun sign. And the fact remains that the poet spends at
least as much time apprenticing medicine as he does apprenticing
and achieving poetry. You might say that the dreamer finds his
gravitas and grounding in the real and mortal heart and brain,

blood and bone, lungs and viscera, earth, air, fire, and water of the body. Keats has lost his father ten years before he writes his first poem; then, in succession, he loses his maternal grandfather (1805); his sea-captain uncle, Midgley John Jennings (1809); his mother (1810)—though she has basically abandoned her children six years before her death; and his maternal grandmother (1811): a legacy he takes with him as he enters Hammond's surgery to begin his exposure to medicine and its life-and-death practicalities and principles. The corporeal—meaning, in this case, Keats's long experience with the health, the frailty, and the grief of the body—underwrites the resonance and richness of his empathic sensual consciousness. Within the compass of the bower is a grave, albeit festooned with flowers.

His four-and-a-half-year apprenticeship to Hammond begins with a range of duties, including looking after the horses (Keats, was, after all, the son of stable keepers), cleaning the surgery, stocking medicine jars, and delivering medicines to patients. Then, after a year or so, once Keats has established himself, his position elevates to something of an assistant, involving learning to pull teeth, setting broken bones, applying plasters and bandages, and bloodletting by means of leeches or venesection. Later, he probably assists in the delivery of babies and learns how to diagnose certain diseases and disorders—knowledge that will allow him to identify, early on, his own illness in spite of ignorant medical opinion and self-delusion to the contrary. In the process, he will as well acquire the skill to compound and administer drugs, such as aconite, digitalis, magnesia, mercury, and opium, these last two of which he will self-administer as he feels the need. Whether he becomes unhappy or outgrows his apprenticeship, as some commentators believe, Keats does see his time with Hammond through. It likely helps that Edmonton, the site of Hammond's surgery, lies in close proximity to Enfield, the site of his old school and home of his dear friend Cowden Clarke. The country walks between places, with open meadows and working fields, hedgerowed and elm-lined lanes, and classic English wildflowers providing texture all anticipate the country walks around Winchester several years in the future and define a setting for Keats's reading of Spenser, Shakespeare, and Milton. "For what has made the sage or poet write / But the fair paradise of Nature's light?" Clarke, in these late teenage years, becomes Keats's other mentor—"That you first taught me all the sweets of song"—parallel to and profoundly different from the functional Hammond. Both early educations prove necessary. From Hammond, Keats will have learned materia medica; with Clarke, he will have opened the book of Chapman's *Homer*.

How far from the pastoral securities of Edmonton and Enfield to the grubby, crowded borough of Dean and Tooley streets—"the Borough is a beastly place in dirt, turnings and windings"—just over the Thames in Southwark. Guy's and St. Thomas's hospitals are linked as "medical schools" and sit across the street from each other, close to London Bridge and the great High Street leading from the city into the open country south. It is a busy, dark, Dickensian part of town, exposed as much to sewage and garbage as to the prison life of the Clink and the new Marshalsea network of jails, and within hailing distance of the infamous Mint. There is an etching of the borough from 1820 that, in artistic perspective, makes it look like nineteenth-century southern Manhattan along the East River, rather like Whitman's ideal picture of it in "Crossing Brooklyn Ferry." But there is nothing ideal about this part of the Thames. The setting seems to suggest a context for the tone and atmosphere of what occurs within the halls of medicine, particularly in reference to and the implications of the arias on the scale of pain produced by the fact that there are no anesthetics.

Although Keats, having entered his medical studies in fall, is almost immediately granted a position as a dresser, he will not assume the actual duties of such until the following spring. In the meantime he attends chemistry and physiology lectures and graphic anatomy demonstrations. Joseph Henry Green, Guy's chief anatomical demonstrator and later Samuel Taylor Coleridge's "doctor" and amanuensis, puts a fine point on the difference between the lectures and demonstrations:

> *It must be recollected that lectures, however necessary, are only calculated to give general ideas; whereas it is required of the practitioner, that his knowledge should be particular and even minute. It is not sufficient that he is merely acquainted with the presence of certain parts, but he must know precisely their situation and extent. The surgeon's knife may give health or death within the space of one hair's breadth. This kind of knowledge is to be acquired by actual dissection alone.*

The lectures, by comparison, must have seemed celestial when placed against the grounding realities of the dissecting room, which Donald C. Goellnicht, in his fine *The Poet-Physician: Keats and Medical Science*, describes as a "gruesome place, with its bodies laid out on tables and its specimens in macerating tubs and bottles." He goes on, "The students seem to have been immune to these sights and smells, for according to tradition they drank, cooked, and indulged in horseplay in the room, which they treated like a common room." He quotes one observer who finds, on entering the room, a stench that "was most abominable. About 20 chaps were at work, carving limbs and bodies, in all stages of putrefaction, & of all colours; black, green, yellow, blue, while the pupils carved them, apparently, with as much pleasure, as they would carve their dinners. One, was pouring 1. Terebinth on his subject, & amused himself with striking with his scalpel at the maggots, as they issued from their retreats."

Goellnicht notes that "Keats must have faced such scenes almost daily." As a dresser, however, Keats must have faced a good deal more. For the combined hospitals, consisting of scores of students, hundreds of patients, and a limited number of physicians and surgeons, there were only twelve dressers, three or four of whom were assigned per surgeon. The job of the dresser—a position somewhere between surgical pupil and surgical apprentice—consisted of walking the wards—or making the rounds—with a whole party of students and the lead surgeon, carrying a box containing plasters, bandages, and linseed meal. Or the job consisted of standing in readiness on the floor of the operating theater while the surgeon in charge performed the "operation," whose cure was too often worse than the disease. The dresser then "dressed" what wound there was and followed up with changes in the dressing in the "post-operative" period. Pain, and the voice of pain, was the hallmark of the operative and post-operative process. (There is a famous painting by the American Thomas Eakins that—although it depicts a moment much later than Keats's experience—brings to life a sense of the operating theater, its almost sideshow element, with the patient on exhibit, in an attitude that hardly draws a line of difference between the operation and a dissecting demonstration. The whole scene is framed as if it were on a stage.) Keats's other dresser duties involve, among other things, emergency room–like incidents such as accidents and broken bones, as well as outpatient issues, drawing of teeth, routine bloodletting, and hernias. He also likely has to serve on occasion as a liaison with local "body-snatchers" or "resurrection men," such as Ben Crouch or the Harnet brothers, in order to secure fresh examples for anatomy and dissecting classes. The bodies are usually only hours old from the grave or sometimes, in anticipation, procured with minimum violence.

Nevertheless, in spite of wide-awake realities and regardless of his growing awareness of his strengths as a poet, why does Keats apparently end this chance at a money-making profession in the spring of 1817, especially when he has invested so much time in it? Perhaps he really believes, as he tells his guardian Richard Abbey, that he has gifts "beyond those of most men"; perhaps he really believes that once the Keats inheritance is clarified in Chancery court he will have just enough means to live independently. One reason, certainly, is the difference in sensibility between what is required in being a poet and in being a doctor, at least by the standards of medicine that Keats is exposed to: anatomy, for example, as practiced in the dissecting room.

He entered himself of St. Thomas's, but he could not knit his faculties to the study of anatomy. He attended the lectures; and he did not retain a word he had heard: all ran from him like water from a duck's back. His thoughts were far away— in the land of Faery. He was with "the lovely Una in a leafy nook"; or with "old Archimago leaning o'er his book." He said to me that a ray of sun-light came across the lecture-room, and he peopled it with the "gay beings of the element," glancing to and fro like the angels in Jacob's dream.

This is from Cowden Clarke's reminiscence for Milnes's biography of Keats, and it echoes a similar memory ("a whole troop of creatures floating in the ray") in Clarke's *Recollections of Writers*, published in 1878. Keats cannot "knit his faculties to the study of anatomy," yet once he begins to act as a dresser, the graphic, even grotesque, attention to the living body—utterly vulnerable and completely unmediated—magnifies. Anatomy demonstrations in a dissecting room are one thing; actual operations on the operating stage under the watching eyes of faculty and students are another.

If Keats had been able to "dress" for Astley Cooper, the finest and most famous surgeon of the day, the practice of medicine might have looked more attractive. Cooper was renowned for his skill and positive bedside manner. His surgeries were medical theater at its best, meaning that the patient not only had a good chance of surviving the experience but of being improved by it. Cooper emphasized that "surgery requires certain qualities, without which no man can arise to celebrity in the Profession,— these are a good Eye, a steady hand, and above all a Mind which is not easily ruffled by circumstances which may occur during the Operation . . . the head must always direct the hand." Unfortunately, Keats does not dress for Cooper; he dresses for perhaps the worse surgeon at Guy's, Billy Lucas, known publicly as "the butcher." As one student later reports in his memoirs (*Memoirs of John Flint South*, 1884), Lucas was a "tall, ungainly man, with stooping shoulders and a shuffling walk, as deaf as a post, not over-burdened with brains of any kind, but very good-natured and easy, and liked by everyone"—a frightening combination of charm and incompetence. Even Cooper himself cannot stay an opinion: "He was neat-handed, but rash in the extreme, cutting amongst most important parts as though they were only skin, and making us all shudder from the apprehension of his opening arteries or committing some other error." Brown notes in his piecemeal *Life of Keats* that the young poet "assured me the muse had no influence over him in his determination, he being compelled, by conscientious motives alone, to quit the profession, upon discovering that he was unfit to perform a surgical operation . . . He ascribed his inability to an overwrought apprehension of every possible chance of doing evil in the wrong direction of the instrument. 'My last operation,' he told me, 'was the opening of a man's temporal artery. I did it with the utmost nicety; but, reflecting on what passed through my mind at the time, my dexterity seemed a miracle, and I never took up the lancet again.' "

6

ON SUNDAY, APRIL 11, 1819—TWO WEEKS BEFORE HE BEGINS the sequence of odes (including "Ode to a Nightingale") that will carry his name into the future, and two months before he restarts his fragment epic *Hyperion*, and several years now into the condition called "a sore throat," and two months after his first serious, "death-warrant" hemorrhage—Keats encounters Samuel Taylor Coleridge on a walk on Hampstead Heath. The wind is high, one of those coastal winds that sweeps far inland and fills the tops of big trees. It is late morning, with an early spring light. Keats has only just been allowed to go out for any length, let alone take a good walk. He is headed north, toward Highgate. Coleridge, that "archangel a little damaged," is headed south toward Hampstead Village, along with his secretary-physician, Joseph Henry Green. The now familiar circumstances of their meeting are nearly as interesting as its afterglow. Coleridge, by this time, though still only in his forties, is thought to be the supreme intellectual senior citizen of England, the man whom Hazlitt has referred to as "the only person I ever knew who answered to the idea of a man of genius," and whose mind he has described as "being clothed with wings" and whose voice "rings in my ears with never dying sounds."

Yet the fact is that Coleridge, to use Keats's phrase for him, is "a great ruin," though still gifted with the jewel of his mariner's eye, which, like his mind, seems to catch all the light. His opium habit is nocturnal. Because Keats has never before met him, he at first does not recognize the famous face and head of Coleridge. When he does, out of shyness he keeps on walking. It is Green, who knows Keats from their days together at Guy's Hospital, who says to Coleridge, once they have all passed by one another, "Is that not the poet Keats?" Green then catches up with Keats and makes the introductions.

There are three versions of this one-and-only meeting between the obscure young poet and the established, renowned figure. Keats's is first, written a few days later, in yet another long journal-letter to George and Georgiana, covering February through early May.

Last Sunday I took a Walk towards highgate and in the lane that winds by the side of Lord Mansfield's park I met Mr Green our Demonstrator at Guy's in conversations with Coleridge—I joined them, after enquiring by a look whether it would be agreeable—I walked with him at his alderman-after dinner pace for near two miles I suppose In those two Miles he broached a thousand things—let me see if I can give you a list—Nightingales, Poetry—on Poetical sensation—Metaphysics— Different genera and species of Dreams—Nightmare—a dream accompanied by a sense of touch—single and double touch—A dream related—First and second consciousness—the difference explained between will and Volition—so many metaphysicians from a want of smoking Southey believes in them—southeys belief too much diluted—A Ghost story—Good morning—I heard

his voice as he came towards me—I heard it as he moved
away—I had heard it all the interval—if it may be
called so. He was civil enough to ask me to call on him at
Highgate . . .

The meeting takes place in Millfield Lane, on the eastern side of the Heath, between Highgate Ponds and Highgate proper, meaning that Keats has already walked a goodly distance from Wentworth Place and Coleridge has really only begun his walk. The two miles that Keats speaks of would likely take them back toward Hampstead and home. At an "alderman-after dinner pace," such a walk, even fueled by Coleridge's monologue, would occupy close to forty-five minutes. In an interview eleven years after the event, the encounter comes up in a conversation between Coleridge and a Mr. John Frere, although the text itself is not published until 1917 ("A Talk with Coleridge," ed. E. M. Green, *Cornhill Magazine*).

> *C. Poor Keats, I saw him once. Mr. Green, whom you have*
> *heard me mention, and I were walking out in these parts, and*
> *we were overtaken by a young man of very striking counte-*
> *nance whom Mr. Green recognized and shook hands with,*
> *mentioning my name; I wish Mr. Green had introduced me for*
> *I did not know who it was. He passed on, but in a few moments*
> *sprung back and said, "Mr. Coleridge, allow me the honour*
> *of shaking your hand." I was struck by the energy of his man-*
> *ner, and gave him my hand. He passed on, and we stood still*
> *looking after him, when Mr. Green said, "Do you know who*
> *that is? That is Keats, the poet." "Heavens!" said I, "when I*
> *shook him by the hand there was death!" That was about two*
> *years before he died.*
> *F. But what was it?*

C. *I cannot describe it. There was heat and a dampness in the hand. To say that his death was caused by the Review is absurd, but at the same time it is impossible adequately to conceive the effect which it must have had on his mind. It is very well for those who have a place in the world and are independent to talk of these things, they can bear such a blow, so can those who have a strong religious principle; but all men are not born Philosophers, and all men have not those advantages of birth and education. Poor Keats had not, and it is impossible I say to conceive the effect which such a Review must have had upon him, knowing as he did that he had his way to make in the world by his own exertions, and conscious of the genius within him.*

How different the emphasis here. For Keats, the meeting is about Coleridge's marvelous and profound gift of gab, meandering, like the walk, over ups and downs, ins and outs, twists and turns, perhaps almost an hour—"all men are not born Philosophers." For Coleridge, the meeting is all in their handshake, the "heat and a dampness," and of that he makes not only prophecy but sympathy and defines exactly Keats's lifelong dilemma: not being born a lord and six feet tall while at the same time born a genius. Three years after this interview, now 1832, when Coleridge is dictating his *Table Talk*, the Keats incident comes up again, diminished—particularly in the length of the visit—but with the same focus.

A loose, slack, not well-dressed youth met Mr._____ and myself in a lane near Highgate. _____ knew him, and spoke. It was Keats. He was introduced to me, and stayed a minute or so. After he had left us a little way, he came back and

said: "Let me carry away the memory, Coleridge, of having
pressed your hand!"—There is death in that hand," I said
to _____, when Keats was gone; yet this was, I believe,
before the consumption showed itself distinctly.

One's attention is drawn back to the healer's mortal hand in that moment when Keats is telling Brown why he thinks he cannot pursue surgery because of "apprehension of every possible chance of doing evil in the wrong direction of the instrument." And we are reminded, in Hunt's memoir, *Lord Byron and His Contemporaries*, of Keats's self-consciousness regarding his body when its wasting is becoming visible: how Keats would often look at his hand, "which was faded, and swollen in the veins, and say it was the hand of a man of fifty." Then there is that final fragment, written in the margin of a larger, last fragment, *The Cap and Bells; or, The Jealousies*, that becomes Keats's final signature.

> *This living hand, now warm and capable*
> *Of earnest grasping, would, if it were cold*
> *And in the icy silence of the tomb,*
> *So haunt thy days and chill thy dreaming nights*
> *That thou would wish thine own heart dry of blood*
> *So in my veins red life might stream again,*
> *And thou be conscience-calmed—see here it is—*
> *I hold it towards you.*

"Whether the dream now purposed to rehearse / Be Poet's or Fanatic's will be known / When this warm scribe my hand is in the grave"—these lines that close the induction to *The Fall of Hyperion* delineate exactly the difference between the surgeon's hand, the faded hand, the death hand, and the poet's hand, whose skill and dexterity are extensions of the mind, the imagination, and not of the machine itself. Keats's dreaming ends and begins in the hand that will soon enough start to fail him and that Coleridge has held and known. Keats's "greeting of the spirit" in his hand-shake with Coleridge adds a certain resonance to a living hand that is "now warm and capable / Of earnest grasping." Capable perhaps, warm absolutely. By the time Keats writes these last, original lines, his hand will be suffering the palsy, the paleness, and the specter-thinness he "ascribes" in the Nightingale ode, "Where but to think is to be full of sorrow / And leaden-eyed despairs. . . ."

7

THE DICHOTOMIES IN KEATS WILL INTENSIFY AS HIS ILLNESS progresses. The distinctions and separations in the kinds of poetry he has practiced and planned will be no less subject to contradiction. Once he and Brown have left Winchester and returned to Hampstead at the beginning of October, just weeks after the full flush of Keats's writing career is, like color in his hand, fading, his real posthumous life begins. Just weeks ago he had written Reynolds that he was "surprised . . . at the pleasure I live alone in." He had said to Brown that he intended to "no longer live upon hopes." He had professed to Woodhouse that once back in London he would "get employment in some of our elegant Periodical Works." And although he had confessed to Dilke that "I am fit for nothing but literature," he had also asked him to help find cheap lodgings in Westminster, a place "tolerably comfitable," so he might strike out on his own, not as a doctor but as a journalist. These self-promises last less than a fortnight, from October 8 until October 20, at which time he returns to reside with Brown at Wentworth Place, next door to Fanny Brawne. Says Brown,

> . . . *we returned to town together. Up to that period he had always expressed himself averse to writing for any periodical work. The only contribution he ever made of this kind was to "The Champion" newspaper, in a short notice of Kean's performance of Luke in "The city madam." As his poems were, to the disgrace of his contemporaries, unprofitable, in which sense alone his time had been spent idly, and as I was well acquainted with his independent feeling, there was no part of his plan, but what met with my concurrence, except the loss of his society. On this subject he heard me patiently, but concluded with insisting on the necessity of his living in a lodging in town, and by himself. He actually carried his plan into effect, not aware, as I was, of his incapability of living in solitude . . .*

This is Brown many years later in his *Life of Keats*. Whatever the personal or psychological reasons for needing to stay with Brown (who is by now well established as a brother-surrogate), health is a major factor. Keats is essentially broke, "lax, unemployed, unmeridian'd, and objectless," despairing ("You had best put me into your Cave of despair," he writes to Severn, playing on the title of Severn's entry in a Royal Academy show) and stuck ("—when I do feel ambitious. I am sorry to say that is very seldom"). In November Keats writes his publisher and states, in the same first sentence, "I have come to a determination not to publish any thing I have now ready written"—meaning, perhaps, since *Endymion*—"but for all that to publish a Poem before long and that I hope to make a fine one"—meaning, probably,

Lamia, which he hopes to revise into stronger shape. *The Fall of Hyperion* seems to be in limbo. And he appears to have little faith in anything he has written after the reviews of *Endymion,* unless "now ready written" refers to a more immediate, local time of finished and fair-copied drafts and not to the spread of nearly a hundred poems post-*Endymion* and including almost all of his best work. "Nothing could have in all its circumstances fallen out worse for me than the last year has done, or could be more damping to my poetical talent—" These words, written to George in this same November, speak to the way the troubles of one brother bear on the options of the other. George is bankrupt. John is broke, unemployed, and in retreat—not into a bower but, in Spenser's fine phrase, a cave of despair. The lingering question of health, however, is behind most of Keats's complaints. Small bothers of more than a year are adding up. By Christmas he says to his sister, "You would have seen me if I had been quite well. I have not, though not unwell enough to have prevented me—not indeed at all—but fearful lest the weather should affect my throat which on exertion or cold continually threatens me—By the advice of my Doctor I have had a warm great Coat made and have ordered some thick shoes. . . ."

With the new year, 1820, the new coat and shoes have come in handy. Winter is in full sail and George has arrived back in London to pursue the funds that are necessary for him to rebuild—though *build* may be the better word—because his and Georgiana's life in America has never gotten well started in the first place. Abbey has still not come through with the additional money he vaguely promised; George, the most practical member of the family, has returned to England to make sure that Abbey fulfills his roles as guardian and money manager of the Keats estate. Unlike John, George commands Abbey's respect. Different biographers have taken different views of the confusing state of the brothers' financial dealings with one another and the sorry state of the inheritance left, first, by the Keatses' maternal grandfather and, second, by their maternal grandmother, the Jenningses. Abbey, as trustee, seems to have contributed to, if not caused, the confusion. The money questions among the three brothers have that fated familial quality of desultory debt without closure, or, as George writes John in Teignmouth in March 1818, "I am about paying your's as well as Tom's bills, of which I shall keep regular accounts and for the sake of justice and a future proper understanding I intend calculating the probable amount Tom and I are indebted to you, something of this kind must be done, or at the end of two or three years we shall be all at sixes and sevens." Now it is two years later, Tom is dead, his part of the inheritance is up in the air, and the surviving brothers are indeed at sixes and sevens. As for the general issue of the inheritance—specifically the grandmother's estate—the complexity and longevity of what becomes a Chancery case is suggested by the fact that in *Bleak House* Dickens alludes to it as an example relevant to the interminable Jarndyce and Jarndyce suit in the High Court. "It's about a Will, and the trust under a Will." Without appealing to the number of pounds involved, it eventually becomes clear—after Tom and John are both dead—that there have been further monies set aside that were to be claimed when each of the Keats children reached age. The obscurantism of these claims has been blamed at different times on Abbey, the court, or problems with the grandmother's will.

At the moment unaware of this other, "latent" inheritance, George has recrossed the ocean to secure funds that he feels he has coming, whether from Abbey, Tom's estate, or money that John may owe him. John is not only ill but, for all intents and purposes, penniless. The beginning of the disintegration of the Keats Circle begins here, in January, just as the beginning of the end of Keats's writing career has the definite date of the autumnal letters written only months before George's arrival. Once Keats, as a unifying figure, is gone, his friends will find any number of things to disagree about: Writing the biography will be one, but George's behavior during his visit regarding the raising of funds will be another. The complications of who owes whom and who needs the money more will ultimately result in bad feeling in every quarter and will turn friend against friend and, almost, brother against brother. Yet at the time, in the month of George's stay, discussions of money, as such, will be secondary to George's busy social schedule, which includes parties and dinners with his in-laws as well as old friends, and only some of which have included John's company. Halfway through the month, Keats comments in a long letter to his sister-in-law, Georgiana, that "It is strange that George having to stop so short a time in England I should not have seen him for nearly two days—He has been to Haslam's and does not encourage me to follow his example." This letter, in itself, is curious in that it starts out intending to reassure Georgiana that George has arrived safely and that his mission has every promise of being fulfilled. But as it goes along, it becomes more and more a confessional, directly and indirectly, with two or three recurring themes: poverty and indolence and not a little self-abnegation, with the anger attached to these sublimated. If Keats sends the letter by post, it will arrive after George has returned; if he sends it with George . . . well, either way George will naturally read it.

I could almost promise that if I had the means I would accompany George back to America and pay you a Visit of a few Months. I should not think much of the time or my absence from my Books, or I have not right to think, for I am very idle: but then I ought to be diligent and at least keep myself within the reach of materials for diligence. Diligence! that I do not mean to say, I should say dreaming over my Books, or rather other peoples books.

If you should have a Boy do not christen him John, and persuade George not to let his partiality for me come across—'T is a bad name, and goes against a Man—If my name had been Edmund I should have been more fortunate—

This is a beautiful day; I hope you will not quarrel with it if I call it an American one. The Sun comes upon the snow and makes a prettier candy than we have on twelvth cakes. George is busy this morning in making copies of my verses—he is making now one of an Ode to the nightingale, which is like reading an account of the black hole at Calcutta on an ice bergh.

The more I know of Men the more I know how to value entire liberality in any of them. Thank God there are a great many who will sacrifice their worldly interest for a friend; I wish there were more who would sacrifice their passions. The worst of Men are those whose self interests are their passion—the next those whose passions are their self-interst. Upon the whole I dislike Mankind . . .

—perhaps by this time you have received my last three letters not one of which had reach'd before George sail'd, I would give two pence to have been over the world as much as he has—I wish I had money enough to do nothing but travel about for years—

To me it is all as dull here as Louisville could be. I am tired of the Theatres. Almost all the parties I may chance to fall into I know by heart . . . When Once a

person has smok'd the vapidness of the routine of Society
he must have either self interest or the love of some sort
of distinction to keep him in good humour with it. All I
can say is that standing at Charing cross and looking east
west north and south I can see nothing but dullness . . .

On January 28, at six o'clock in the morning, in the dark, George leaves London on the Liverpool coach with seven hundred pounds in his pocket, and leaves John with something under seventy pounds, ten—perhaps more—pounds fewer than Keats owes, which comes to less than nothing. Later, Keats would say to Fanny Brawne that "having a family makes a man selfish." And he would say to Brown, "he ought not to have asked me," meaning that whatever funds and advances George had secured from Abbey and his part of Tom's inheritance, George was of the opinion that John was in his debt. George could not afford, apparently, to permit any money within his sphere of influence to go ungathered. He must not have perceived how strapped his brother was, or how ill. Keats, neurotic about money, could not confront George as to his situation. Eight months into the future, when Keats is desperate for funds for the voyage to Italy, Abbey will bluff him with the remark, "You know that it was very much against my will that you lent your money to George," money that Tom has left him. After the falling-out among the friends, George will write Dilke in 1824 that "John himself was ignorant of the real state of his funds, it was so painful a subject and in our private communications he was so extremely melancholy that I always had to show him the pleasing side of things; when I left London I had not the courage to say that the 700L I had obtained was not all ours by right." Money, when it relates to families, is not only a complexity but an opacity, and no one and everyone is usually to blame. Keats lives for another year and a month, and after George's departure from Liverpool on February 1 never writes his brother—who has been his mainstay and confidant—again.

Two days after George's departure from Liverpool, on February 3, a Thursday, Keats goes into town to spend the day. The weather has brightened and warmed, and even though it is still the middle of winter, Keats, like a boy anticipating spring, leaves his new great coat at home. He is late coming back; it is eleven o'clock before he reaches Wentworth Place. He has spent the entire day in the city, old sore throat and all, moving from place to place more or less exposed to cold London damp. Worse, to save, he returns "on the outside of the stage this bitter day until I was severely chilled." But "now I don't feel it," he says to Brown. "Fevered!—of course, a little," as he stumbles into the house. Fifteen years later, as he is remembering the incident, Brown cannot recall the date: "(I have no record of the date, but it was either at the end of December or the beginning of January)": He is off by a month and therefore makes no connection between the date of Keats's first major, life-threatening hemorrhage and George's difficult visit and departure, though if he had remembered right, connecting George to John's "death-warrant" blood-spitting would have been an easy judgment for him. Aileen Ward implies that, indeed, there is a connection between Keats's withheld anger with his brother and the arterial "blood from my mouth." Whatever the emotional, psychological cause and effect—the psychosomatic cause—Keats's vulnerable physical condition is by itself dangerous enough, perhaps requiring only some single inciting force to start the explosion of blood from the lungs. The coach from town out to Hampstead, a ride of about four miles, would have deposited Keats at the top of Pond Street off the High Street. The names of these streets, like so much else in the English imagination, are literal. The High Street is not only the main through way but sits well above Hampstead's primary residential areas and the Heath itself. Wentworth Place, right off East Heath Road, would have been a good walk down Pond Street hill, then a left turn. Naturally, at the bottom of Pond Street lay Hampstead Ponds, which, at this moment, on a wet, cold night, means there is a knife-sharp wind coming up from the Heath across the ponds. Spending the day in winter London without a coat, riding the coach home on top, and having to walk downhill against the night wind would be enough for any-one. For Keats, it was as if he had yielded to something inside himself and given in to what he felt was fated.

Keats the Poet will, on this night, be replaced by Keats the Patient and, at times, Keats the Physician. The dreamer, the sleeper inside, will awake. Brown describes Keats as "in a state that looked like fierce intoxication." Keats goes up to bed, and, "before his head was on the pillow," coughs blood. "I went towards him; he was examining a single drop of blood upon the sheet. 'Bring me the candle, Brown; and let me see this blood.' After regarding it steadfastly, he looked up into my face, with a calmness of countenance that I can never forget, and said,—'I know that colour of that blood;—it is arterial blood;—I cannot be deceived in that colour . . .' " Brown here is observing both the patient and physician, dual roles that Keats will have to play for the rest of his short life, often against the "sage" advice of his doctors. And it is the physician in Keats, the realist, who sees in the absolute color of this blood—" 'my death-warrant;—I must die' "—the same "calmness of countenance," the same healer consciousness that Severn will see at the end.

Brown "runs" for a surgeon, a Dr. George Rodd, who, like

the two doctors who follow—Doctors Sawrey and Bree—immediately relieves Keats of more blood—a lot more—and puts him on a meatless, nearly nutritionless "pseudo-victuals" diet, recommending as well no activity that might excite the patient, such as the writing of poems. Bloodletting in the nineteenth century is still a first-response reaction to illnesses that before the discovery of the microscope and bacteria and the invisible world of the body's interior were understood by inference and speculation, confirming Keats's once expressed opinion that when it comes to disease, "medical men guess." Keats's fevered mental state—meaning his nerves—must have also contributed to the conviction of letting his blood, because venesection, from the Egyptians on, was seen as a way of drawing off the corrupt matter that causes an imbalance among the four humors, or temperaments, representing the sanguineous, melancholic, choleric, or phlegmatic. Blood would have been taken from one of three of the major veins in one of Keats's arms (likely the left to start)—the cephalic vein, the median, or the basilica—then varied over time. If nothing else, bloodletting tends to exhaust the patient into the appearance of calm and stability. In this invalid-convalescing state, tucked away in the now famous small bedroom of what is now the Keats House, he remains until he is well enough to be repositioned on a sofa bed in the front parlor, allowing him a view of the garden and the street. This "pleasant prison" is made all the more pleasant because the Brawnes have, since fall, lived in the Dilkes' half of the house.

Although he is a pulmonary specialist, Dr. Bree decides that Keats's trouble is in his stomach, caused by various nervous disorders, which was a common reading of the diseases of the day. Only when something such as consumption reached conclusive, late stages—namely the obvious, visible wasting away of the body—would a more definite diagnosis be made. In Keats's case, Bree dismisses the possibility of anything pulmonary let alone consumptive. This is, of course, stunning news, considering Keats's own diagnosis to Brown the night he coughs up the arterial blood. Yet this disparity between what the patient is experiencing and what his doctors observe will continue until the end. And the bloodletting—of which Keats himself has been a practitioner—and the "starvation" diet continue, though once Keats seems to be regaining some of his old robustness, his fast will abate.

By March he is not or is doing better. On March 8, 1820, Brown writes to Keats's publisher, John Taylor, of Taylor and Hessey, that

> *Poor Keats will be unable to prepare his Poems for the Press for a long time. He was taken on Monday evening with violent palpitations of the heart, and has since remained too weak to get up. I expect Dr Bree every hour. I am wretchedly depressed.*
>
> *Your's sincerely,*
> *Chas Brown*
>
> *If you come, do not let him hear your voice, as the slightest circumstances tending to create surprise, or any other emotion, must be avoided.*
>
> *CB*

Two days later, Brown writes to Taylor again.

> *After my dismal note I am glad to be able to give you good news. Keats is so well as to be out of danger. We*

*intend, if the weather remain kindly, to go to the coast
of Hants. He walked in the Garden to-day. You will
suspect that I gave you a useless alarm, but I wrote at
the time I was told that it was possible he might sud-
denly be lost to us in one of those fits. Hessey's letter
came, & I opened it, for Keats could not endure even the
circumstance of a letter being put in his hands,—nor
can he bear it even yet, tho' I consider him perfectly out
of danger, & no pulmonary affection, no organic defect
whatever,—the disease is on his mind, and there I hope
he will soon be cured.*

Your's sincerely,
Chas Brown

Back in the autumn, when there seemed no imminent dan-
ger regarding his health, Keats had said to Taylor that he had
no intention of publishing another selection of poems—none, at
least, that he had written since *Endymion*. He wanted to write
something large and salable, something new, something like a
Lamia or even bigger and more exotic that would hit the public
just right, à la Byron. But the reality of his ambition has, by early
spring, changed profoundly. Taylor and Hessey have encour-
aged him to rethink his situation. Hence these March notes to
Taylor, and thus the "preparation" of a new collection that will
become an on-again, off-again project for the next three months,
until July, when *Lamia, Isabella, The Eve of St. Agnes, and Other
Poems* (1820) appears. On his good days, Keats will tinker with
revisions of the poems that he plans to include; on his less good
days, he withdraws into a mood where poetry is far away, and
love and Fanny Brawne are near. "Illness is a long lane, but I see
you at the end of it, and shall mend my pace as well as possible."

The disease is *on* his mind, as Brown malaproply says, but it is not *of* his mind.

Of the some ninety-six poems written since *Endymion*—that is, from the autumn of 1817 to the autumn of 1819—including long poems, lyric poems, and light and incidental poems, only thirteen make it into the last selection. And even at that small figure, it is interesting to note the balance and number of pieces from each category as well as the order in the sequence. The odes, for instance, which will ultimately rank Keats among the English poets, are separated into two "groups" and arranged within the frame of the longer narrative pieces and set next to the lighter poems, so that *Lamia, Isabella,* and *The Eve of St. Agnes* begin the collection and *Hyperion: A Fragment* ends it, whereas the "Nightingale," "Grecian Urn," and Psyche" odes are followed by "Fancy," "Bards of Passion and of Mirth," "Lines on the Mermaid Tavern," and "Robin Hood," which are in turn followed by "To Autumn" and "Ode on Melancholy," making the table of contents look like this:

Lamia
Isabella
The Eve of St. Agnes
Ode to a Nightingale
Ode on a Grecian Urn
Ode to Psyche
Fancy
Ode ("Bards of Passion and of Mirth")
Lines on the Mermaid Tavern
Robin Hood
To Autumn
Ode on Melancholy
Hyperion: A Fragment

(Amy Lowell, in her marvelous personalist biography of Keats, notes that "Taylor and Hessey seem to have had some idea of printing the poems in the *Lamia* volume as separate books or pamphlets. On the back of one of the pages of a manuscript of *Lamia*, a manuscript in Keats's handwriting, is a faint pencil memorandum (not by Keats) to this effect":

Isabella	500	32
Lamia	600	35
St Agnes	500	29

This day are published in 8 vo. form 3 shillings each Five Poems:

1 Isabella
2 Lamia
3 St Agnes
4 Poems, Miscellaneous
5 Hyperion, a fragment.
The whole in 1 Vol. 8vo., price 12 & 6.

Keats more than likely concurred in the idea of separate publication, with the thought of profit, but then reconsidered.)

The arrangement of the poems seems more collaborative than single-minded, and it is clearly aimed at an audience, in an order in which the romance narratives are featured, the serious lyrics are subordinated, the lighter fare is elevated, and the fragment epic is emphasized. It is a selection meant to sell; Keats's voice—though certainly not against making money from his book—was doubtless heard, but it was one of three, along with Taylor's and Woodhouse's. (Keats at one point wants to start off with *The Eve of St. Agnes*; at the time, *Lamia* was still being revised.) One could form a considerable collection from what was left out of this last book. There are no sonnets, among which the list includes "After Dark Vapours," "On Sitting Down to Read King Lear," "When I Have Fears," "What the Thrush Said," "On Seeing the Elgin Marbles," and "Bright Star." Nor is "La Belle Dame sans Merci" included, nor *The Fall of Hyperion. A Dream*, and obviously none of the poems from the Northern tour. Keats is ill and distracted but not—to use his favorite word—"disinterested." Like so much else in his life from now on, the vote of the majority will prevail. The "Advertisement" written for the book by his publishers is an example.

> *If any apology be thought necessary for the appearance of the unfinished poem Hyperion, the publishers beg to state that they alone are responsible, as it was printed at their particular request, and contrary to the wish of the author. The poem was intended to have been of equal length with Endymion, but the reception given to that work discouraged the author from proceeding.*
>
> FLEET STREET, 26 JUNE, 1820

Other than the title page, these are the first words to greet the reader of *Lamia, Isabella, The Eve of St. Agnes, and Other Poems*, "in many ways perhaps the most remarkable single volume to be published by any poet during the past century and a half, if we leave aside collected works published by poets in their old age," to quote Bate. The last sentence of the "apology" is particularly hurtful to Keats, and in one of the book's gift copies he strikes out the entire paragraph with cross-hatching and writes at the top of the page that "This is none of my doing—I was ill at the time," then, for emphasis, right under the *Endymion* part of the sentence, adds, "This is a lie." *Hyperion. A Fragment* was not going where and how he wanted it to go; it was an artistic decision to quit the poem, just as it was an artistic decision to start it up again later as *The Fall* and as *A Dream*. But Taylor, Hessey, and Woodhouse recognize the new level of writing that the first *Hyperion* achieves, especially as an antidote to the soft passages in *Endymion* that the Tory critics have so taken to task. Keats's publishers' motives are clear: They want the book to be read as an advance and to be seen for what it is: a rare range of writing. They do not want it tied to the past. Keats, on the other hand, as the maker, sees his poems in process and about process, and about progress, about arrivals and departures and necessary connections to the past—not only in the line of his own development but, he hopes, in the lineage of the great poets he admires. The rewrite of *Hyperion* is exactly what his work is about, just as the spring odes require return and return to the form he has discovered, and just as "To Autumn," written months later, is a farewell to that form. The more insidious aspect of the final sentence of the "Advertisement" is that in addition to its distortion of artistic motives, it also confirms an implication of the lie that some weakness of character prevented Keats from meeting his ambition, that he is a flower too frail for the harsh winds of enemy criticism. This is the notion that will be picked up and promulgated well into Keats's immortality, and like his gravestone epitaph and Shelley's elegy will be the legacy not of his enemies but of his friends.

Although modern taste has gone in a different direction, Woodhouse preferred the first version of *Hyperion* to the second. He likely felt that, even as a fragment, it better met the test of an epic than the more "lyrical" dream version. Indeed, in trying to persuade us that the crucial passage of lines 187 through 210 in *The Fall*, in which Keats debates the role of the poet versus the role of the dreamer, was "intended" to be erased, Woodhouse allows that Keats seems to have had no answer to the argument. Are the poet and the dreamer necessarily distinct, as Moneta asserts? Is the healer that different from the dreamer? Keats at his medical lectures drew flowers, yet a mind as negatively capable as his could surely be in more than one place at once, even opposite places. "What am I then?" Keats's speaker asks the goddess, "whose face I cannot see," whose face is to be revealed as "bright-blanched / By an immortal sickness which kills not . . . which happy death / Can put no end to." Such a face is not only the face of memory of his mother and of the fine-boned Tom, it is Keats's own projected death mask. Now, with his great work emerging in print, whether or not it is quite what he wants, Keats is neither healer nor poet but a patient whose own face will become a memory. Ten days after his "death-warrant" hemorrhage, still in the midst of winter, Keats writes his friend James Rice,

> *How astonishingly does the chance of leaving the world*
> *impress a sense of its natural beauties on us. Like poor*
> *Falstaff, though I do not babble, I think of green fields.*
> *I muse with the greatest affection on every flower I have*
> *known from my infancy—their shapes and colours are as*
> *new to me as if I had just created them with a superhu-*
> *man fancy—It is because they are connected with the*
> *most thoughtless and happiest moments of our Lives—I*
> *have seen foreign flowers in hothouses of the most beauti-*
> *ful nature, but I do not care a straw for them. The simple*
> *flowers of our spring are what I want to see again.*

PHYSICIAN NATURE

...

Physician Nature! let my spirit blood!
O ease my heart of verse and let me rest...

1

Shall I give you Miss Brawne? She is about my height—
with a fine style of countenance of the lengthen'd sort—
she wants sentiment in every feature—she manages to
make her hair look well—her nostrills are fine—though
a little painful—her mouth is bad and good—her Profil
is better than her full-face which indeed is not full but
pale and thin without showing any bone—Her shape
is very graceful and so are her movements—her Arms
are good her hands badish—her feet tolerable—she is
not seventeen—but she is ignorant—monstrous in her
behaviour flying out in all directions, calling people such
names—that I was forced lately to make use of the term
Minx—this is I think not from any innate vice but from a
penchant she has for acting stylishly. I am however tired
of such style and shall decline any more of it—

If this is a portrait, it is a very real one, representing the good
and the "badish" of appearance and character. Yet it is also a
portrait in the round of—to Keats—a compelling figure against
whom he protests too much. To the contrary, he is *not* tired
of such style and will *not* decline any more of it. This much-
quoted paragraph is Keats's introduction of Fanny Brawne to
George and Georgiana in his Christmas–New Year's journal-
letter of 1819, spanning a little over two weeks. Exactly when
he first officially meets "Miss Brawne" is unclear, though there

are probably many serious encounters over the course of the fall of 1818 leading up to the burst of his portrait comment. Earlier in the letter, rather offhandedly, Keats mentions that "Mrs Brawne who took Brown's house for the Summer, still resides in Hampstead—she is a very nice woman—and her daughter senior is I think beautiful and elegant, graceful, silly, fashionable and strange we have a little tiff now and then—and she behaves a little better, or I must have sheered off—" "Now and then" implies not only meetings absent the "occasional tiff" but a deal of something more when the tiffs occur. Like other aspects of his personal life, Keats prefers privileged silence over anything resembling publicity. What is odd is that in these months Keats remains unclear about Fanny's age: She is eighteen, not sixteen, and is not simply "stylish" but smart, and versed in languages and literature, not just fashion, manners, and dancing.

Their relationship has been developing for about six weeks when Keats first mentions Fanny to George and Georgiana. Fanny B., you might say, is part of how he inaugurates the new year, his best year of writing. The fantasy of her—if the dates of their coming together are correct—cannot help but inform the light and richness behind the beauty of *The Eve of St. Agnes*, composed in the month after he speaks of her in the journal-letter—that is, the anticipation of romance, an acknowledgment of foreplay, is acted out in the poem in Keats's most representative terms. Already, by Christmas—"the happiest day I had ever then spent," Fanny later states—the two of them have an "understanding," which means that Keats's various commitment to Fanny coincides exactly with the period of grief following Tom's December 1818 death and lasts—through all kinds of absences and distances—until Keats himself dies in February 1821. By the calendar, this looks like a fair reach of time, especially when we consider how little time Keats has after Tom. The fact is, though, most of the Keats-Brawne romance will happen in separation, by mail, and during a failed convalescence; it will happen in tandem with the rest of Keats's life, never to rid itself of the nagging ambivalence that Keats feels toward women in general and himself in love in particular. Added to these tensions will be the near-yet-far syndrome of lovers who live next door or down the road from each other, with almost always a wall of some kind between them.

After the introduction, by letter, of Fanny to what is left of Keats's family, mention of her goes underground for the remainder of the winter and spring. Proximity seems, for the moment, to preclude the need for correspondence. Keats is now living with Brown, while Fanny, in three months, will move from Elm Cottage, around the corner, to the Dilkes' half of Wentworth Place, less than a step or two away. Their relationship will become an open secret, though their actual engagement will be kept between them until close to the end. Keats's near pathology for secrecy regarding their relationship adds to its at-once intensity and distancing, as if he and Fanny were together in a parallel circumstance to what else is going on in their lives. The secrecy is mostly, but not entirely, in Keats's mind, like his moods and complaints of indolence. By 1819 he is beginning to feel the implications of Tom's tubercular legacy: periods of intense creativity juxtaposed with those of lassitude. As usual, too, he has no money, making him potentially a "Parson-romeo," unable to support himself let alone a possible wife. Still, with the first version of *Hyperion* put in recess, this new year holds promise as well as secrets. Immediately following *St. Agnes* (January), he writes the abortive *The Eve of St. Mark* (February), the poem adored by the

Pre-Raphaelites, then once the weather picks up and the birds return in March, he writes and revises, in succession, "La Belle Dame sans Merci" (April), "Ode to Psyche" (April), "Ode on a Grecian Urn" (May), "Ode to a Nightingale" (May), "Ode on Melancholy" (May), "Ode on Indolence" (June), plus, in between, a couple of sonnets on "Fame" and a sonnet "To Sleep," all to be followed over the summer by *Lamia*, *The Fall of Hyperion*, and "To Autumn." There is no written word about or word to Fanny until he has chosen to move to the Isle of Wight at the end of June (Brown has again sublet his half of Wentworth Place for the season). Absence and distance make a fonder heart, so on July 1 Keats writes his first surviving letter to the young woman whom he has so glowingly spoken of seven months before, if you do not count the poems as secret letters.

Keats writes Fanny Brawne some thirty-seven letters and notes that have survived. He himself destroyed or was buried with her last letters to him. The Keats-Brawne "correspondence"—if it can be called that, because, on record, it is one-sided—falls into three distinct periods: those letters from far and near beginning in the summer of 1819 when, with his usual search for the "solitude" in which to write, Keats moves from the Isle of Wight to Winchester to Fleet Street to College Street in Westminster; the paragraph and half-page letter-notes written during his recovery following his February 4, 1820, hemorrhage and lasting through the spring, until he is forced once again to leave Brown's half of Wentworth Place and move to nearby Kentish Town for the summer; and those few final, darkest letters written from just a mile or two away yet at an emotional distance of illness and anger. Perhaps the most effective way to see the arc, the rise and fall, of Keats's state of mind regarding Fanny, starting many months after their "quiet" engagement, is to read excerpts of the implicit narrative of what he writes to her, addressed variously as "My dearest Lady" or "My sweet Girl" or "My love" or "Dearest Fanny."

I am glad I had not an opportunity of sending off a Letter which I wrote for you on Tuesday night—'twas too much like one out of Rousseau's Heloise. I am more reasonable this morning . . .

I would not have you see those Rapsoides which I once thought it impossible I should ever give way to, and which I have often laughed at in another, for fear you should think me either too unhappy or perhaps a little mad.

I have never known any unalloy'd Happiness for many days together: the death or sickness of some one has always spoilt my hours—and now when none such troubles oppress me, it is you must confess very hard that another sort of pain should haunt me.

In case of the worst that can happen I shall still love you—but what hatred shall I have for another!

ISLE OF WIGHT, JULY 1

Your Letter gave me more delight, than any thing in the world but yourself could do . . .

You mention "horrid people" and ask me whether it depend upon them, whether I see you again . . .

Why may I not speak of your Beauty, since without that I could never have lov'd you—I cannot conceive any beginning of such love as I have for you but Beauty.

I have met with women whom I really think would like to be married to a Poem and to be given away by a Novel.

*I kiss'd your writing over in the hope you had indulg'd
me by leaving a trace of honey . . .*

ISLE OF WIGHT, JULY 8

*I have been in so irritable a state of health these two or
three last days . . . You say you might have made me bet-
ter: you would then have made me worse: now you could
quite effect a cure: What fee my sweet Physician would I
not give you to do so.*

*. . . Poems are as common as newspaper and I do not
see why it is a greater crime in me than in another to let
the verses of an half-fledged brain trumble in to reading-
rooms and drawing room windows.*

*I will say I will see you in a month at most, though no
one but yourself should see me; if it be but for an hour. I
should not like to be so near you as London without being
continually with you . . .*

ISLE OF WIGHT, JULY 15

*. . . you say speaking of Mr. Severn "but you must be
satisfied in knowing that I admired you much more than
your friend." My dear love, I cannot believe there ever
was or ever could be any thing to admire in me especially
as far as sight goes—I cannot be admired, I am not a
thing to be admired. You are, I love you; all I can bring
you is a swooning admiration of your Beauty.*

*I have two luxuries to brood over in my walks, your
Loveliness and the hour of my death. O that I could have
possession of them both in the same minute. I hate the world;
it batters too much the wings of my self-will, and would I
could take a sweet poison from your lips to send me out of it.*

ISLE OF WIGHT, JULY 25

*You say you must not have any more such Letters as the
last . . . I am not idle enough for proper downright love-
letters—I leave this minute scene in our Tragedy and see
you (think it not blasphemy) through the mist of Plots
speeches, counterplots and counter speeches—The Lover
is madder than I am—I am nothing to him—he has a
figure like the Statue of Maleager and double distilled
fire in his heart.*

Isle of Wight, August 5

*—what shall I say for myself? I have been here four days
and not yet written you—*

 *I must remain some days in a Mist—I see you
through a Mist: as I dare say you do me by this time—
Believe in the first Letters I wrote you: I assure you I felt
as I wrote—I could not write so now—The thousand
images I have had pass through my brain—my uneasy
spirits—my unguess'd fate—all spread as a veil between
me and you—*

 *This Page as my eye skims over it I see is excessively
unloverlike and ungallant—I cannot help it!—I am
no officer in yawning quarters; no Parson-romeo—My
Mind is heap'd to the full; stuff'd like a cricket ball—*

Winchester, August 16

*I came by the Friday night coach—and have not yet been
to Hamstead. Upon my soul it is not my fault, I cannot
resolve to mix any pleasure with my days: they go one
like another undistinguishable. If I were to see you to day
it would destroy the half comfortable sullenness I enjoy at
present into downright perplexities. I love you too much to
venture to Hampstead . . .*

Knowing well that my life must be passed in fatigue
and trouble, I have been endeavouring to wean myself from
you: for to myself alone what can be much of a misery?

FLEET STREET, SEPTEMBER 13

I cannot exist without you . . . I should be afraid to sepa-
rate myself far from you . . . I could be martyr'd for my
Religion—Love is my religion—I could die for that—I
could die for you—

COLLEGE STREET, OCTOBER 13

Mrs Dilke I should think will tell you that I purpose liv-
ing in Hampstead—I must impose chains upon myself—
I shall be able to do nothing—I should like to cast the die
for Love or death—

COLLEGE STREET, OCTOBER 19

They say I must remain confined to this room for some
time. The consciousness that you love me will make a
pleasant prison of the house next to yours.

On the night I was taken ill when so violent a rush of
blood came to my Lungs that I felt nearly suffocated—I
assure you I felt it possible I might not survive and at that
moment thought of nothing but you—

According to all appearances I am to be separated from
you as much as possible . . . there may be no end to this
emprisoning of you . . . I am recommended not even to read
poetry much less write it. I wish I had even a little hope.

. . . how could it ever have been my wish to forget you?
how could I have ever said such a thing?

I read your note in bed last night, and that might be
the reason of my sleeping so much better . . . Be very

*careful of open doors and windows and going without
your duffle grey.*

*Do not let your mother suppose that you hurt me by
writing at night. For some reason or other your last night's
note was not so treasureable as former ones . . . I am
nervous, I own, and may think myself worse than I really
am; if so you must indulge me, and pamper with that sort
of tenderness you have manifested towards me in differ-
ent Letters . . . "If I should die," said I to myself, "I have
left no immortal work behind me—nothing to make my
friends proud of my memory—but I have lov'd the prin-
ciple of beauty in all things, and if I had had time would
have made myself remember'd."*

*I have been confined three weeks and am not yet
well—this proves that there is something wrong about me
which my constitution will either conquer or give way to-
Let us hope for the best. Do you hear the Thrush singing
over the field? I think it is a sign of mild weather—so
much the better for me. Like all Sinners now I am ill I
philosophise aye out of my attachment to every thing,
Trees, flowers, Thrushes, Spring, Summer, Claret & c &
c aye every thing but you—*

I will not sing in a cage—

*I do not love you so much as you wish? . . . in the hot-
test fit I ever had I would have died for you . . . Do you
not see a heart naturally furnish'd with wings imprison
itself with me? . . . When you are in the room my thoughts
never fly out of the window: you always concentrate my
whole senses. The anxiety shown about our Loves in your
last note is an immense pleasure to me . . .*

*I improve a little every day. I rely upon taking a walk
with you upon the first of may . . .*

Perhaps on your account I have imagined my illness more serious than it is: how horrid was the chance of slipping into the ground instead of into your arms—the difference is amazing Love—Death must come at last; Man must die, as what more pleasures than you have given so sweet a creature as you can give.

What a horrid climate this is? or what careless inhabitants it has? You are one of them. My dear girl do not make a joke of it: do not expose yourself to the cold. There's the Thrush again—I can't afford it—he'll run me up a pretty Bill for Music—

. . . if I were a little less selfish and more enthousiastic I should run around and surprise you with a knock at the door. I fear I am too prudent for a dying kind of Lover. Yet, there is a great difference between going off in warm blood like Romeo, and making one's exit like a frog in a frost . . . Illness is a long lane, but I see you at the end of it, and shall mend my pace as well as possible . . .

HAMPSTEAD, FEBRUARY 4–
MARCH 22

I wrote a Letter for you yesterday expecting to have seen your mother. I shall be selfish enough to send it though I know it may give you a little pain, because I wish you to see how unhappy I am for love of you, and endeavour as much as I can to entice you to give up your whole heart to me whose existence hangs upon you. You could not step or move an eyelid but it would shoot to my heart—

. . . I think a real Love is enough to occupy the widest heart—Your going to town alone, when I heard of it was a shock to me—yet I expected it—promise me you will not for some time, till I am better.

—if you can smile in peoples faces, and wish them to admire you now, you never have nor ever will love me—I see life in nothing but the certainty of your Love—convince me of it my sweetest. If I am not somehow convinc'd I shall die of agony. If we must not live as other men and women do—I cannot brook the wolfbane of fashion foppery and tattle. You must be mine to die upon the rack if I want you.

I am tormented day and night. They talk of my going to Italy. 'Tis certain I shall never recover if I am to be so long separate from you: yet with all this devotion to you I cannot persuade myself into any confidence of you. Past experience connected with the fact of my long separation from you gives me agonies which are scarcely to be talked of.

When you were in the habit of flirting with Brown you would have left off, could your own heart have felt half of one pang mine did. Brown is a good sort of Man—he did not know he was doing me to death by inches . . . I will never see or speak to him until we are both old men, if we are to be. I will resent my heart having been made a football. You will call this madness.

— you do not know what it is to love—one day you may—your time is not come. Ask yourself how many unhappy hours Keats has caused you in Loneliness. For myself I have been a Martyr the whole time . . . I cannot live without you, and not only you but chaste you; virtuous you.

WESLEYAN PLACE, MAY

I see you come down in the morning: I see you meet me at the Window—I see every thing over again eternally that

I have ever seen . . . My friends laugh at you! I know
some of them—when I know them all I shall never think
of them again as friends or even acquaintance . . . how
short is the longest life . . . Your name never passes my
Lips—do not let mine pass yours—
　　How could I slight you? How threaten to leave you?
not in the spirit of a Threat to you—no—but in the spirit
of Wretchedness in myself. My fairest, my delicious, my
angel Fanny! do not believe me such a vulgar fellow. I
will be as patient in illness and as believing in Love as I
am able—

WESLEYAN PLACE, JUNE

I feel it almost impossible to go to Italy—the fact is
I cannot leave you, and shall never taste one minute's
content until it pleases chance to let me live with you for
good. But I will not go on at this rate. A person in health
as you are can have no conception of the horrors that
nerves and a temper like mine go through.

　　I shall never be able any more to endure the society of
any of those who used to meet at Elm Cottage and Went-
worth Place. The last two years taste like brass upon my
Palate. If I cannot live with you I will live alone. I do not
think my health will improve much while I am separated
from you. For all this I am averse to seeing you—I cannot
bear flashes of light and return into my glooms again.

　　Hamlet's heart was full of such Misery as mine when
he said to Ophelia "Go to a Nunnery, go, go!" Indeed I
should like to give up the matter at once—I should like
to die. I am sickened at the brute world which you are
smiling with. I hate men and women more. I see nothing

but thorns for the future—wherever I may be next winter in Italy or nowhere Brown will be living near you with his indecencies . . . Suppose me in Rome—well, I should there see you as in a magic glass going to and from town at all hours . . . the world is too brutal for me—I am glad there is such a thing as the grave—I am sure I shall never have any rest till I get there.

MORTIMER TERRACE, AUGUST

2

WHEN KEATS'S LETTERS TO FANNY BRAWNE WERE FINALLY published in 1878, well over a decade after her death and almost six decades after his, the Victorians, through a major spokesman such as Matthew Arnold, could not help but judge them as at once sensuous and sniveling and the sad work of a "badly bred surgeon's apprentice." For some the letters also proved that Fanny was the minx—the superficial and sharp-tongued flirt—that Keats was originally attracted to, the young woman whom most of his friends found wanting in depth. For others the letters proved Keats's weakness of character, the "puling boy" whom Brown had accused Hunt of invoking in his memoir of the Romantics. Keats's "love" letters do stand out—no question—especially from the profound and beautiful letters to his friends—letters without equal in their intuitive genius about making poetry. They even stand out from the letters that he is writing to Reynolds, Brown, his sister Fanny, George Keats, and Dilke at the same time as the love letters. Within days, in fact, of his last ever and most extreme letter to Fanny B. (in

August), he writes, on August 16, one of the most thoughtful and poignant of all his letters, his famous response to Shelley's invitation to join the Shelleys on the northwest coast of Italy. If he had, he would have likely died in Shelley's arms, an image beyond contriving, particularly considering that when Shelley drowned off the coast of Viareggio, he had Keats's last book open in his pocket.

"You I am sure," he writes to Shelley, "will forgive me for sincerely remarking that you might curb your magnanimity and be more of an artist, and 'load every rift' of your subject with ore. The thought of such discipline must fall like cold chains upon you, who perhaps never sat with your wings furl'd for six Months together." As already noted, this exquisite evaluation of Shelley's high poetic style is only a sidebar to Keats's thanks but no thanks to the invitation to convalesce with the expatriate. As for his own mood, Keats's singular comment that "I am pick'd up and sorted to a pip. My Imagination is a Monastery and I am its Monk" is wonderfully self-possessed. It is as if Keats were operating in at least two, perhaps three, worlds simultaneously: the one in which he speaks fairly and honestly to his friends about his existential situation; the one in which he speaks to Fanny in contradictory, crazy, and sometimes abusive ways; and, ultimately, the one in which he speaks to himself, in silence, about dying, day in, day out.

The emotional arc of the love letters speaks for itself. By the time of the first letters to Fanny, Keats is off on the Isle of Wight trying to complete great long poems (*Lamia, The Fall of Hyperion*) and salable drama (*Otho the Great*). Except for "To Autumn," all his important, immortal work is behind him— work he thinks of as all too mortal. This extended, exhausting summer marks a vital transition in Keats's life, not just his work.

This is the summer of Brown's marvelous and accurate drawing of the face of early fatigue, Keats at his most handsome, male, serious, and disinterested. Every issue in his life has come into focus in this July–September period: no money, no prospects, no family, no home. He could turn to his medical training, which is what Fanny's mother hopes he will do; he could follow Abbey's suggestion and try his luck as a hatter; he could compromise and write as a journalist, a notion that Brown talks him out of. He could, if he felt better, attempt any number of options, assuming whatever he chose sorted well enough with the muse. To a mind and spirit as active and contemplative as Keats's, and within a context of so short a life, it is remarkable, when all is said and done, just how little time he spends writing the poems that rescue his name from being written in water. In terms of the very best writing, about a semester's worth, say from the beginning of 1819 (*Eve of St. Agnes*) to the end of that summer ("To Autumn," *The Fall of Hyperion*), no time at all. Which means, even with his five years of medical training, his busy social schedule, his traveling, his capacity for playing at poems, and his commitment to his correspondence, he has time on his hands, time he often feels he is wasting. The letters to Fanny Brawne essentially pick up his creative energies at just the moment when his true creative era ends. However we look at it, Fanny B. is like a figure in lieu of the poetry; even those worthy fragments and pieces, such as *The Fall of Hyperion*, a few middling sonnets, and "To Autumn" must be written out of her sight and hearing.

This psychological fact helps explain—beyond the peaks and valleys associated with the fevers and cooldowns of consumption—the hyperbole, the paranoia, the self-recrimination, jealousy, fantasy, and deathwatch of the love letters. Keats is acting out in literal terms what has been sublimated, transformed, and configured in the poems leading up to the intensification of his "engagement" with Fanny and the real sickness inflicted upon him. The "mad boy" whom Mrs. Brawne has nervously characterized *is* often a little mad—isolated, frustrated, muted, then, within the cell of his and Fanny's intimacy, explosive. The power that Keats assigns to Fanny is the power of life and death; she becomes, inside the burn of his imagination, more than mortal and, on his bad days, less than real. Jealousy is the most crippling of emotions, and perhaps the most involuntary. From the time of his first hemorrhage, when he is forced into two months of confinement and convalescence, until his last month in England, when he becomes again a patient and "a dying kind of lover," under the care of Mrs. Brawne and her daughter, Keats's nerves will be raw and his temper unpredictable, and Fanny will be seen as both his savior and tormentor. Just about the last serious poem he writes, in February 1820, at the true beginning of his decline, is a dialogic ode "To Fanny" in which jealousy ("Ah! dearest love, sweet home of all my fears") and inconstancy ("Must not a woman be / A feather on the sea, / Swayed to and fro by every wind and tide?") are the keynotes. The poem begins better than it ends.

> *Physician Nature! let my spirit blood!*
> *O ease my heart of verse and let me rest;*
> *Throw me upon thy tripod till the flood*
> *Of stifling numbers ebbs from my full breast.*
> *A theme! a theme! Great nature! give a theme;*
> *Let me begin my dream.*
> *I come—I see there, as thou standest there,*
> *Beckon me out into the wintry air.*

The last request here—to "beckon me out into the wintry air"—suggests the state of mind—suicidal—that Keats has succumbed to once he has recognized the "death warrant" of the arterial blood he has coughed up days before. This request from the same man who keeps telling both the Fannys in his life—his lover and his sister—to bundle up against the cold. By the second stanza of the poem, nature—his nature—has given him his theme, which he hits hard for almost fifty more lines. John Bernard, in the notes to his fine edition of Keats's poems, comments that "After his first haemorrhage on 3 February 1820, Keats was confined indoors, and sometime in February he offered Fanny Brawne the opportunity to free herself from their engagement. Her refusal to do so did not quiet his jealousy for long, and it was exacerbated by his own helplessness, and the fact that she was living next door at Wentworth Place."

Even more than the burden of being tormentor is the burden of being a savior, a symbol, a repository of longing. Fanny Brawne's most presiding role becomes that of life's promise—not simply the promise of faithfulness, the promise of honor, but the promise of the future, the promise of life itself. Keats is not only ill, he is ambiguously ill; he is not only poor, he is ambiguously poor; he is not only—except to his friends—obscure, he is ambiguously obscure. Promise "dost tease" him "out of thought." Promise is only that, a promise. Fanny is Keats's promise—to live, to marry, to be happy, to have a life. The apparent hyperbole of "I cannot live without you," "I will die without you," turns into less of an exaggeration when looked at in the light of Keats's limited mortality. In his heart of hearts he may know he is doomed, yet the doctors keep assuring him that consumption is not what is ailing him. In the depths of his soul, he may realize Fanny's commitment to him, yet he seems able to be neither near her nor far, next door nor down the road, without suspicions. And at his best, he may sense the value of the "fine passages" he has been "cheated into," yet too little too late is the public acknowledgment of his genius. Love is now life to Keats, yet love seems to be part of what is killing him, piecemeal, part-time.

3

NO WONDER WENTWORTH PLACE HAS COME TO BE CALLED Keats House, though by rights it may have as well become the Keats-Brawne House. Until 1839, when the house is joined into a single, uninterrupted dwelling, Keats and the Brawne family are alone in their having occupied, made a home, in both Brown's and the Dilkes' halves. Once the Dilkes, at the end of March 1819, decide to move to town to be close to their son's school, the Brawnes leave Elm Cottage and move in (April 3). They have already rented Brown's half of the double the summer before, the summer of Keats's and Brown's Northern tour, the summer that George leaves for America and Tom takes a turn for the worse. Now three days after Keats writes his last letter to Fanny Brawne, in the middle of August 1820, in which he opens by saying that "every thing else"—except the thought of her—"tastes like chaff in my Mouth" and closes by saying that "I am glad there is such a thing as the grave," he is sitting at the window at Hunt's Mortimer Terrace address awaiting a reply. The Hunt household, ever in chaos, has somehow misplaced Fanny's answer; in fact, the maid seems to have broken the seal and read the reply, which has arrived two days before. For Keats, for all he has and feels he has endured this final, fateful summer, this is a last straw. Hunt's kindness and solicitude become pointless. Keats, in tears and in a rush, heads for Hampstead, but exactly where he is not sure. By instinct he tries the brothers' old haunt at the Bentleys, the place where he nursed Tom and began his great year of poetry. But no one is at home. Home—Keats must realize at this moment—does not really exist for him. He is what we might call an adult orphan. Almost from habit, he ends up at Wentworth Place, at the Brawnes', wasted, on the edge. Mrs. Brawne comprehends and acts on the situation immediately. Here, at the door, is a sick, adrift young man. In this farewell month, from the rest of August through mid-September, Keats at last finds a kind of home, a surrogate mother, a family, and Fanny. The Keats-Brawne House.

Keats's doctor of the day is George Darling, a Scotsman educated at the medical school in Aberdeen. He, along with Dr. Robert Bree, has recommended wintering in Italy; he has attended Keats at both Wesleyan Place and Mortimer Terrace. Dr. William Lamb has also seen Keats at the Hunts, is a friend of Bree's, and as an albino as well as a vegetarian is among the more eccentric medical men in London. He has kept Keats— or tried to—on a strict vegetarian diet. It seems only logical that he is Shelley's doctor, too. But before Darling and Lambe comes Bree, an Oxford man and a specialist in the lungs and what was referred to in those days as "palpitations," meaning breathing problems related to the heart. Bree has been called in by Dr. George Rodd, who was brought to Keats's bedside by Brown the night of the first hemorrhage, or "haemoptysis." (Rodd's wife, it turns out, is a close friend of Fanny Brawne.) Also on the list is Tom's physician, a Dr. Solomon Sawrey, who has helped facilitate Tom in the fiction that, off and on in his last six months, he has been improving. And we must not forget that Keats himself is trained in recognition and diagnosis. Yet as if we are dealing with a conspiracy, not a single one of these early nineteenth-century physicians is willing or able to commit to an opinion that Keats is suffering from consumption, a disease that has killed his mother, her brother, and Tom. Keats's problem is either nerves or of his mind, a view that even he, in blinder moments, subscribes to. It is true that consumption, at this time, is a generic medical label associated with paleness, loss of weight and energy, and severe hectic spells; it is true that many symptoms might fit the bill. More than one acquaintance alludes to the possibility of "Keats's consumption" over the course of his last two years. Both Severn and Haslam worry that he has made himself vulnerable when he shuts himself up with Tom at Well Walk, windows closed against the dangerous night air. But hearsay and word of mouth are not medical evidence. Besides, much of the time Keats, the pugilist, appears to be robust, in fighting form, until the first dark blood rises from his lungs.

The question is, how long does one have once the evidence is clear, regardless of its opacity to the medical powers that be? By 1815, when Keats has not yet turned twenty, a Dr. Thomas Young has already concluded that "of all the hectic affections, by far the most important is pulmonary consumption, a disease so frequent as to carry off one-fourth the inhabitants of Europe and so fatal as often to deter the practioners from attempting a cure." In Keats's time consumption was commonly referred to as "the poet's disease"; by Dickens's time it was known as "the white plague," signifying not race but paleness, the wasting disease, the disease of the slum. In our time, tuberculosis of the lungs has morphed into something abbreviated as XDRTB, Extensive Drug Resistant TB. Of course, "consumption" goes back to the beginning of civilization and congregation, when large numbers of people live in close proximity. Does consumption's popularity necessarily mean its inevitability? Tom Keats, from the start, has the body and chemistry of a tubercular—bird chested, slight limbed, high-strung. John Keats, however, is hale, exuding ruddy health as well as charm. George, somewhere between in body type, survives healthy until trauma—bankruptcy—kicks in the latent TB inside him. Still, he lives to be forty-four, just as Pope, Austen, Elizabeth Browning, Stevenson, D. H. Lawrence, Molière, Dostoevsky, Chekhov, and Chopin live to be close to or into their forties and fifties—all tubercular, like Eugene O'Neill, but creative until the end. Propensity naturally has a good deal to do with vulnerability. Keats closes himself up with Tom in order to act as his nurse; Severn closes himself up with Keats in the same role. How different, though, the result.

The lily or the snow or pale fire or the thin gray ash of the flesh withdrawing from the bone—these are some of the manifestations of the deadly consumptive illness that was known by many names, such as phthisis, scrofula, asthenia, tabes, bronchitis, hectic and gastric fever, even lupus. The pet phrase for all such conditions was that one was "going into a decline." The term *tuberculosis* was not employed until the 1840s, and the tubercle bacillus not discovered until 1882 by Robert Koch. In the nineteenth century in particular, consumption is the number-one killer, especially in crowded, poorer sections of emerging industrial cities or within the intimacies of families. Tuberculosis is, and was, a social disease in every sense: airborne, invisible, insidious, breath to breath, touch to touch. For those who at one time wished to ignore it or moralize it or classify it according to class, Dickens's answer was that generic consumption was a disease "that medicine never cured, wealth never warded off." English medicine, well into the Victorian era, could not accept the notion of a contagious, airborne disease. It had trouble accepting the fact that the invisible world of germs existed at all—hence the filthy conditions of the "operating theater." One might intuit the danger of proximity to a person coughing up blood, but the truth of the danger was unestablished. One might imagine that fresh air and clean linen might make a difference, but the difference was unclear. One might long for the protein taste of meat, but blood could corrupt blood. One might sense that bit by bit the flesh clothing the spirit was wasting away, but the cause could be anything, imaginary or real. On the other hand, appearances counted for almost everything. People looked consumptive or bright, they acted healthy or ill, they had an appetite or they were melancholic, they needed to be starved or they needed to be stuffed, they needed broth or they needed to be bled. Determining the personality of health was based on physical presence, just as diagnosing the personality of sickness was based on supposition and extrapolation, on a kind of mind-reading of the body, as if the humoral fluids of blood, choler, black bile, and phlegm were actual evidence rather than hypothetical tempers, as if humoral pathology were science rather than a metaphor for metabolic balance.

Within the liver, for example, via chyle borne from the stomach, certain distinct fluids accounted for different temperaments. Black bile could account for despondency or melancholy; too much phlegm for indolence. An abundance of "richness" in the blood might make a person too sanguine. Blood was the vehicle for such tempers, just as blood carried disease. Blood was therefore the victim as well as the medium of illness. Corruption of the blood suggested a surfeit of a particular humor, an excess that perforce had to be relieved, the way any pressure that causes an internal imbalance must be leaked in order to restore balance. And although this might be ancient and inadequate medical theory, it still had power into the eighteenth century and well after. The imagination of humors was an interesting way of making palpable and immediate what was invisible and psychological, of investing the somatic with psychic force, and of confusing, unintentionally, the causes of sickness, whether a disease was of the mind, the heart, or a bad chill. In attempting to explain aggressiveness, pugnacity, indolence, or laziness, the humors were graphics of how the mind in tension with the body might work, or not work, of how the mind and body, though distinct, were interdependent.

To enact the humoral theory, to give substance, reality, and specifics to the humoral tempers, there had to be a method of healing. There had to be a technique of treatment. The imbalance of the fluids had to be able to be treated, physically, visibly, blood exposed, blood relieved. A disposition toward too much bile or phlegm, too much melancholy or indolence, had to be ministered to in the same way that a body otherwise diseased could be cured. The most popular and direct method, by default, was bloodletting, or wounding, by which a vein in an arm or leg would be opened to let the superfluidities slip out, drop by drop, into a pan of sand or sawdust. The patient would lie or sit there, as if a disinterested third party, watching his or her supposed illness and vital energy evaporate. Leeches were sometimes used in lieu of the knife, usually by those medical men given to more organic methods. This "primitive" practice, whether by surgery or suction, was as old as the theory of humors and remained in vogue as late as the Victorians. As a centuries-old practice, bloodletting must have seemed, to both suffering patient and limited doctor, the best that could be done, which is to say better than doing nothing. As a stay against the troubles of the moment, or even of fatal illness, bloodletting was hands-on and intimate. It allowed immediate treatment and relief, if only through exhaustion. It salved the mind as well as stilling the body. It also depleted reserves of resistance and stamina. Yet to have lasted so long, its methods and effects must have held powerful sway over the sympathetic imagination, if not the literalist mind.

Because it was intended to relieve both physical and psychological impasse, if indeed the difference could be told, bloodletting—or venesection—was accepted as logical and universal medicine. It was one means, short of clumsy surgery, to enter—however minimally—the sick body and release—it was assumed—the pathology of the sickness. It seemed benign, because it not only calmed the nerves but, by draining carrier blood, allowed the imagined negative vapors to separate from the conductive fluid. Bloodletting, like the unrecommended practice of taking mercury—also drop by drop—was seen by most practioners as a panacea. The treatment of more evident diseases, such as consumption, therefore tended to duplicate the treatment of the more nebulous humoral disorders—so much so that symptoms of consumption and melancholy were subject to the same curative bloodletting. Both were considered wasting diseases regardless of their different sources. Consumption was thought to be no less generic an ailment than melancholy, because it covered physical illnesses as variant as cancer, silicosis, lung abscess, and apparent heart conditions. The Greek word for consumption—*phthisis*, from *phthoe*—refers to a melting away under intense heat—the fever of melancholy or consumptive fever. It would have been hard to find a social gathering in nineteenth-century England without at least one potentially pale, fatal figure.

4

KEATS'S CONSUMPTION IS CONCOMITANT WITH—AND CER-tainly predated by—his well-known melancholy, or (his own words) his "morbidity of temperament." Melancholy (or an imagined excess of bile in the blood) proves to be one of the poles of his personality. "Always in extreme," to quote one of his Enfield classmates, "always in extreme in passions of tears or outrageous fits of laughter." George remembers, after Keats's death, how quickly his "oversensitive" nature could sink with his "blue devils" or rise to the "most generous heights of fellow-ship and friendship," a polarity that mirrors the passion and para-noia of the love letters. Keats's penchant for "hypochondriasm" (George's word) is another manifestation of the same "extremes" and suggests another reason why Drs. Rodd and Bree placed his illness in his mind. His illness had so affected his nerves that his ulcerous stomach (not his lungs) is named the source of the first bad blood he spits up. Even at the end, in Rome, Keats's sixth doctor, the redoubtable Scot James Clark, agrees with the mind/ nerves/stomach diagnosis—until an autopsy. Or is it that all the doctors cannot bear to tell Keats the truth, the truth that he him-self seems to recognize on the winter night when he sees how dark his blood is against the whiteness of the sheet, after which the question is not if but how long.

Doctors aside, once Keats enters, in mid-August, the now

Brawne half of Wentworth Place, he moves into a space, relatively speaking, of some serenity, and resignation. Aileen Ward, in her exceptional narrative of Keats's "making" as a poet, summarizes best the tone that this final month in England would take: "Mrs. Brawne must have been overcome by the sight of his wretchedness when he appeared on her doorstep that evening, for she drew him in and insisted that he stay with them. Keats had come home at last. His remaining days in England were to be spent at Wentworth Place under her nursing, and for this brief spell he was secure in the motherly tenderness that he had lacked so long. Fanny later wrote that Keats and her mother became deeply attached in these weeks; to Severn he seemed like a child in his surrender to her care. As for Fanny, the nightmare of the summer"—the period of the worst, most abusive of the "love" letters—"was over. She was now simply and truly herself to him again, his young love, his beauty, his own, no longer a figure of bale. From this time on, every word Keats wrote or spoke of her turned on one thought alone—that she had been life to him and parting from her now would be death. For now he finally admitted the necessity which he could not bear to face at Hunt's. He realized at last he must agree to the plan for sending him to Italy."

It is well that Ward puts the Italy plan into the passive: the medical opinion, his brother George's opinion, his friends' opinions, particularly Brown's, the popular opinion is that Italy in winter can be a place of healing and restoration, certainly compared with an English winter. Keats, however, in his opinion, is not so sure, yet is also not, not so sure. He writes his sister, just after he arrives at the Brawnes, that he is "staying a short time with Mrs Brawne who lives in the House which was Mr Dilke's. I am excessively nervous: a person I am not quite used to entering the room half choaks me—'Tis not yet Consumption I believe, but it would be were I to remain in this climate all the Winter; so I am thinking of either voyageing or travelling to Italy." On the same day, August 13, as this letter to Fanny Keats, he writes his publisher Taylor that "My Chest is in so nervous a State, that any thing extra such as speaking to an unaccustomed Person or writing a Note half suffocates me. This Journey to Italy wakes me at daylight every morning and haunts me horribly. I shall endeavour to go though it be with the sensation of marching up against a Battery." In other words, possible suicide.

Although everyone seems to want him to go to Italy, no one seems to have an awareness of how to pay for it. Motives, too, seem mixed. Keats is loved, but he also presents a problem. He is essentially homeless; he is, as a few of his friends intuit, contagious; and he is church poor. On some level Italy makes sense; on another level Italy is exile, a potential, truly undiscovered country. Brown, for one—who has served as benefactor, nurse, and compatriot for some time now—has his own life and appears to be tired of the burden of Keats's friendship—at least for this interim—and has once again gone off to the North for the summer, seemingly out of reach. Haydon has become an antagonist to Keats largely over money owed; Hunt, as always, is mired in domestic life. Reynolds and Haslam now have marriages and duties, employment and responsibilities. Friends seem to be growing in different directions. Keats, if he were healthy, would be going his way too. But he is stuck in time, locked inside his own mortal world, isolated. He knows this; he knows that his moment with the Brawnes, with Fanny, is terminal, transitional, though he has a fleeting fantasy that his lover and her mother might be able to accompany him on his journey.

Otherwise, he will have to travel alone, be alone—or, God forbid, stay with the Shelleys. He even entertains the notion that Italy will indeed be a restorer, Rome—the Eternal City—a renewer. As he says to his sister, "I have been improving lately, and have very good hopes of 'turning a Neuk' and cheating the Consumption," a consumption that he may or may not have—he apparently believes—already contracted. "Cheating the consumption" is ambiguous. He also tells her that he has written to Brown somewhere in Scotland to the effect of having Brown join him on the fateful trip to Italy. Brown later claims to have belatedly received this letter, and when he does receive it he edits so as not to recognize the request. Keats's request to Taylor for an advance on any profits from his new book of poems *is* recognized and honored. So if not flush for what lies ahead, he will at least now not be a journeyman pauper. As for traveling alone: Haslam, the Keats brothers' "oak friend," comes to the conclusion that John—if he is well enough at all—is not well enough to journey to Italy by boat by himself, and clearly not well enough to make a land trek north from the port of Naples to Rome—140 miles—without company. At this stage Keats is on-again, off-again so feeble that he is not even well enough to write his sister a farewell letter.

Thus, it is in this context that Fanny Brawne starts her four-year correspondence with Fanny Keats, a correspondence that begins with a dictation. "In the hope of entirely re-establishing my health I shall leave England for Italy this week and, of course I shall not be able to see you before my departure. It is not illness that prevents me from writing but as I am recommended to avoid every sort of fatigue I have accepted the assistance of a friend, who I have desired to write to you when I am gone and to communicate any intelligence she may hear of me. I am as well as I can expect and feel very impatient to get on board as the sea air is expected to be of great benefit to me. My present intention is to stay some time in Naples and then to proceed to Rome where I shall find several friends or at least several acquaintances." He will find a doctor waiting for him, but without companionable company he will not likely find a full-time nurse.

5

WILLIAM HASLAM IS THE SAME AGE AS KEATS AND, DATING from Enfield, one of Keats's oldest friends. He is a link among the brothers and a few of Keats's most valuable friends (including Severn); it could be argued that, along with Woodhouse, Haslam will best serve the life and immediate memory of Keats. Trained as a solicitor, devoted to Keats's posthumous reputation, correspondent with Severn during the poet's last days in Rome, Haslam becomes a basic resource for Milne's 1848 biography of the poet. Keats loved him, though he thought Haslam cut a sorry figure in love. Near the end, when Haslam sides with Brown and others on what they perceive to be George's "brutality and dishonesty," he writes to Severn that he should "Avoid speaking of George to him"—meaning Keats. "George is a scoundrel! but talk of his friends in England, of their love, their hopes of him. Keats must get himself well again, Severn, if but for us. I, for one, cannot afford to lose him. If I know what it is to love, I truly love John Keats."

It is no surprise, then, when there seems to be no one available or willing to accompany Keats on this difficult and dubious voyage—literally into the unknown—it is Haslam who comes up with the idea, however compromising, of Severn as a traveling companion. The idea is compromised because Severn's innocence about the project—and it will become a project—is double edged if not many sided. Although Severn adores Keats, he has never been part of the inner circle, but more like an admirer looking in. And although Severn is an artist—a miniaturist with large-picture ambition—he is only rather good. If Rome is the art capital of the world and Severn sees its opportunity, it may be wishful thinking to imagine success there. Severn has long been aware of Keats's slide in health, but he has no clue as to the degree of the decline or what might be expected of him once they are far from home and even farther from help.

Severn's gift for surfaces, from the very moment of the Italian departure, will stay him in good stead, though it will also cause him much angst. Because his nature has always been to read the character of a situation through appearance, this habit will be magnified in a new and strange environment. In the case of Keats, when he looks well enough and seems well enough, he is—to Severn—improving; when he sinks, and especially in the last two months begins to fall, he is—to Severn—suddenly tragic. This innocence in judgment will play out in every aspect of Severn's various commentary on the sea, the land, and the spiritual journey of the middle of September 1820 through the third week in February 1821. Yet Severn, for all his excitability, is no milquetoast. He is a survivor, and a faithful friend. But before the test of friendship and survival comes due, the process of fare-wells must take place.

The most problematic good-bye has to be the leaving of Fanny Brawne, the equivalent, in Keats's mind, of leaving life and enter-ing what he will now call, in earnest, his posthumous existence. Amy Lowell, in the first great biography of Keats, places this farewell in truly sympathetic light: "Many and long must have been the talks between the lovers, and between the lovers and the mother . . . Keats wished fervently that not only Fanny, but her mother as well, could go with him to Italy. Yet it was his chivalry even more than Mrs. Brawne's prudence which denied him the peace of marriage under the circumstances. Still, hoping against hope, cheating themselves in the light of a false dawn, Keats and Fanny made their impossible plans. Mrs. Brawne was to live with them when they married, which was to be just beyond the fatal journey to Italy. So Keats, refusing to sacrifice Fanny, pictured out a future which, in reality, he never believed in. All his petty selfishness in little things fades away before the spectacle of his immolation on the spear of his all-embracing chivalry. He denied himself life to spare her the intimate experience of death."

This experience will not be denied to Severn. Or as Fanny herself years later puts it, that Keats's "sensibility was most acute, is true, and his passions were very strong, but not violent, if by that term, violence of temper is implied. His was no doubt susceptible, but his anger seemed rather to turn on himself than on others, and in moments of greatest irritation, it was only by a sort of savage despondency that he sometimes grieved and wounded his friends . . . For more than a twelvemonth before quitting England, I saw him every day, often witnessed his sufferings, both mental and bodily, and I do not hesitate to say that he never could have addressed an unkind expression, much less a violent one, to any human being. During the last few months before leaving his native country, his mind underwent a severe conflict; for whatever in moments of grief or disappointment he might say or think, his most ardent desire was to live to redeem his name from the obloquy cast upon it; nor was it till he knew his death was inevitable, that he eagerly wished to die . . . I believe that the fever which consumed him, might have brought on temporary species of delirium, that made his friend Mr. Severn's task a painful one."

In addition to the many farewells, there are necessary "foreclosures." On September 11, Taylor sends Keats what amounts to a contract of copyright for all the work that Taylor and Hessey have published or will publish, a contract assigning financial value to *Endymion* and the *Lamia* volume, or, put another way, a promissory note for monies advanced. "Before you go out of the country I am desirous of explaining to you what Terms we conceive ourselves to be acting as your Publishers," so begins Taylor's statement of what he hopes will become a positive return of investment, though "promissory" here represents faith—but only to a degree—in Keats's public promise as a poet. With Brown and George far away, Taylor's advance—that is, his letter of credit for 150 pounds—is Keats's only resource. (As for cash, Severn has 25 pounds from the sale of a miniature seemingly hours before they embark; and oak Haslam has donated 50 pounds out of pocket.) Taylor also witnesses Keats's Last Will and Testament, a document blessed by its simplicity.

> *In case of my death this scrap of Paper may be service-*
> *able in your possession.*
>   *All my estate real and personal consists in the hope of*
> *the sale of books publish'd and unpublish'd. Now I wish*
> Brown *and you to be the first paid Creditors—the rest is*
> *in nubibus—but in case it should shower pay my Taylor*
> *the few pounds I owe him.*
>   *My Chest of Books divide among my friends—*

This modest declaration says all that needs to be said about ultimate value. A writer is the words. All that Keats is or will ever be is his poems, a fact of life he is all too well aware of. Even the implicit pun on "Taylor" is about the haunting value of words. Place this testament next to the epitaph of the no-name writ in water and you begin to understand the despair that Keats comes to in his coffin of a room in Rome. His "estate" consists of the clothes on his back, a few valued books, and the "hopes" of books—his books—published and unpublished.

On September 13, a few days before departure, Taylor answers news from Haslam, which has confirmed Severn's willingness to make the voyage with Keats. "Your Letter has given me the greatest Pleasure, and to Keats it is most cheering. He has come here today to be ready to go by the Vessel, but we have just now learnt that it does not sail till Sunday Morning. The Vessel is the Maria Crowther"—a 127-ton brigantine rig—"lying off the Tower,—the Master, Thomas Walsh—Messrs. R. & H. Richardson are the Agents, No. 3 Howford Buildings—It will give me much Pleasure to see you here whenever you can make it convenient.—We dine at 5 today, & shall be happy to have your Company—"

So four days later, in a chill gray September dawn, almost to the day of the year before when Keats writes "To Autumn," he and Taylor go by carriage to the London Docks, where soon after they are joined by the excitable Severn (who has literally had to fight his father to travel on this "mad journey"), Severn's brother Tom, Woodhouse, Haslam, and perhaps others—a loose assembly not unlike the group that gathers in dawn light six months into the future at Keats's funeral. If you visit the Morgan Collection on Madison Avenue in Manhattan, you will see there, under glass, the "Lock of hair of John Keats which I cut off at Gravesend on Sunday the Sept 1820 on board the Maria Crowther just prior to leaving him. He was to sail for Naples for the benefit of his health on the following day. RD Woodhouse." Woodhouse, curiously, leaves the date blank, though in a note to Fanny Keats on Tuesday, September 19, Taylor reports that "On Sunday Morning Mr Keats went on board the Maria Crowther, for Naples, and about Noon reached Gravesend.—He did not go ashore, but entered at once on the kind of Life which he will have to lead for about a Month to come, dining in the Cabin with the Captain, and another Passenger (a Lady) besides Severn the Friend who is gone with him.—The Vessel waited at Gravesend for another Lady who was coming on board there.—Mr Taylor Mr Haslam & Mr Woodhouse accompanied Mr Keats to Gravesend, and left him at 4 oClock on Sunday afternoon." Thus Woodhouse needed only to write the 17th as the date on which he took a cut from Keats's hair.

At this point, once Taylor and Haslam and Woodhouse leave the little ship, now docked for the night at Gravesend, Severn becomes Keats's only witness. Severn's letters to Haslam, his journal entries, his letters to Brown and others, his later reminiscences—some published, most not—become the sole written record of Keats's last six months, including the voyage, the land trip north from Naples to Rome, and the daily company and watch at 26 Piazza di Spagna. (Severn's memories of Keats, in both prose and portraits, will continue into his old age with evermore mixed results. Keats in Rome will remain the subject.)

Perhaps the best that can be said of Severn's sometimes contradictory, often vivid, meandering, disclaiming, nervous prose style is that it almost always is on top of the moment, the moment of his range of emotion, from excessively heartfelt seriousness to surprised, unabashed innocence. His feel for things, whether exaggerated or misperceived, speaks nevertheless to the truth between the lines and also presents an intimate, fair reading of Keats's moon-like phases. Severn is ignorant—until right at the end—of Fanny Brawne's role and the degree to which Keats's consumption has destroyed the lungs. But then few know of the depth of Keats's attachment, and almost none seems aware or will admit how fatally ill he is. Severn, therefore, must judge from the outside, which only reinforces his habit of drawing—literally and otherwise—conclusions from the refractions of sur-

faces. When, for example, Keats copies "for me on a blank leaf in
a folio volume of Shakespeare's 'Poems' . . . the following mag-
nificent sonnet," Severn assumes that the poet has recently writ-
ten "Bright Star" and it is still fresh in his mind. More than likely,
it is Fanny B. who is on Keats's mind, and the dated sonnet is an
indirect way of acknowledging her presence here at the start of
his leave-taking, now only a couple of days into the Italian jour-
ney. "Bright Star" is not, as Severn's observation implies, Keats's
last poem; it is the last poem that he fair-copies, because he has
probably composed it, according to Brown's mix of manuscripts,
sometime in 1819. Yet surfaces can also be revealing. When a
fourth passenger, a Miss Cotterell, joins the two young English-
men and middle-aged Mrs. Pidgeon (who was apparently under
the impression that just the two women would be making this
voyage), Severn comments that "I could not have made much
of a figure, for before we left Gravesend a lady-friend of one
of those on board looked hesitatingly at Keats and myself and
inquired which was the dying man. I was suffering at the time
from a liver complaint, and was very pale and wan." Miss Cot-
terell has perhaps a vested interest in her question, as she, too, is
dying of consumption—is, in fact, worse off than Keats—and is
on her way to live with her brother in Naples.

The 1,260-mile voyage to Naples should, with good wind
and good weather, take no longer than three weeks, less or more
depending. But because the vessel is a small, two-masted brig,
fitted primarily for cargo and "coasting on the Cardiff-Liverpool
run," the *Maria Crowther* is vulnerable to conditions that might
not burden a larger, more expensive ship. Just getting going,
therefore, will prove a problem. Storms and rough seas followed
by dead calms will prevail until the end of September, inducing
the *Crowther* to do what she does best: hug the coast in sight of
land along the Strait of Dover and the ragged shoreline of Kent

and Hampshire, sometimes anchoring close enough for Severn and Keats to go ashore. On September 28, the two of them manage to make it to Bedhampton, an impulsive inland trip meant to surprise Keats's old friends the Snooks, who are more than happy to see him and hear about the "sea-voyage" so far. It is not, of course, far at all, though in terms of the gale-force winds, high seas, seasickness, and stifling conditions on board that they have already endured, it feels *far*.

Now comes the kind of news into which moment complexity pours and becomes painfully simple—not unlike the way the mist clearing over the harvest in Winchester distills, or the veil lifting from the muse's face in the meeting with Moneta reveals. Brown, it seems, as reported by the Snooks, has come back from Scotland, and, because his half of Wentworth Place is rented until October, is visiting Dilke's parents in Chichester, only twenty miles away. There is no question of Keats "dashing over" to see him. Even by carriage the distance is too great for the time that he and Severn have before they must return with the tide to the *Crowther*. Surely Brown has received Keats's letters imploring him to join the journey to Italy. Surely. To add to the irony of nearness and distance is the fact that ten days before, on the overnight that the *Crowther* spends at Gravesend, the Dundee smack that has brought Brown from the North anchors within "shouting distance" of the boat bearing Keats, who, exhausted, has gone to bed early and risen late, too late before these ships passing in the night have parted.

Perhaps the good thing is that both times of these potential encounters nothing happens. Keats may know in his heart that Brown does not want to continue as—or at least needs a break from being—an absolute friend—that is, nurse and moneylender. But the near-miss opportunities for meeting—or not meeting—allow Keats, at this eleventh hour, to maintain the fiction of the old friendship. (Most of Brown's guilt regarding Keats will come from this fateful time when he fails his friend and will manifest itself in the stupid words he composes for Keats's epitaph and the crazy anger he finally aims at George.) Brown is Brown. For Keats's part, sitting there in the warmth of a friendly Bedhampton home must make him extremely homesick, ill as he is. As Severn notes, it was tempting not to reverse course and head back to Hampstead and the Brawnes, except what would be the use? The last thing that Keats wants is to compound suffering by dying in Fanny Brawne's arms. She stands for life and the future; he is now the past without a future, posthumous. Or if the future is our ultimate father, then Keats, by ancient definition, is fatherless, because Posthumous is the child born after the death of the father. Or is it that a life lived after the death of promise can also be posthumous? To be dead and alive at once requires a negative capability that Keats up until now has only dreamed of.

On September 30, when the *Crowther* is still "in a calm" and not yet able to begin to cross the Channel toward the Bay of Biscay, Keats writes Brown the first of his final four letters.

> *I thought I would write "while I was in some liking"*
> *or I might become too ill to write at all . . . We are in a*
> *calm and I am easy enough this morning. If my spirits*
> *seem too low you may in some degree impute it to our*
> *having been at sea a fortnight without making any way.*
> *I was very disappointed at not meeting you at bedhamp-*
> *ton, and very provoked at the thought of you being at*
> *Chichester today. I should have delighted in setting off*
> *for London for the sensation merely—for what should I*
> *do there? I could not leave my lungs or stomach or other*
> *worse things behind me . . . The very thing which I want*
> *to live most for will be a great occasion of my death . . .*

*I wish for death every day and night to deliver me from
these pains, and then I wish death away, for death would
destroy even those pains which are better than nothing.
Land and Sea, weakness and decline are great seperators,
but death is the great divorcer forever.*

Keats closes this letter by asking Brown to be "a friend to Miss
Brawne." "The thought of leaving Miss Brawne is beyond every
thing horrible—the sense of darkness coming over me—I eter-
nally see her figure eternally vanishing . . . Is there another Life?
Shall I awake and find all this a dream?"

IN THE BAY OF BISCAY "WE ENCOUNTERED A THREE DAYS'
storm. The sea swept over the ship all day and night, and the
rushing up and down of the water in the cabin was a frightful
sound in the darkness. I was afraid that Keats might die." So
writes Severn well after, remembering that "the waves were of
an enormous length, and so high that the effect was like a moun-
tainous country." Keats obviously does not die, and they both
come to appreciate the skill of ship and captain. It "was a cheer-
ing sight to see how nicely the ship met each wave and rode over
it diagonally."

Daylight on the ocean is one thing; confined in the closets of
the undercabin at night, listening to the chaos of a storm above,
is another. Daylight puts the undifferentiated sea and sky into
some perspective. "When off Cape St. Vincent the weather
changed . . . a great relief it was . . . Once more we were all in
each other's company at dinner, and congratulated ourselves the

more heartily when we heard from the captain that he had had fears for the ship, which had laboured heavily in the trough of the seas. Keats was greatly impressed by the beauty of the ocean off Cape St. Vincent."

Severn, painter and miniaturist, as always good at literal surface and detail, in this new calm sees the water as "smooth as oil, and all one undulating motion, and with the bright sun shining on it we saw many large and strange fish; and once, to our delight and excitement, a whale appeared." Then the next day "we found ourselves in proximity to some Portuguese men-of-war, particularly a large four-decker, the *San Joesef.* We were leaning over the taffrail, looking at this unwieldy monster in the distance flapping on the idle waves, when a shot passed close under the cabin-window. The captain, who was shaving, rushed on deck, to discover that a gun had been fired at us for not answering the signals on board the Portuguese man-of-war." Severn pursues the character of this experience for a further vaguely relevant page or two in one of his reminiscences, suggesting all manner of high drama on the high seas ("genuine fear and trembling on the part of our captain, who held the Portuguese in dire distrust") and no small amount of danger ("the Portuguese admiral was not so much on the look-out for South American privateers as cruising about to intercept vessels going to the aid of Spain").

Mostly, however, beyond the glitter and possible danger, the voyage to Italy is uneventful, even tedious, with Keats acting as physician and confidant to Miss Cotterell—"a sad martyr to her illness," says Severn—and sometimes willing—to Severn's unease—to compare symptoms and feelings concerning their respective "wasting diseases." Cotterell surely reminds Keats of Tom—frail, sensitive, fading. The sleeping quarters of the boat are so small that the genders can be separated only by a makeshift curtain that means to inhibit sight but certainly not sound. Much of the conversation, medical and otherwise, occurs right before sleep, which may be therapy for the ill but for those in relative health becomes an irritation. Proximity creates a kind of family, for better and worse. Keats, the stoic, keeps his bad days to himself as much as possible; Cotterell, subject to fainting and exhaustion, cannot help being apparent.

Finally, after nearly four weeks, "We passed Gilbratar before dawn, and could but just see the enormous outline; a little later, however, we saw the coast of Barbary lit up by the sun's fiery rays—a scene of great beauty, by which Keats was deeply impressed." Severn's sea narrative gets a bit carried away with his painter's eye at this point as the ocean begins "glowing like a vast topaz" and the "sunlit waste of dancing shimmering wavelets" turns golden and "blue as a sapphire, stretching away in to a pearly haze." A few days later, "we entered the beautiful Bay of Naples," completing a journey that, had the autumn weather been more cooperative and the size and quality of the ship more substantial, would have taken half the time with half the stress and physical consequence. Severn's penchant for high prose rarely abates regardless. "It would be difficult to depict in words the first sight of this Paradise as it appears from the sea. The white houses were lit up with the rising sun, which had just begun to touch them, and being tier above tier upon the hill-slopes, they had a lovely appearance, with so much green verdure and the many vineyards and olive grounds about them." He and Keats seem always to be arriving at dawn, as if night passage had worked part of a miracle. "Vesuvius had an immense line of smoke-clouds built up, which every now and then opened and changed with the sun's golden light, edging and composing all kinds of groups and shapes in lengths and masses for miles. Then the mountains of Sorrento to the right seemed like lapis lazuli and gold; the sea between being of a very deep blue such as we had not seen elsewhere, and so rich and beautiful that it gave great splendour to all the objects on shore."

The objects on shore, though doubtless beautiful in southern Italian morning light, will remain just out of reach for a while. An epidemic of typhus has broken out in London, and the *Crowther*, after what must feel like a double journey, is to be held in quarantine, along with a whole bay full of boats of various sizes and purposes, for another ten days' delay—a painted ship, indeed, upon a painted ocean. At first, with the *Crowther* come to rest, and with new supplies of fruit and vegetables being brought aboard, this true dead calm does not seem so bad, especially with the views. "Keats was simply entranced with the unsurpassable beauty of the panorama, and looked longingly at the splendid city of Naples and her terraced gardens and vineyards, upon the long range of the Apennines, with majestic Vesuvius emitting strange writhing columns of smoke, golden at their sunlit fringes, and upon the azure foreground covered with ships and all manner of white-sailed small craft." But as time wears on, such "golden" moments disappear into the reality that Miss Cotterell "had become much worse" and Keats is "often so distraught, with so sad a look in his eyes" and "a starved, haunting expression that bewildered me." Consumption, Severn will later realize, is not the only ailment afflicting Keats. "At that time I never fully understood how terrible were his mental sufferings, for so excruciating was the grief that was eating away his life that he could speak of it to no one." (Except to Brown: "As I have gone thus far into it, I must go on a little;—perhaps it may relieve the load of WRETCHEDNESS which presses upon me. The persuasion that I shall see her no more will kill me . . . My dear Brown, I should have had her when I was in health, and I should have remained well . . . O that

I could be buried near where she lives!" This written on November 1, the first day out of quarantine and on land.)

The consumption, though, is enough by itself, with visitations of fever, coughing, vomiting, "blue devils," and blood from the lungs, which continues to be ascribed to "the blood came from his stomach." Yet before crew and passengers can leave their boat and receive appropriate civil and/or medical attention on shore, they must endure additional passengers, such as a boat's crew headed by a Lieutenant Sullivan from an English fleet rowing over to say hello, then stuck on board. After which arrives Miss Cotterell's brother, anxious to see how his sister is doing. ("Mr. Cotterell, concerned about the delicate state of his sister, made arrangements in Naples, and then came aboard to share our enforced isolation. Not only was he unbounded in his direct kindness to Keats and myself, and a boon to all, for he kept the company supplied with every delicacy in fruit, fish, and fowl that could be procured . . . he was also most welcome, for he knew Italian thoroughly, and . . . the Neopolitan lazzaroni-patois.") Brother Cotterell is at least entertaining, knowledgable, and a good supplier—"The fun, the laughing, the singing, all contributed to increase the brilliant holiday scene, so much so that at the expiry of our 'isolation' I could not help feeling regret." Keats, with his puns, jokes, and sometimes general good spirits, contributes to the shipboard party atmosphere, if only to keep up appearances and stave off the dark gods. He is trying hard to fit into this strange new world, which, however fleeting and wholly other, is the only world he has now. "Give my love to Fanny," he writes Mrs. Brawne on October 24, "and tell her, if I were well there is enough in this Port of Naples to fill a quire of Paper—but it looks like a dream—every man who can row his boat and walk and talk seems a different being from myself—I do not feel in the world—"

On October 31, Keats's twenty-fifth birthday, the quarantine is at last lifted and crew and passengers of the *Maria Crowther* are permitted to go ashore. In English, the visé on the back of Keats's passport reads: "Registered with the Council of Public Security, Naples, 31, Oct. 1820. / At the office of the 3rd Department. / J.NADIA." What has looked "so beautiful from the sea," the perspective of the bay, turns out to be a different reality on land. "We were taken aback by the dirt, the noise, and the smell," writes Severn. "Everything seemed offensive, except the glorious autumnal atmosphere . . . With songs and laughter and cries, and endless coming and going, the whole city seemed in motion. The men ran to and fro with their baskets of grapes, bawling and screaming with mere delight apparently, not one here and there, but everywhere and all at once. The city itself, with its indiscriminate noises and bewildering smells, struck us as one great kitchen, for cooking was going on in every street and at almost every house—*at*, not *in*, for it was done out-of-doors or upon the thresholds." Eating and singing and hawking carry on all day and all night, the two pale Englishmen discover. Miss Cotterell's brother, full of thanks for Keats's kindnesses to his ailing sister throughout the voyage, takes the two under his wing, finds them rooms in the Hotel d'Inghilterra—or the Villa da Londra, depending on which version Severn is offering—and for the week they spend in Naples becomes their guide. For a brief moment they even consider, once they have their land legs, staying in Naples, though when they realize the political situation of a city-state torn between revolution and tyranny, Keats cannot wait to leave.

Two details from their brief encounter with Naples speak to Keats's "adjustment" to his new world. They are anecdotal and arrive aslant from one Charles MacFarlane, a member of Naples's

English community and an acquaintance of Cotterell's. Like most stories that achieve a certain immortality, they are second-, then third-hand—from Cotterell to MacFarlane (*Reminiscences of a Literary Life*) to Amy Lowell, who quotes directly.

. . . he was driving with my friend Charles Cotterell from the Bourbon Museum, up the beautiful open road which leads up to Capo di Monte and the Ponte Rossi. On the way, in front of a villa or cottage, he was struck and moved by the sight of some rose-trees in full bearing. Thinking to gratify the invalid, Cotterell, a ci-devant officer in the British Navy, jumped out of the carriage, spoke to somebody about the house or garden, and was back in a trice with a bouquet of roses.

"How late in the year! What an exquisite climate!" *said the Poet; but on putting them to his nose, he threw the flowers down on the opposite seat, and exclaimed: "Humbugs! They have no scent! What is a rose without its fragrance? I hate and abhor all humbug, whether in a flower or in a man or woman!" And having worked himself strongly up in the anti-humbug humour, he cast the bouquet out on the road. I suppose that the flowers were China roses, which have little odour at any time, and hardly any at the approach of winter.*

Returning from that drive, he had intense enjoyment in halting close to the Capuan Gate, and in watching a group of lazzaroni or labouring men, as, at a stall with fire and cauldron by the roadside in the open air, they were disposing of an incredible quantity of macaroni, introducing it in long, unbroken strings into their capacious mouths, without the intermediary of anything but their hands. "I like this," said he; "these hearty fellows scorn the humbug of knives

and forks. Fingers were invented first. Give them some car-
lini *that they may eat more! Glorious sight! How they take
it in!"*

The exclamatory speech assigned to Keats here has the stilted
quality of dated fiction, though the feeling behind the language
is probably accurate. MacFarlane slips into making Keats sound
like a humbug himself—hence, the hand-me-down effect of
hearsay. Yet implicit in the episode of the roses is the home-
sick longing for a rich English rose, and implied in the pasta
episode is the passion of health. Each of these details will be
reinvoked when Severn fills the little carriage with wildflowers
on their way to Rome and when Keats, tired of the bad-to-awful
food sent up by the Italian landlady, dumps his plate of spaghetti
from his second-floor bedroom window onto the tidal steps of
the Piazza di Spagna.

7

THERE ARE TWO CHARACTERIZATIONS OF KEATS IN MACFAR-
lane's account: one, that Keats is an invalid; the other, that Keats
is "the Poet." Curious word that "invalid," because it refers not
only to the disabled but to the non-valid as well—Keats is clearly
an invalid poet, one disabled, but he may be—and in his own
mind now is—an invalid poet, one "inabled" or "falsely based,"
whose name deserves to be disappeared. Losing Fanny Brawne,
losing the future, losing his life, disabled by illness, this is one
thing; losing the possibility for immortality, an afterlife as a poet,
invalidated by the very work itself, is another. Keats is alive, but
here in this moment, in Naples, among aliens, he has entered a

different dimension, a kind of existential interregnum, an in-between state of states of being. He knows, as he tells Severn, "that I shall not last long," yet saying a thing, the worst thing, does not dispel the wish, the hope that it is not so. And what if a winter in Rome does have an ultimate healing effect, a miracle reversal; what if, as all the doctors seem to be suggesting, it is nerves, the stomach, the temperament, the diet that is the cause? What if John Keats recovers, albeit wounded, will he ever write again, write on scraps of paper, as if to stave off the indictment of the gods? Because if what he has written so far is no better than words written in water, if his critics are correct, then what of the work of someone who has come through, though marked an invalid? The involuntary—even voluntary—chance of letting go is certainly one way to relieve the anxiety of ambition; without ambition, however, life alive would nevertheless still be anxious, posthumous.

Keats and Severn spend their last couple of days in Naples preparing to leave it. In addition to thank-yous and a farewell dinner with the Cotterells, visas must be had, first from the British Legation, second from the Papal Consul General, because traveling from Naples to Rome requires the crossing of borders. They depart on a Wednesday morning, November 8, in an after-rain, which means that when the roads are wet they are thick with mud and when they are dried hard they are rough with ruts and when they are stone, as on the Appian Way, they are unforgiving. The travelers will move, therefore, at a very slow pace, in a small carriage known as a *vettura*. (Small spaces are a signature of Keats, relative perhaps to his size: his small bedroom at Wentworth Place where he has his first major hemorrhage; the small garden adjacent to the house where he writes the odes; the small couch space at the Hunts' where he often has spent the night; the bedroom at Well Walk where he nurses Tom; the hammock-and-pulled-curtain sleeping space on the *Maria Crowther* where, in the half-dark, he advises and commiserates as a doctor; the space of quarantine where he is forced to act as if there were nothing wrong with him; and the "coffin-like" space of his bedroom in Rome where he looks out the window, stares at the high rosette ceiling, and slips away.) Good thing that the weather improves almost immediately, with the golden Italian autumnal light pouring down blessings.

"The season was delightful, and as the carriage did little more than crawl along, I was able to walk nearly the whole way," so remembers Severn many years later. He adds that "I gained strength by my pedestrian trip, and got to Rome considerably stronger than when I left England." The image, then, is of Keats alone in the close carriage, tossed and turned as if he were caught in a small boat at sea; Keats alone and lunar, "very listless, and seldom . . . even relatively happy, except when an unusually fine prospect opened before us, or the breeze bore to us exquisite hill fragrances or breaths from the distant blue seas, and particularly when I literally filled the little carriage with flowers." Indeed, "at frequent intervals," writes Severn, he "delighted Keats by gathering the wild flowers which in some parts grew in profusion." Severn does not name the wildflowers, but more than likely, at that time of year, they were versions of yarrow, Queen Anne's lace, possibly tansy, hawkweed and goldenrod, dominant in off-whites and yellows. The further image of a pale Keats, in the bob and weave of his ride, surrounded, then re-surrounded, with wildflowers graduates to something more ominous than delight and begins to resemble death in his funeral carriage. Severn, the artist, will not see this implication, perhaps because it is too unsettling. And perhaps because the discomfort of the bump and shock of the ride and the isolation of their mere figures on the landscape are too distracting. And not only are the roads "bad, and the accommodation at the wayside inns villainously coarse and unpalatable," the stress of travel itself is worse, in wear and tear, than the long voyage to Naples.

The landscape and proximity to the sea are the compensations, both in their beauty and surprise. The coastal route means stopping at such places as Capua, Santa Agata, Mola, and Fondi; it means moving in and out of sight of the sea among lush hills of olive trees and vineyards and Lombardy poplars and stone pines. It means pure blue air to take into the lungs. They are moving along at about fifteen to sixteen miles a day, which means that it takes at least four days, maybe five, to reach Terracina, "the boundary"—as Amy Lowell notes in her early biography of Keats—"between the Kingdom of the Two Sicilies and the Papal States." Here at the boundary post, Keats's passport is stamped for the last time. From now on they move inland, first over the Pontine Marshes, which, by November and after a frost, are likely safe enough from mosquito-carrying "mal'aria," then into the Campagna, "whose vast billowy wastes, Keats said, were like an island ocean, only more monotonous than that we had lately left." This moorland-like open ground, in spite of a scattering of sheep and goats, with its "billowy" but often ill wind, cannot be more opposed to the close-in pastorals in Keats's memory. It is a different planet from anything that he or Severn knows. In the distance looms a giant aqueduct, one of the great land bridges for water that the ancient Romans have engineered, just as they have engineered the well-worn road they are traveling. The aqueduct's otherworldly presence gives off the effect of ruins, of a massive, fantastic twilight structure lost between realities. More than once they encounter leftover gibbets for the crucifixion of thieves, whose ruin includes in some cases the ragged bones of their bodies—Childe Roland to the dark tower come. These "vertical" surprises are ranged among numerous carcasses and skeletons of wild horses and the odd domestic animal. The most unusual sighting, however, is when Severn's "attention was attracted by a large crimson cloak, and on approaching nearer I discovered it to be around no less a dignity than a cardinal, engaged in what seemed to us the extra-ordinary sport of shooting small birds. He had an owl tied loosely to a stick, and a small looking-glass was annexed to move about with the owl, the light of which attracted numerous birds. The whole merit of this sport seemed to be in not shooting the owl. Two footmen in livery kept loading the fowling-pieces for the cardinal, and it was astonishing the great number of birds he killed."

They enter Rome "by the Lateran Gate, and almost immediately came upon the Colosseum, superb in its stupendous size and rugged grandeur of outline. It is the best way," says Severn on reflection, "to approach and enter Rome, and far more striking than the route from the north"—which is surely less striking than the last Roman mile of the Appian Way, marked on either side with more crucifixions of criminals, and juxtaposed with another newer scene of execution, even slaughter. Shelley, that lover of ruins both natural and man-made, makes the Colosseum sound as big as Mont Blanc: "of enormous height and extent . . . and the arches built of massy stones are piled on one another, and jut into the blue air, battered into the form of overhanging rocks . . . changed by time into an image of an amphitheatre of rocky hills, overgrown by the wild olive, the myrtle and the fig-tree, and threaded by little paths which wind among its ruined stairs and immeasurable galleries." The "little paths" part is especially Piranesian, bringing the interiority of the carnal and corporeal wild outside of the Campagna, with its near-invisible line between brutal death and survival, chance and luck, within the "civility" of the old Aurelian Wall. Rome at this time is a small city, the countryside at the gates. Evidence of the past, the deep past, is everywhere, not just the Colosseum but the Forum itself, broken, half-standing, skeletal, haunted. Eternal, as in Eternal City, has a multiple meaning here. Ruins represent the wilding of civilization, the visitation of destruction by increments, the breaking down of order and culture into preternatural chaos. The emblem of this process of disintegration can be taken as a sign, ironically, of eternity, because we can see it, now, all at once, the ancient and the recent side by side, one indebted to the other. The eternal is history, piled, or plied, against time. It is not ethereal, but stone, whatever form it has fallen to. The eternal is to stone what the immortal is to paper, made manifest by what breathes life into it.

As they enter the city, Keats and Severn are headed for what is called the English Quarter, in and around what is known in English as the Spanish Steps. Dr. James Clark, a Scotsman, has found rooms for them across the Steps from his own apartments; in fact, wondering as to their whereabouts, he is in the middle of a letter of inquiry to a friend in Naples when he hears their carriage arrive. Clark, in keeping with Keats's physician karma, is a better judge of character than of consumption. Twelve days later he writes Taylor that Keats "has a friend with him who seems very attentive to him but between you & I is not the best suited for his companion, but I suppose poor fellow he has no choice." Then Clark continues. "I fear much there is something operating on his mind—at least so it appears to me—he either feels that he is now living at the expence of some one else or something of that kind. If my opinion be correct we may throw medicine to the dogs." Clark's diagnosis, like his several predecessors, is that Keats's trouble lies in his stomach, sourced in his mind—to wit, his nerves: "The chief part of his disease, as far as I can see, seems seated in his stomach. I have some suspicion of the heart and it may be of the lungs, but of this say nothing to his friends as in my next I shall be able to give you something more satisfactory. His mental exertions and application have I think been the sources of his complaints . . ." Ironically, Clark is supposed to be a specialist on consumption, having studied its causes and effects at university in Edinburgh and in residency in Switzerland, after which he begins, according to Lowell, "to collect data on the effects of climate on phthisis," hence his stay in Rome and forays in Germany before returning to London. Keats, if Clark could but recognize it, makes an excellent example of consumption's causes and effects.

The important thing for now is that Clark is a kind and thoughtful man, however ordinary he is as a doctor. At 26 Piazza di Spagna, second floor, Keats can look from his bedroom window across the magnificent wavy lines of the Steps to Dr. Clark's own windows. He can also lean out and look up at the dominating perspective of the church SS. Trinita dei Monti, which looms at the top of the 130 steps; or he can look down, to the left, at Bernini's famous *Barcaccia*—Old Boat—fountain, sinking day and night in its perpetual pale green waters. He may or may not want to leave the window open for all the street life attracted to the area, ranging from tourists to artists' models to gypsies to beggars, all on the make. He may, though, sometimes want to hear the street noise or he may other times want to hear the soft waters of the fountain. He may not have a choice, being so close to everything. Then there are the various vendors hawking their wares, especially the flower sellers, who bring their goods each day from the Campagna: the same flowers—and no more colorful at this time of the year—that Severn has picked along the way in order to fill Keats's carriage with joy. But window open or shut, during the morning and afternoon hours Keats will want the late autumnal sun to warm, and fill, this small space of a room he has traveled so far to, as if it were a realm of gold.

SEASON OF MISTS

...

Where are the songs of Spring? Ay, where are they?
Think not of them, thou hast thy music too—

1

NOW ON THE MAPS AS PART OF CENTRAL MEGALOPOLITAN LON-
don, the hillside village of Hampstead in Keats's day was a long
four miles from the city that had formed around the Thames. It
was a slow-climbing four miles at that, because the Heath, which
borders Hampstead on the north, is still the highest point in the
metropolitan area. Heath is the softer word for and softer sense
of a rich moorland, rich by way of its variable pasture, meadow,
shrub, and forested combination of landscape. In this case it is
not only high but large, the largest open space in the south of
England until the wild country of Exmoor and Dartmoor, to the
west. During the reign of Charles II, the Heath was a hunting
ground not unlike the more manicured Hyde Park; then it got to
be domesticated with a few farms and manor houses and in some
parts became, like the later Protestant Cemetery in Rome, a place
of recreation for commoners wanting to escape the crowds and
bad air of the city proper. Hampstead Village, with its healing
waters of iron salts, started off as a spa, reinforced in its healthy
atmosphere by its proximity to much greenland and woodland,
"the lungs of London." Owned originally by the Abbot of St.
Peter, the "town" itself boasted one plow and a hundred pigs.
The medieval or "irregular" maze of narrow streets, stepped
lanes, and tucked alleyways was already established by the late
eighteenth century when Keats was born, within a two-hour walk
away. By 1819, the year Keats writes the odes, another notable
artist, John Constable, has moved to Hampstead, first at Abion

Cottage, Upper Heath, then on the other side of the village from Wentworth Place, at 2 Lower Terrace, from which garden he paints his unique cloud studies, all fifty or so of them, of the same skies, day in and day out, that Keats has looked up at hundreds of times. ("It will be difficult to name a class of landscape in which the sky is not the keynote, the standard of scale, and the chief organ of sentiment"—from a letter that Constable writes to an Archdeacon Fisher.) Keats and Constable seem to have never met, and it is Constable, not Keats, who is buried in Hampstead.

As for Wentworth Place, now Keats House, Keats Grove, Hampstead, London Borough of Camden, Keats, like the orphan he is, is more like a visitor than a long-term resident—though here he does write much of the work we remember. He rents rooms from Brown for a few months, then come summer has to leave, because Brown sorely needs the exceptional income he can secure from seasonal visitors to the warm, healthy air of this village next to the Heath. Then Keats "re-rents" the rooms after the season. The summer of 1819, when Keats travels to the Isle of Wight and Winchester, is such a summer, as is the summer following when Keats is failing and losing direction, staying here and there, drifting on the edges of Hampstead. His last month in England is spent at Wentworth Place with the Brawnes, who are themselves renting from the Dilkes, Brown's immediate neighbors on the west side of the two semi-detached houses that form the single residence. At the time, the double house is barely four years old. Brown and the Dilkes have pooled their resources and become among the first all-year owners in Hampstead, building a place in what was then still country, with the Heath just across the street and open fields lying just behind and leading to the Ponds. When Keats's nightingale flies from its nest near the house that late April 1819, it has a choice of flying "past the near meadows, over the still stream, / Up the hill-side" . . . into "the next valley-glades" or gliding east over Hampstead Ponds into the countryside. The setting, the situation, the garden context of Wentworth Place make it special, make it—in spite of all the mixture of love, separation, and living drama associated with its history—a welcoming, caring place, a place where one might heal or die as if falling into a deep Endymion sleep surrounded by lawns of fruit trees, of pear and plum and mulberry, and laurel hedges and patches of roses, a place two tiered above a kitchen wine cellar and bread baking in an oven. Wentworth Place and Hampstead are, as much as possible, Keats's home.

Rome in 1820, in the autumn of Keats's arrival, is—as it is now—a city of layers, from its beginnings in the middle of the eighth century BC to its establishment as an empire in 27 BC to its Christianization in the early fourth century AD to its papalization in the eighth century AD and on through its poverty in the Middle Ages to its rebirth in the Renaissance to its Catholic Reformation in the 1500s. And so on, layer upon visible layer, like a great graveyard to be claimed and reclaimed, the living among the dead, risen and rerisen. No accident, too, that the Vatican lies on a direct diagonal across the Tiber from the Coliseum (or the Colosseum), the spiritual embodiment juxtaposed with the incarnate, the wine and the wafer with the actual blood and body. Pantheon, Forum, Palatine, Vatican—not only a monumental sequence but the ruins and preservations of the civilized in the hierarchy of the immortals, the Roman gods superimposed on those of the Greek, the papal gods in even rarer air. Heaven, in the high cerulean blue yet invisible dome over the city, is ever becoming a place of contention between the Christian God on His Throne and the ghosts of the pagan gods drinking from a fountain. Rome is the gravity under and holds together this various Italian heaven and earth.

Keats and Severn enter the city from the southeast, on the "pagan" side of the river, and make their way north toward the

area of the Piazza del Popolo, known to the Italians as the For-
eigners' Quarter—including the Piazza di Spagna—but thought
of by the English as theirs.

When Keats and Severn move in 26 Piazza di Spagna is
almost a hundred years old, as old as the grand waterfall of the
Rococo Spanish Steps themselves. The landlady, Signora Anna
Angeletti, along with her daughter and son-in-law, occupy the
back of the house on the first and second floors; another English-
man, Thomas Gibson, lives at the front of the first floor facing
the piazza. Keats and Severn are more or less above him, in a
"suite" of rooms consisting of a sitting room/bedroom combi-
nation for Severn, and a closet-size space where Severn paints,
and the "tall grave" of the bedroom where Keats spends most
of his time and from where he can look out on the comings and
goings and meetings on the Steps, listen—when he can hear it—
to the soft underscore of Bernini's stone-boat fountain and see
across the way the residence of his doctor. Because of his window
proximity to the Steps and the square they spill into, Keats can
also take in the considerable business of the day, which includes
shops belonging to printmakers, engravers, artists in mosaic, as
well as the carts of flower vendors and hawkers and the assorted
parades of artists' models, loungers, curious tourists, and nobility
in carriages. It is colorful, sensual, and utterly exotic compared
to quiet Hampstead and the proper parts of London. One aspect
that may appeal to Keats is the pastoral habit of shepherds usher-
ing through the open square flocks of sheep and goats and small
herds of cattle, whose hooves on the cobblestones must have a
special ring clattering to and from market. Past the nearby Piazza
del Popolo, the countryside begins, where the wildflowers never
seem to stop filling the fields, and small farms mark the land-
scape—a landscape, if he could spend time there, Keats might
recognize as different yet reminiscent of Enfield Chace and the

walks there between Edmonton and his old school, farms and cottages scattered among meadow, hedgerow, and pasture.

By the start of the twentieth century, 26 Piazza di Spagna is scheduled to become a hotel, but an organization calling itself the Keats-Shelley Association manages, in 1906, to raise enough funds to buy it and transform it into a Memorial House for the English Romantic poets of the second generation. Chilly Wordsworth, mindful Coleridge, and popular Southy made up the first generation and were therefore not included. In the spring of 1909, what becomes the Keats-Shelly Memorial House is officially opened to the public, with renovations meant to enhance its museum character without compromising—too much—the original integrity of where and how Keats and Severn lived. Shelley never lived there, nor did Byron, though they are represented by letters and manuscripts. Under the category of poetry-this-and-that is a reliquary once belonging to Pius V (the pope, according to the *Guide*, who excommunicated Queen Elizabeth I) that contains locks of hair from Milton and Elizabeth Barrett Browning. The pamphlet *Guide* to the house states that "Leigh Hunt showed this reliquary to Keats who was inspired to write his famous 'Lines on Seeing a Lock of Milton's Hair.' " Not famous enough, apparently. The poem is actually Keats's first named-as-such ode and is entitled "On Seeing a Lock of Milton's Hair. Ode." It is a young man's homage, and asks the implied question "Will I, grey-gone in passion, / Leave to an after-time / Hymning and harmony / Of thee, and of thy works, and of thy life"—to which answer is, well, no, or not exactly; *The Fall of Hyperion* is abandoned, according to Keats in a letter to Reynolds, because there are those "too many Miltonic inversions" in it. Doubtless Elizabeth Barrett Browning's hair was not part of the original relic. It is in the nature of museums to be relative catch-alls, repositories, and revivers. It is perhaps appropriate then that the one room in the

Rome Keats House that is most preserved is Keats's bedroom, where visitors are met immediately by the rather severe rectangular shape of the space, a decorative fireplace on the right, the two windows on the left, the bed in the far left corner, and, above, the faded blue-and-white painted rows of rosettes on the ceiling. It is not hard to imagine Keats feeling the enclosure of the walls and the press of the flowers bearing down.

As for the address itself, all marble and mahogany-dark woods inside—cool against the summer, cold in winter—and travertine stone and rosso Romano outside, befitting a neighborhood of buildings either salmon colored or yellow ocher or old neutral, it could not be, in 1820, more well placed than at this north edge of the city, palm trees and pines included. It grants the complex commerce of the street, the square, and the Steps an added dignity, beauty, and a more modern history. The day before D day, June 1944, A. C. Sedgwick, a *New York Times* correspondent attached to the American Fifth Army, writes the following dispatch:

> *There was to be a great deal more fighting. The decisive phase had not yet been reached. The attack in Northern France, which actually began on the morrow, was awaited: none knew how it would prosper. Yet for us, or some of us, who entered Rome with the Allied columns that bright morning, 5th June, 1944, there was a surprise emotion in so abrupt a descent of peace.*
>
> *Rome, during the years of world-madness, had, perhaps for the only time in all her venerable history, lapsed from being a world-city, and instead had become merely the capital of one country—a country that because of a silly whim had decided to wage war against us.*

Rome conquered at last was Rome instantaneously restored: Rome taken was Rome, handed back. In one spot, anyway, on this warring and war-torn planet things were once more as they should be. With time over whose healing process Rome seemed to have a monopoly the recent regrettable past would soon be fused with other tragic episodes generally lamented by the very stones.

My good companion Captain Mason, attached to British Army Public Relations, had the imagination to halt our jeep on the Piazza di Spagna. I think it was the first time he had ever seen it. For me it was familiar from childhood. I believe, had times been normal and had I arrived in Rome by train, I should have come to this scene of touching beauty directly from the railroad station to look about me and to visit the Keats-Shelley Museum which adjoins it.

For the Keats-Shelley House is less of a museum than a house of contemplation, itself brooding inwardly upon its tenant the poet who died in one of its rooms about a century and a quarter before, and outwardly upon the very view which was before his eyes during the last days of his sad life.

We climbed the stairs. The Italian Curator, whom we were to find refreshing and charming company, came to the door in delayed response to our knocking and opened it cautiously. I believe we were the first in four years who sought entrance, not to loot or to search for incriminating documents, but to peruse the wealth of material the house has to offer— things that can be carried away only in the spirit.

There, intact, were various objects all familiar. The furnishings were as they used to be. Severn's little study of the dying Keats was in place and there too was Severn's portrait of Shelley sitting among ruins, lost in the world he was in *the very process of constructing. There was the smell—more of England than of Italy, or so one thinks—of leather bindings that bewitched Henry James. There was quiet, peace, pause in our lives in which to think, reflect and be thankful that such a haven had been spared, it would appear, by a miracle. Outside—it seemed very far away—we heard the clatter of our mechanized cavalry.*

2

DR. JAMES CLARK—LATER, SIR JAMES CLARK—IS ONLY SEVEN years older than the young Keats. Yet he is not without experience. Having taken his medical degree at the University of Edinburgh and, the following year, traveled in Switzerland in charge of a consumptive, where he becomes interested in climatic effects on consumption—the fact that warm weather is positive, cold and damp weather negative—he heads south to the warmer, convalescing climes of Italy. Rome is where he settles, although he leaves the city in the sultry summers for more climate study in Germany. Clark is, therefore, knowledgeable about phthisis, both in its early stages and its ugly endings, and understands the roles played by the sun and the quality of the air. Nevertheless, as we are aware, like all of Keats's previous doctors he seems incapable of an accurate diagnosis. Where is all the blood that Keats is now regularly coughing up coming from—the stomach, apparently, not the lungs, as if he were suffering from some terrible ulcer? Clark follows the usual contrarian routine when the symptoms are bad: starvation diets, isolation, and, just when whole pints of blood have passed from Keats's body through his

mouth, more bloodletting. The confusing state of English medi-
cine in the early nineteenth century is such that Clark goes on to
become a doctor to royalty (achieving the status of Physician-
in-Ordinary to Queen Victoria), yet also twice receives public
censure for serious faulty diagnosis (of Lady Flora Hastings and
the Prince Consort). Clark is not exactly incompetent; he is sim-
ply trying to read the signs. In Keats's case, the patient seems to
be overwrought, distracted, and despairing—conditions that his
secret, invisible body seems to be directly responding to. Clark
presumably is capable of reading between these lines. Perhaps the
problem is Keats himself—the fierceness of his mind, the inten-
sity of his personality, the strength of his will. He does not easily
fit the popular profile of a tubercular consumptive. His profile
too often fits someone psychosomatic. A month before the end,
in yet another lull in the progression of the disease, Severn writes
Fanny Brawne's mother that Keats has for the moment "changed
to calmness and quietude, as singular as productive of good, for
his mind was most certainly killing him," echoing Brown's famil-
iar assertion that "poor Keats's disease is in his mind," adding, in
a late letter to Severn, that "he is dying broken-hearted."

So the would-be-doctor-turned-poet, who draws flowers
in the margins of his medical lecture notes and who in death,
according to Shelley, is "like a pale flower," dies of love, or if
not love alone then of "the London world, which was striving
to drag him down in his poetic career," as Severn himself writes
in 1863—forty-two years after the poet's death—in his *Atlantic
Monthly* article on the "Vicissitudes of Keats's Fame." The state
of Keats's mind is apparently the seat of his consumption, the
start of his wasting away, as if the periodic "deathly dews upon
the forehead" were secretions from that mind. But the mind, as
we know, is a metaphor, just as the heart is; they stand for more

than what they literally are. Keats's physical state seems to level off during the first few weeks in Rome. To calm his mind, Clark recommends the world immediately outside the confinements of the second-story rooms. Walking, of course, becomes one form of exercise, though nothing grand. "We went out in a quiet way, not to see sights, but just for him to breathe the sunny air . . . The fine public walk on the Pincio was our principal place of resort, particularly as it was sheltered from the north wind, and was warm like summer, with a balmy air." The Pincio—now subject to all kinds of traffic—was then one of Rome's popular parades, so the air and light were filled with faces and voices. To reach it, one had to climb the entire of the Spanish Steps.

By this time we had made the acquaintance of a Lieutenant Elton, a gentlemanly young officer, tall and handsome, though consumptive, yet, despite his complaint, always an excellent companion for Keats. He regularly joined us for our stroll on the Pincio, and at first we were invariably a trio, for, until Keats seemed to be really gaining in resistive power, I could not bring myself to leave him even for my art. On the fashionable promenade we frequently met the celebrated beauty and grand dame, *the Princess Buonaparte, Prince Borghese. She was still very handsome, both in countenance and person, and had a very haughty air, save that it was at times unbent by such coquettish glances that we all agreed the sight was uncommon . . . Canova had just done a nude statue from her, which we went to see, and thought it "beautiful bad taste." It was Keats who gave this statue its lasting name, "The Aeolian Harp."*

Severn adds to this scenic memory that "this eminent lady" had "a quick eye for a handsome figure . . . hence it came about that she cast languishing glances upon Lieutenant Elton each time we encountered her. At last this so jarred upon Keats's nerves . . . that we were obliged to go and take our walks in another place." Keats's "mind"—his fantasy imagination—can doubtless not not make the association with a once-possible life with Fanny Brawne, whose very name he cannot bear to hear. (He is clearly, even at this leveling-off moment, psychologically and spiritually without reserves.)

Besides walking, Clark recommends horseback riding, another kind of outing that Keats can share with fellow-consumptive Elton. "Their rides were never anything else than slow walks," whose "snail-pace" allows Severn to "stroll at my own pace"— not unlike his sometime walks beside Keats's carriage when they trekked from Naples to Rome. The circumference of the rides takes the three of them as far as the Coliseum ("How well I remember risking my life in getting a wildflower on a ledge of the Colosseum, for Keats to feel how all the air could be scented by its keen perfume!") and along the tree-lined high banks of the Tiber, "beyond the Porta del Popolo" ("I was even rash enough to again cherish a faint hope"). Clark also recommends music, so a piano is hired—carried at no little trouble up the cornered marble staircase—and Haydn played in the evenings. Severn's family background is in music; had his own nerves been less hectic, Severn might have become a better pianist than painter. Music, though, like the walks and the rides, will work only as long as Keats's health holds up enough to make them useful. "This Indian summer period" is how Amy Lowell describes this brief phase. Severn puts it more precisely: "These bright moments were sadly counterbalanced by the sad and pathetic poignancy of his mental sufferings and forlorn hopes . . . He always explained his own case so clearly and convincingly, and so calmly described just how he would die and when, that I had no answer but silence, and he knew it . . . He wrote nothing, but we talked on many themes, and even on poetry. Once, when I was talking of Tasso, my great favourite, he said that he anticipated 'he should become a greater poet if he were allowed to live'; but immediately he shook his head, and bewailed his cruel fate that he was about to be cut off before he had completed anything great."

The diagnosis of the mind-stomach matrix finds comic respite in an incident often cited as a detail only. The fuller story is that after a week or so of indifferent pasta and occasional meat (he is again allowed an appetite at this point), Keats loses patience. The meals have been sent up from a trattoria on the ground floor of 26 Piazza di Spagna, a trattoria that happens to be owned by their landlady. "Complaints to her being of no avail, Keats hit upon a plan to mend matters which he would not reveal to his friend. When next the porter came up with the food Keats went forward smiling roughishly at Severn and saying: 'Now, Severn, you'll see it!' Taking the large square tin box which contained the dishes he opened the window, and thus disappeared a fowl, a rice pudding, cauliflower, a dish of macaroni, etc. The *padrona* was present but she joined good-naturedly in the shout of laughter which went up from the astonished porter. 'Now,' said Keats, 'you'll see, Severn, that we'll have a decent dinner.' In less than half an hour an excellent meal came up and without extra charge." Thus reports Dorothy Hewlett in her 1937 biography of Keats. By December, however, twenty-five days after their Rome arrival, meals and everything else will change dramatically for the worse. December 10 is a Sunday, a day they would "normally" take extra advantage of, because Rome, as a Sunday city, becomes quieter, more reflective, less hectic. Keats and Severn never make it outside. By that early afternoon, the first in a series of escalating hemorrhages occurs, lasting days and pushing Keats almost past endurance. The fevers alone are bad enough. Clark immediately draws blood, "black and thick in the extreme," according to Severn, and puts his patient back on another version of the severe diet, one anchovy and a small piece of toast daily.

By the middle of December, Severn writes Brown that "our poor Keats is at his worst.—a most unlooked for relapse has confined him to his bed—with every chance against him:—it has been so sudden upon what I almost thought convalescence—and without any seeming cause that I cannot calculate on the next change." The "almost" is important here because Severn, as the singular witness to Keats's decline, is at once reliable and unreliable, depending on his own emotional state and on his blind hopes for a recovery. It can take up to three weeks for a letter to reach England; therefore, the news, whether good or bad, subjective or objective, is perpetually out of date. Perhaps with this in mind, Severn constructs a diary within his letter to Brown, so as to follow the facts of these near-fatal days.

This is the fifth day and I see him get worse, but stop—I will tell you the manner of this relapse from the first.

Dec. 17—4—morning. Not a moment can I be from him—I sit by his bed and read all day—and at night I humour him in all his wanderings. he has fallen asleep— the first for 8 nights, and now from mere exhaustion . . . I had seen him wake on the morning of this attack, and to all appearances he was going on merrily and had unusual good spirits—when in an instant a Cough seized him and he vomited near two Cupfuls of blood. —In a moment I got Dr. Clark, who saw the manner of it, and immediately took away about 8 ounces of blood from the Arm— it was black and thick in the extreme . . .

O what an awful day I had with him!—he rushed out of bed and said "this day shall be my last."

This is the 9th day, and no change for the better— five times the blood has come up in coughing in large quantities . . . this is the lesser evil when compared with his Stomach. Not a single thing will he digest, yet he keeps on craving for food. Every day he raves he will die from hunger . . .

Then his mind is worse than all—despair in every shape—his imagination and memory present every image in horror so strong that morning and night I tremble for his Intellect. The recollection of England—of his "good friend Brown"—and his happy few weeks in Mrs. Brawne's care—his sister and brother—O he will mourn over every circumstance to me whilst I cool his burning forehead—until I tremble through every vein in concealing my tears from his staring glassy eyes . . .

Severn closes his long, exhausted—and exhausting—letter with the comment that "I wish you were here my dear Brown."

3

MY DEAR BROWN. CHARLES BROWN——LATER CHARLES ARMITAGE Brown, as his interest in a literary career increases—is the most complex figure of those comprising the intimate Keats circle— Keats's best friend by almost all accounts. This does not mean that Brown was always best for Keats, only that he was the one who was there, close. Nor does it mean that he was always there, but there in times of crisis. Nor does it mean that he was there for every crisis. He is there when Keats needs to "stretch his legs" and literally seek the sublime in nature on their mutual walking tour of the North in the summer of 1818; he is there in the moments immediately after Tom's death in December 1818 with an offer of friendship (as a surrogate brother) and a place to live; he is there "to rescue" when Keats writes the 1819 spring odes on "scraps of paper"; he is there to comfort and nurse Keats after the first terrible hemorrhage on the night of February 3, 1820; he is there when Keats needs money; but he is not there—after May 7, 1820—through the trial of Keats's lost and last summer, nor there when the question of a traveling companion must be answered for the journey to Italy.

Hyder Edward Rollins, in his invaluable *The Keats Circle*, comments that "Brown was a strange mixture of coarseness, kindliness, cold-bloodedness, and calculation." He was a Scot, and—by stereotype—a fundamentally practical man. Up to a point, this made him a stable counterpart to Keats, who was, to a fault, at a loss concerning money. Brown essentially replaces George as Keats's counter-stay in matters of business and dailiness; by at least his own acknowledgment he also "Saves" much of Keats's lyric work—including the odes—from the banishment of indifference, though Brown's old friend Dilke will later refute the former's version of the deliverance of the nightingale ode from its "thrusting behind the books." We do not thrust scraps of paper behind books, Dilke will maintain, even "fugitive pieces." Brown's proprietary interest in Keats extends not only to his work ("Thus I rescued that *Ode* and other valuable short poems, which might otherwise have been lost") but to those areas of advice that George represents—pragmatic matters, of course, but also as to who among Keats's friends is most worthy, be they Haydon or Hunt, Taylor or Woodhouse, Fanny Brawne or no one. George himself will become Brown's chief antagonist insofar as Brown, near the end of Keats's life, needs a scapegoat for his guilt and denials before the crowing of the cock. Brown becomes, within the Keats circle, an everyman figure, elevated through his importance to Keats to something between pathetic and tragic status. He is one of those men who is either utterly inarticulate when confronted with his true feelings or consciously unaware of them. He is, for nearly two years, Keats's great friend, after which he becomes Keats's great betrayer. And if "betrayer" sounds too strong a note, it is only because Brown's failures of friendship are all too human and played as good intentions.

Brown's human side naturally has a history. According to an 1890 sketch of his father's life by Charles Brown Jr. (nicknamed Carlino), Brown is a sixth son on whose shoulders falls a tradition of responsibilities handed down from brother to brother, so that, for instance, not yet a teenager yet the last son still left in the house in Lambeth, one of his jobs is the protection of the property from burglars. His weapon is a blunderbuss. "On one occasion," writes Carlino, "he stopped the washing copper and chain from going over the garden wall, and on another occasion the burglars were boring holes in the front door, to take a piece out, and insert a boy to undo the fastenings, before they were stopped." At fourteen he is already "occupying a stool in a merchant's office"; at eighteen he is in St. Petersburg working in partnership with his elder brother John in the manufacture of bristles, a business that goes bust when a cheaper substitute of split whalebone is introduced by the competition.

This bankruptcy, when Brown is still in his early twenties, has a profound effect. "He suffered great privation after this, as he was too independent to ask for any assistance, often living on one meal a day, where he got it for four pence, and the knives and forks were chained to the table." Finally, another brother, James, finds Brown employment in the East India Company in London. Soon after, this brother succumbs to "Malay poison" and dies, leaving Brown enough of an inheritance to begin a life of literary ambition and social choice. This literate Brown is the man to whom Charles Dilke introduces Keats at Wentworth Place in the summer of 1817, right after the publication of Keats's first book. One personal detail suggests a qualification in all of Brown's relationships with both men and women. "While in Petersburg, he became engaged to a Miss Kennedy, whose mother was governess to the Grand Duke Michael; the lady jilted him for an apparently wealthier English merchant, who became a bankrupt and died, a year or two after. Brown received an intimation afterwards at Hampstead, through a mutual friend, that he could be introduced to the widow, if he desired it, but he had suffered too keenly to forget or forgive the injury; and it was his intention in after life, to gibbet the lady in a novel that he commenced, but which was not completed."

The one literary piece that Brown does complete, *Narensky or the Road to Yaroslaff*, a comic opera, he later disavows, though it runs for a while at Drury Lane. His relationships, likewise, are either often incomplete or later disavowed. Carlino's mother, Abigail Donohoo, who starts off as Brown's Hampstead housekeeper, becomes kept herself, but at some arm's length, because Brown seems to want a son more than he wants a wife. "The marriage was performed," states Carlino, "by a catholic priest, and therefore not legal, but as she was a bigoted catholic, and Irish, she was satisfied with the blessing of the priest, and cared not for the illegality." Brown, then, chooses well. He "marries" a woman in a marriage, by mutual consent, that does not count, and fathers a son who becomes his alone, estranged from the mother. Brown, ever practical, every wary, quick to anger, "a melancholy carle" (Keats's phrase for him), is in his bones a loner, which is to say someone who has learned and embraced self-sufficiency as a way not to be hurt. It is that seeming independence that Keats finds so attractive in a man of the world. Independence can also mean an intolerance, sooner or later, for dependence, which is what happens to the Keats-Brown friendship a full year after the great odes are written by Keats and "saved" by Brown. By May 1820, anyone can see that Keats is in dire straits—no money, no home, and declining health. But to Brown, Keats's sickness is of his mind and his penchant for melancholy, and not physically organic; therefore, the young friend he appears to be leaving in the lurch in May 1820 is not ill in a mortally incapacitating sense. After all, as if to prove his medical diagnosis, Brown has asked Keats to join him once again on his walks into the North Country, walks that two years before mark the start of Keats's current decline. And short of that, after all, he has advanced Keats even more funds to help get him through the summer. Brown is good at playing roles, less good at following through. He has, for example, played well the role of Keats's older brother, replacing the younger George, who now seems lost in the wilds of the middle of America. (Brown has played the role of husband, up to a point, and will be playing the role of father, if an all-controlling one.) Indeed, he has played the brother role beyond what might have been expected. Then—not unlike George—when money becomes the crucial question, when survival, even, becomes a possible issue, when a psychological wall is reached, Brown— like George—disappears. And like George, when Brown sees Keats for the last time on May 7, his parting words might as well be: "You, John, have so many friends, they will be sure to take care of you!"

If character cuts its own allegorical figure, Brown's dilemma regarding Keats demonstrates the human limitation to do good. Even more, it reveals to us especially and specifically what those limitations are, however limited our response. Keats's two anxious letters to Brown at the end of the summer of 1820 never reach Brown in time. Both letters pointedly ask Brown to accompany Keats to Italy; both are forwarded just behind Brown's footsteps as he treks through the Highlands and eastern Scotland. When the letters finally reach him and he can make his way south by boat, it is too late: Keats and Severn have already started their journey and are, in fact, lying off Gravesend for the night before they sail out to sea. Remember: Brown's Dundee smack is also lying off Gravesend for the night, at shouting distance, before it docks in the morning. And days later the same ironic proximity occurs on land. The *Maria Crowther* has been driven back to shore by Channel storms, and Keats and Severn have gone inland to visit friends in Hampshire, where they discover that Brown has just passed through on his way back to London. These near meetings are what we might call almost accidents; they feel more fated than chanced. In his memoir of Keats, Brown excises all reference to Keats's requests from the letters and from his own commentary. He makes much, however, of the cruel timing that causes them to just miss each other. "And so you wish me to follow you to Rome?" Brown writes on December 21—five weeks after Keats's Roman arrival and a week after the close-to-fatal first of a sequence of hemorrhages (which Brown would be unaware of)—"and I truly wish to go,—nothing detains me but prudence. Little could be gained, if any thing, by letting my house at this time of year, and the consequence would be a heavy additional expense which I cannot possibly afford,— unless it were a matter of necessity, and I see none while you are in such good hands as Severn's." Hyder Rollins's footnote on these words is that Brown "afforded it later when such a move was not necessary." Rollins, editor of the standard edition of Keats's *Letters*, is alluding to the fact that within a year of Keats's passing, Brown has sailed to Italy and set up house, and renamed his young son an Italian equivalent, Carlino.

George, too, is a willing conspirator; he and Brown make an odd-couple brothers-in-confidence. Based on a June 1820 letter to John, which he never sees except as Brown's censored paraphrase, George believes that Keats is not only on the mend but will fully recover if he goes to Italy the following winter. George is led in this opinion by Brown, suggesting that the two of them have been discussing Keats's future before Keats himself has given it much definite thought—certainly not the thought of risking his life sailing to Italy. "Brown says you are really recovered, that you eat, drink, sleep, and walk five miles without weariness . . . Since your health requires it to Italy you must go." Brown's is the overvoice behind these words. In effect, he can see the summer coming, he can see what will be expected of him, he can see himself stuck as nurse and banker. He has, over the spring, been trying to enlist George in a plan to ship Keats out; there is no other way to read it. He has done enough; he has been responsible long enough. He has his routine and requirements. He must rent his house for the warm season and he must take his leave. Yet, to his credit or not, he feels great guilt, the kind that will turn him against George and cause him to flatter his friendship with Keats. But are his rationalizations all that different from, say, someone like Taylor, Keats's friend and publisher, who, two days after Keats's departure for Italy, writes to Fanny Keats that "Mr Taylor, Mr Haslam & Mr Woodhouse accompanied Mr Keats to Gravesend, and left him at 4 oClock on Sunday afternoon.—He was then comfortably settled in his new Habitation with every prospect of having a pleasant Voyage.—His Health was already much improved by the Air of the River, & by the Exercise & amusement which the Sailing afforded.—He was provided with everything that could contribute to make the Time pass agreeably, and with all that his Health required; and his Friends have the Satisfaction to think that from the Time he leaves England he will probably have to date the Commencement of many Pleasures & Benefits not the least of which, they trust, will be his Restoration to perfect Health."

4

ON NOVEMBER 30, MIDWAY IN THE "INDIAN SUMMER" PERIOD between his arrival in Rome and the beginning of the final two months of his life, Keats writes his last letter, whose substance is:

My dear Brown,

'Tis the most difficult thing in the world for me to write a letter. My stomach continues so bad, that I feel it worse on opening any book,—yet I am much better than I was in Quarantine. Then I am afraid to encounter the proing and conning of any thing interesting to me in England. I have an habitual feeling of my real life having past, and that I am leading a posthumous existence. God knows how it would have been—but it appears to me—however, I will not speak of that subject. I must have been at Bedhampton nearly at the time you were writing to me from Chichester—how unfortunate—and

to pass on the river too! There was my star predominant! I cannot answer any thing in your letter, which followed me from Naples to Rome, because I am afraid to look it over again. I am so weak (in mind) that I cannot bear the sight of any hand writing of a friend I love so much as I do you. Yet I ride the little horse,— and, at my worst, even in Quaratine, summon up more puns, in a sort of desperation, in one week than in any year of my life. There is one thought enough to kill me—I have been well, healthy, alert &c, walking with her—and now—the knowledge of contrast, feeling for light & shade, all that information (primitive sense) necessary for a poem are great enemies to the recovery of the stomach . . . Dr. Clark is very attentive to me; he says, there is very little the matter with my lungs, but my stomach, he says, is very bad. I am well disappointed in hearing good news from George,—for it runs in my head we shall all die young . . . If I recover, I will do all in my power to correct the mistakes made during sickness; and if I should not, all my faults will be forgiven . . . Severn is very well, though he leads so dull a life with me. Remember me to all friends, and tell xxxx I should not have left London without taking leave of him, but from being so low in body and mind. Write to George as soon as you receive this, and tell him how I am, as far as you can guess;—and also a note to my sister—who walks about my imagination like a ghost—she is so like Tom. I can scarcely bid you good bye even in a letter. I always made an awkward bow.

God bless you!
John Keats

Two weeks after Keats sends his letter, he experiences the series of hemorrhages that mark the beginning of the end. This profound, poignant, and thoughtful letter is rich in the range of ground it covers. First he disclaims even being able to write a letter, though its difficulty clearly implies that there may be no more. But as bad off as he is, it was worse on the boat stuck in the Bay of Naples. The "proing and conning" part, referring to news of home, is quietly compelling not only because it invokes the name of the one whose name he cannot bear being spoken, but because any news of "that country" is like news from life, and he cannot hear it, short of torture, because he has already passed into a "posthumous existence." He confuses, in fact, "past" with "passed," doting on the time or mortal sense in the sounding of the word. Then he remembers his "star predominant," whose meaning carries with it the fated terms of near misses—ships in the night, yes, but also families that are cursed, brothers unfortunate, love at the lip of the cup. Words themselves, in books, in poems, in letters, are like punishments; even to look over again the letter from Brown that this one is responding to is too much, the sight "of any hand writing of a friend." He stays busy, as physically busy as possible; he tries to maintain his mental balance in spite of his memory of Fanny (whose name Brown later changed to "her") in particular. The negatively capable knowledge of "light and shade" that once so enriched his poetry is now knowledge that turns on him. Clark still believes that Keats's stomach is his problem—hence his mind and nerves. Nothing seems to be the matter with his lungs. "It runs in my head we shall all die young"—George, yes, but perhaps you too, Brown, and maybe Keats's sister, maybe Fanny Brawne herself, and all of you back there in life. Can we correct our mistakes? Yet if we die before they can be corrected, they will be forgiven. Death is forgiving. "I can scarcely bid you good bye." Keats's exit line, "I always made an awkward bow," is not unlike his desired epitaph: "Here lies one whose name was writ in water." Both make a gesture, a memorable gesture; both, thus, are poetry; both close without closure; both elevate the moment; and both speak in the past tense, the posthumous tense.

5

BY CHRISTMAS, KEATS'S PATTERN IS SET. HEMORRHAGES OF varying intensity, cupfuls of blood mixed with expectoration, fevers, endless nights of sleeplessness and exhaustion, bloodletting, "starvation diet," then periods of calm, a sort of body sanity, a willingness and an ability to go outside and walk a bit on the upper terrace of the Steps or along the ilex- and olive-groved Pincio, the countryside alive just beyond the trees. There is a foolish moment when Severn is so deceived by what seems like a recovery that he makes Fanny Brawne's mother an impossible promise: "I said that 'the first good news I had should be for the kind Mrs. Brawne.' I am thankful and delighted to make good my promise, to be able at all to do it, for amid all the horrors hovering over poor Keats this was the most dreadful—that I could see no possible way, and but a fallacious hope for his recovery; but now, thank God, I have a real one. I most certainly think I shall bring him back to England." Severn, however, adds the qualification that "at least my anxiety for his recovery and comfort made me think this—for half the cause of his danger has arisen for the loss of England, from the dread of never seeing it more." Of course, the calms are followed by deeper, longer storms of a magnitude that to a neutral observer make it look as though the body—Keats's small body—must break apart. And if the body, the mind, too, is in jeopardy. Or is the breaking of the mind itself the cause, the real source of the "cancer"?

Whatever their different points of view, whatever their separate reasons, Brown (the now-distant friend), Severn (the now-intimate friend), and Clark (the now-present physician) have all shared the opinion that the source of Keats's physical suffering is somehow psychological—his over-finely tuned nerves attacking his oversensitive stomach. "Now he has changed to calmness and quietude, as singular as productive of good, for his mind was most certainly killing him," Severn continues in his letter to Mrs. Brawne. By early January, Clark is still clinging to the mind diagnosis, especially because Keats seems, off and on, to fall into and rise out of the depths of his consumption. But with the help of an Italian consultant, Clark also begins to recognize that whatever the source, Keats's "digestive organs are sadly deranged and his lungs are also diseased." The bleeding, Clark realizes, is coming from the lungs, though his "stomach is ruined and the state of his mind is the worst possible for one in his condition." Clark then unwittingly confesses to a remarkable judgment on a patient who happens to be a poet: "I fear he has long been governed by his imagination & feelings." Indeed! This use by a scientist of the term "imagination" is different from Severn's equation of the mind with mixed memories—"his memory presented to him everything that was dear and delightful, even to the minutiae, and with it all the persecution, and I may say villainy, practiced upon him." And it is certainly different from Keats's own comment that complexity of thought—the juxtaposition of light and shade—is now too painful to conjure and "the continued stretch of . . . imagination" is torture. Even Brown sees the connection between Keats's powerful if "diseased" mind and his capacity for grieving. "He is dying broken-hearted"—and Brown blames everyone—George, *Blackwood's*, Taylor, whomever—except himself. "I will have no mercy; the world will cry aloud for the cause of Keats's untimely death, and I will give it." George has left his brother penniless; the vicious reviews have poisoned the career and future of Keats; Taylor is a mere publisher and will likely try to exploit or abandon posthumous Keats.

Keats's imaginative genius, his gift for empathy, his perfect sense of otherness—these qualities and more may have written his great poetry, but they have also now placed him in a void. "I cannot see—but darkness, death and darkness." Now that his poetry is gone, Fanny Brawne gone, the long walks on the Heath gone, family gone, friends gone, England gone, "despair is forced upon me as a habit." The mind has become the mirror of the body, and death—"untimely death"— entirely timely, because the source is entirely, as it always has been, in the lungs. Tubercle bacillus. Only a year and a half earlier, "I cannot see what flowers are at my feet" is spoken out of a whole and living world, as dusk, blue dark, descends on the green space of Hampstead, Wentworth Place, "verdurous glooms and winding mossy ways." ("O! I would my unfortunate friend had never left your Wentworth Place—for the hopeless advantages of this comfortless Italy.") But now that the newness of Rome has worn off and the reality of his illness escalated, Keats has entered not only his posthumous time but a posthumous space. He is beginning to realize that memory is all he has, and that memory, too, is killing him. He has been sent into exile, in effect alone with and among images of Tom and his sister and Fanny Brawne and friends he has disappointed and who have disappointed him. And now that, more and more, the small circumference of his outside, present world is getting smaller and smaller—like his window on

the Spanish Steps and the lapping boat fountain and the noise
of life in motion—and now that Rome itself—looming in its
timelessness and ruins—feels like the afterlife and now that
the very shape of his bedroom is taking on the shape and depth
of a grave, with the patterned roses on the ceiling emblemizing
what he will see there, now that his confinement is nearly com-
plete, it is his mind that is all he has, because his body, within
itself, is disappearing.

"But the fatal prospect of consumption hangs before his
mind's eye," writes Severn. Then for a moment at the end of Jan-
uary, a slight leveling off, another calm, some hope, then again
a relapse back into hemorrhaging and bloodletting. Except it is
no relapse but an unremitting progress. At least the question of
Keats's lungs is no longer in debate.

*Dr. Clark was taken by surprise at the suddenness of the col-
lapse, as he had a favourable opinion of his patient, and
had encouraged me in thinking that Keats might recover.
But now I saw that the doctor no longer had any hope, for
he ordered the scanty food of a single anchovy a day, with
a morsel of bread. Although he was kept down in a starving
state, yet there was always the fear of his ulcerated lungs
resuming their late dangerous condition. This shortly hap-
pened, and at once threw him back to the blackest despair.
He had no hope for himself save a speedy death, and this
now seemed denied to him, for he believed that he might be
doomed to linger on all through the spring. His despair was
more on my account, for, as he explained, his death might
be a long and lingering one, attended with a slow deliri-
ous death-stage. This was in apprehension his greatest pain,
and having been forseen had been prepared for. One day,
tormented by the pangs of hunger, he broke down suddenly*

and demanded that this "forseen resource" should be given
him. The demand was for a vial of laudanum I had bought
at his request at Gravesend.

If the tone here sounds a bit distant from Severn's hyper tone
in his letters, it is because this prose comes much later in the
form of commentary. The content, however, is present tense.
Had Keats actually been successful in his suicide, the Keats
story changes considerably—how it changes is uncertain, but
it changes. (Compare Henry Wallis's painting of the death of
Chatterton to Severn's deathbed drawing of Keats.) The fact
that Severn, at the start of their Italian journey, seems to have
had no clue as to why Keats might want laudanum—particu-
larly in some quantity—should not be surprising. Keats has
managed all along to maintain his balance before losing it
altogether, regardless of how exactly—in mind and body—
he might be feeling. The laudanum is handed over to Clark,
prompting Keats—echoing his last letter to Brown—to ask
with some heat, "How long is this *posthumous* life of mine to
last?" "Ever after the loss of the laudanum he talked of his life
as posthumous," says Severn

The abortive contemplated suicide—one wonders if Keats
could have followed through with taking his life, no matter how
"wrecked" that life—kicks off a new phase of anger in Keats.
"He grew more and more violent against me," says Severn. "I
was afraid he might die in the midst of his despairing rage . . .
We contended—he for his death, and I for his life." (We are
reminded that a month before departure, Keats twice character-
izes his unhappy journey to Italy as "the sensation of marching
up against a Battery" [to Taylor] and "as a soldier marches up
to a battery" [to Shelley].) "I made him some coffee, and he

threw it away. I then made some more coffee, and he threw it away also. But when I cheerfully made it a third time, he was deeply affected . . . he at last became sensible of his own want of dignity, such as he said 'every man should have in his dying moments.' " But even in Keats's calm, Severn is "harrowed" by his "recounting the minutest details of his approaching death." Two of those signature details involve the expectoration of thicker mucus with darker blood and constant diarrhea. "Keats sees all this—his knowledge of anatomy makes every change tenfold worse." It is not, of course, Keats's medical knowledge alone or even his medical experience at Guy's that forces this perspective on himself—as if he were doctor and patient at once—but his long nursing of Tom, shut up as in a tomb of two brothers, the one handing an inheritance to the other. On the best of Keats's bad, last days, he lives on milk—"sometimes a pint and a half a day"—like a child regressing. On the worst of these days, "his very nature" is "torn to pieces."

Severn's remarkable stamina and commitment to Keats in this terrible time are well established. In the final weeks these virtues are tested again and again, particularly during the night watches, when cleaning up and companionship are the most difficult. Fatigue and worry become Severn's chief enemies, though some nights he can read Keats to sleep, and one night, the accidental way these things happen, he produces what is probably his best work of art. Dated January 28, 3:00 a.m., under which is written, "Drawn to keep me awake—a deadly sweat was on him," Severn, in a matter of minutes, with pencil, pen, and ink, evokes the dying poet in beautiful, vital, accurate terms, as if to make meaning of what he unwillingly comprehends. Among Severn's various choices of reading matter (ranging, with Keats's consent, from Dacier's *Plato* to Bunyan's

Pilgrim's Progress) is Jeremy Taylor's *Holy Living and Holy Dying*, a text that must have seemed utterly pointless to Keats except to fall asleep to. Severn himself does doze off on more than one occasion, which means that if Keats wakes first, the candle will be seen to have disappeared into darkness. "To remedy this, one night I tried the experiment of fixing a thread from the bottom of a lighted candle to the wick of an unlighted one, that the flame might be conducted, all of which I did without telling Keats. When he awoke and found the first candle nearly out, he was reluctant to wake me, and while doubting, suddenly cried out, 'Severn, Severn! here's a little fairy lamplighter actually lit up the other candle.' "

In the often golden Roman winter daylight hours, Severn reads from those letters from England that Keats can bear to hear—nothing, though, from Fanny Brawne. Her letters are saved to be placed "on his heart within his winding sheet." Her presence is acknowledged by silence and "a polished, oval, white cornelian, the gift of his widowing love" that he keeps "continually in his hand." The day before Keats's death, Severn writes their "oak friend" Haslam:

> *O! how anxious I am to hear from you—none of yours*
> *has come—but in answer to mine from Naples—I have*
> *nothing to break this dreadful solitude—but Letters—*
> *day after day—night after night—here I am by our*
> *poor dying friend—my spirits—my intellect and my*
> *health are breaking down—I can get no one to change*
> *me—no one will relieve me—they all run away—and*
> *even if they did not poor Keats could not do without*
> *me—I prepare everything he eats—*
>   *Last night I thought he was going—I could hear*
> *the Phlegm in his throat—he bade me lift him up*

in the bed—or he would die with pain—I watched
him all night—at every cough I expected he would
suffocate—death is very fast approaching for this
Morning by the pale daylight—the change to him
frightened me—he has sunk in the last three days to
a most ghastly look—I have these three nights sat
up with him from the apprehension of his dying—Dr
Clark has prepared me for it—but I shall be but little
able to bear it—

6

ON FEBRUARY 12, WITH THE END NEARING, SEVERN WRITES
to Fanny Brawne's mother that had "he come here alone he
would have plunged into the grave in secret—we should never
have known one syllable about him." Severn closes this part of
the letter by adding (which is its first mention) that "among the
many things he requested of me to-night, this is the principal,
that on his grave shall be this—'Here lies one whose name was
writ in water.'" This suggests that, in cold reflection, had Keats
traveled to Rome by himself, such an exit—assuming he would
have survived the sea voyage and/or thoughts of suicide—
would have itself written his name in water. And he almost did
have to make the journey alone; given that option, he might
have stayed and died in Hampstead. This possibility echoes
James Clark's opinion on the day of Keats's death, as reported
by Severn: "he says Keats should never have left England—
the disorder had made too great a progress to receive benefit
from this Climate—he says nothing in the world could ever
cure him even when he left England—by this journey his life

has been shortened—and rendered more painful—" Thus in this city built on ruins, by water, by fire, by earth, Keats does, piece by part, disappear: no name on the Protestant tombstone; everything in and of his sickroom burned in the street outside 26 Piazza di Spagna; and under fresh violets the deep, eternal Roman ground turning his body back to bone. And by air, too, he disappears, or at the least is transformed. If the idea of the imagined bower defines Keats's secret, recurrent, intimate, and contemplative space, images of the air represent his means of erasure, chameleon adaptation, anonymity, mystery, spirit, the veil, the mist, himself absorbed. Posthumous in all four elements comes to mean, for Keats, disappearance. But air, for him, returns a special provenance.

In Book I of *Endymion*, air is not only weightless but the very substance of dreams—"how light / Must dreams themselves be, seeing they're more slight / Than the mere nothing that engenders them." A few lines later, "light" takes on other senses—"at the tip-top, / There hangs by unseen film, an orbed drop / Of light, and that is love"; "in the end, / Melting into its radiance, we blend, / Mingle, and so become party of it"; and "that moment have we stepped / Into a sort of oneness, and our state / Is like a floating spirit." Air, then, becomes us as we become spirit, the way breath itself is spirit, to aspire and be inspired. And air is the element that bears voices, especially the voice of birdsong, as in Book IV—"there's not a breath / Will mingle kindly with the meadow air, / Till it has parted round, and stolen a share / Of passion from the heart!" By the time of *The Fall of Hyperion*, air is less vocal than visual, and less reassuring. Moneta's image is "huge of feature like a cloud"; her altar is "clouded . . . with soft smoke"; she herself is veiled and to be revealed, and what is revealed compounds the mystery of her "wan face," white air. Of all the aspects of air that speak most to Keats, the veil that is the mist—the mist that conceals in order to reveal—holds the most power in the imagination. "To Autumn" is the obvious example here of a "darkness" and richness "made visible," and "To Autumn" is the great lyric written in phase with *The Fall*. The entire accumulating, working landscape of its harvest scene is "wrapped" and observed through a veil—morning mist succeeding to the afternoon autumnal "drowsy" angle of the light followed by the smoky gold refraction of the "soft-dying" end of the day. "To Autumn" is, in sum, in its thirty-three measured lines, the exalted example of the season of mists—a vision of the air transformed into transforming air.

Early on, in his reading of Milton, Keats comments on lines 318 to 321 of *Paradise Lost*—lines that go "or have ye chosen in its place / After the toil of battle to repose / Your wearied virtue, for the ease you find / To slumber here, as in the vales of Heaven?"—that there "is a cool pleasure in the very sound of vale. The English word is of the happiest chance. Milton has put vales in heaven and hell with the every utter affection and yearning of a great Poet. It is a sort of Delphic Abstraction— a beautiful thing made more beautiful by being reflected and put in a Mist." A vale in a veil, if you will, or, in terms of a "Delphic Abstraction," a rich ambiguity. Autumn is finally a paradise lost—the grain harvested, the leaf fallen. "How beautiful the season is now—How fine the air. A temperate sharpness about it. Really, without joking, chaste weather— Dian skies—I never liked stubble fields so much as now—Aye better than the chilly green of the spring. Somehow a stubble plain looks warm—in the same way that some pictures look warm—" So Keats has written to Reynolds at the beginning of his last autumn in England. Then moments later he adds, "To night I am all in a mist; I scarcely know what's what."

The transforming medium of the air that he sees through, that balances "light and shade," that creates distance, that separates detail from detritus, that values the "temperate sharpness," that makes possible a certain negative capability is the autumnal, mature vision that writes the best and last of the great poems, poems that scarcely know what is what, and that thrive in that "scarcely." In this same year, in the middle of a long letter to George, Keats says that even "here though I myself am pursueing the same instinctive course as the veriest human animal you can think of—I am however young writing at random—straining at particles of light in the midst of darkness." And the year before this, even younger, in the midst of his famous "Chamber of Maiden Thought" letter to Reynolds, with "dark passages . . . on all sides," he says that "We see not the ballance of good and evil. We are in a Mist—*We* are now in that state—We feel the 'burden of the Mystery.' " Much of Keats's maturation as a person and as a poet is the coming to terms with the ambiguities and accepting the "burden" of the bending of the light written on water in the air.

"To Autumn," the perfection of Keats's mode of disappearance into the text, is not only his last great lyric, it is what we could call the "apotheosis" of elemental conversion—of the earth harvest, yes; of the ending fire of the sun; of the arcing anticipation of spring rain; but mostly of the separating veil, the mist, the angular vision, the airy archetype, the symbolist voice. But be careful of what you wish for. Disappearance as a figure is one thing; disappearance as a fact is another. Keats's true disappearance as a poet and a man begins here, a full year and a half before he dies. It is a death by increments, of course, and it will test the community around him. Disappearance will come to mean posthumous, a slow wearing away, the wasting of body and, at times, it seems, of soul, a true consumption, a conversion into air, into breath, in the nothing that is poetry. No wonder the doctors were confused as to what was ailing Keats: in a way it was neither this nor that but everything, manna as well as matter. And it starts with his most perfect poem, as if an open circle had been drawn to close. That is to say, the recognition of what has been true and fated for years arrives like a vision, and that vision is "To Autumn," whose emotional and spiritual realities represent both a full cup and exhaustion, their sequence and consequence. It is as if Keats's only choice after "To Autumn" is to die, to fail, to disappear completely, perfectly, and leave "no immortal work behind." It is as if, having more or less perfected the meditative lyric form, having become at one with its text and texture, he confuses what is great in his art with what is going from his life. The "Delphic Abstraction" of the air, the "beautiful thing made more beautiful by being reflected and put in a Mist," becomes the immortal life of the poem, yet also the abstract substance and fleeting "mist" of the life of the poet. Keats, at the end, is unable to separate, in the worst way, himself from his art—a skill, if he could but see it, he has already won. His mortality becomes, in his last mind, less the mortality *in* than the mortality *of* his poetry. As he says to Fanny Brawne a year before he dies, "If I had had time I would have made myself remember'd"—a prediction that at once misunderstands what is valuable already in his work and assumes what value will be found in a wished-for future of work still unwritten. At one level, Keats's final ode recapitulates the pastoral daylight hours: the "ripeness to the core" of "mellow fruitfulness," the languor after the harvesting and storing of the grain, and the rich melancholy of the "stubble-plains" in the warm light of the "soft-dying" sun. At another level, it is a poem of farewells, full to the core, weighted with endings yet lifted, suspended in air, "reflected and put in a Mist." The voice of its absences seems to be preparing for and anticipating what follows the failing, autumnal light—the dusk, then the real sleep of night.

7

FIVE DAYS AFTER KEATS DIES, SEVERN IS FINALLY ABLE TO write someone—in this case, an unsent fragment of a letter to Brown—as to what has happened. "My dear Brown,"

> *He is gone. He died with the most perfect ease. He seemed to go to sleep. On February 23rd, Friday, at half-past four, the approach of death came on. "Severn— I—lift me up, for I am dying. I shall die easy. Don't be frightened! Thank God it has come." I lifted him up in my arms, and the phlegm seemed boiling in his throat. This increased until eleven at night, when he gradually sank into death, so quiet, that I still thought he slept— but I cannot say more now. I am broken down beyond my strength. I cannot be left alone. I have not slept for nine days, I will say the days since—On Saturday a gentleman came to cast the face, hand, and foot. On Sunday his body was opened; the lungs were completely gone, the doctors could not conceive how he had lived in the last two months . . .*

Memory sends us back nine months to the tea at Mortimer Terrace with the Hunts and the visiting Gisbornes. Keats has arrived as if stricken unannounced, having just, on the street, suffered another attack of blood-spitting. It is a hot June day. It is as if he has been struck by the sun. Pale, nerves on edge, he is welcomed without comment as a member of Hunt's extended family. The conversation goes back and forth with little contribution—save one—from Keats. "We talked of music, and of Italian and English singing," to reiterate what Mrs. Gisborne notes in her diary the next day. "I mentioned that Farinelli had the art of taking breath imperceptibly, while he continued to hold one single note, alternately swelling out and diminished the power of his voice like waves. Keats observed that this music in some degree must be painful to the hearer, as when a diver descends into the hidden depths of the sea you feel an apprehension lest he may never rise again. These may not be his exact words as he spoke in a low tone." Keats, whose powers of empathy are unmatched, becomes both diver and hearer in this story, and at the moment he sinks into death, breathing intermittently as well as imperceptibly, he is drowning within his own fluids.

The casting of body parts of the deceased is normal for the time, as is the thoracic autopsy, which proves what Keats, almost alone, suspected and understood about his tubercular condition from the beginning, however much he wanted to believe his deficient doctors. This body that Severn could carry as if it were a child's from bedroom to living room, this body barely five feet and part of an inch in length, this once robust bantam fighter's body whose face afire Haydon has so beautifully rendered in his panoramic Jerusalem painting, "this mortal body of a thousand days," this boy's body curled as in the womb under his school desk mourning his mother's death, this body among the bodies at Guy's at the anatomical demonstrations, the surgeries, and the surgical mistakes, this body opened and emptied—this body that you wonder how at the end it held itself and soul together is the body to be borne into what Keats thinks is anonymous ground, his spirit having long since returned to the air. And this ghost's face, now immortalized by Severn in his deathwatch drawing and by Gherardi in the white plaster of a death mask, is the face of Tom and the face of their mother, and Moneta's "bright-blanched" face, made vivid in their representations by "an immortal sickness which kills not." A skeletal face returned to the shape of its skull.

Three days after his death, Keats is laid to rest in what is now perhaps the most visited grave in Rome, if we excuse saints and popes from the tally. He is buried on February 26 in the Il Cimitero Acattolico, still at the time a public and picnic area just outside the ancient Aurelian Wall, at a safe distance from true believers. Clark has managed to secure dispensation from the dawn curfew usually required of non-Catholics, so that the funeral—consisting of Clark and Severn and a few of the English community, most of whom do not know Keats—lasts until well past sunrise, 9 a.m. or so. Meanwhile, back at 26 Piazza di Spagna, the landlady has called in the authorities, who are in the process of purging Keats's sickroom: first by burning all its furniture, then by scraping clean and replacing its wall covering. These are facts worth repeating, because they represent a dark line drawn between the distance of Keats's isolation and obscurity in 1821 and his "popularity" now. Like the grave site, the address of the small conflagration is now memorialized and stands as a respite in the busy commercial life of the Popolo and Spanish Steps areas of Rome. But on that day of interment and survival, Severn—the survivor—has little interest in or sense of posterity. "Then the walls were all done up afresh, and I had scarcely paid the shameful demand when the brute of a landlady sent for me to pay for the crockery broken in our service, and I was at once indignant and amused to find a long table covered with the broken crockery of what must have been the debris of the whole parish. I assumed to be in a mad rage, and with my stick I dashed and smashed everything that was on the table, and singularly enough I frightened the vile creature of a landlady, with the result that I never heard any more about the crockery."

Would that Severn had been able to smash "these infernal scoundrels"—Keats's well-established critics at *Blackwood's* and *The Quarterly*—with equal force and result, and with equal (for Brown and Taylor and George as well) value as therapy. Or to smash death and all those incremental, incalculable bits and bites of illness and loss that slowly and inexorably brought Keats down. Severn will later love the Italians, but for now Signora Anna Angeletti and the Roman authorities who are about "their monstrous business" of eliminating—disappearing—all physical memory of Keats from the house that will eventually take on his name are serving as surrogates for much of Severn's frustration and anger at the gods and at all those far away who have, at one time or another, inflicted wounds on Keats. Yet Keats himself, at the end, has passed beyond caring for the losses of a world he is leaving behind. "Four days before poor Keats died the change was so great that I passed dark moments of dread. He was unaware of it himself. He made me lift him up in bed many times. The apprehension of death was strong upon him, but its effect was only that of giving him comfort. He seemed only affected when the morning came and still found him alive, and he grieved inwardly until some further change made him hope that the night would bring death. Each day he would look up on the doctor's face . . . This look was more than we could ever bear. The extreme brightness of his eyes with his poor pallid face were dreadful beyond description. These our last nights I watched him; on the fifth the doctor prepared me for his death—this day I cannot dare think on."

Much of Severn's recovery from his long journey with the dying Keats—from the initial confusions and delays of the depar-

ture from England to the tedium of the voyage and quarantine in
the Bay of Naples to the land trip north through the Campagna
to, most of all, the day and night attendance to a dying man—is
in the company of the dead Keats: "hours of contemplation and
rest in the valley of Monte Testaccio," as Severn's biographer,
William Sharp, puts it. For many months after, Severn finds him-
self standing over Keats's unnamed grave in the meadow area of
this future Protestant Cemetery. Part of his mind's healing pro-
cess is to return to and rehearse the perceived wrongs visited on
Keats, as if he is performing—for both himself and his friend—a
ritual cleansing. "I walked there a few days ago," Severn writes to
Haslam, "and found the daisies had grown all over it. It is in one
of the most lovely retired spots in Rome. You cannot have such
a place in England. I visit it with a delicious melancholy which
relieves my sadness. When I recollect for how long Keats had
never been one day free from ferment and torture of mind and
body, and that now he lies at rest with the flowers he so desired
above him, with no sound in the air but the tinkling bells of a
few simple sheep and goats, I feel indeed grateful that he is here,
and remember how earnestly I prayed that his sufferings might
end, and that he might be removed from a world where no one
grain of comfort remained for him." Keats's "sufferings," in the
time ahead, will become inseparable from his signature identity,
depending on the when, how, why, and what were its causes, and
depending on who is attached to, responsible for, or concerned
with those sufferings.

Is it what kills Keats or who kills Keats? Is it both? Or is
his death too drawn out a process, too incremental, too part
and piecemeal, too invisible to the daily eye, too disguised for
any word as abrupt as *kill*—and therefore too detailed, too
divided, too separated into too many sources, psychological,
physical, spiritual? Among the candidates are, of course, the

Tory reviewers of Keats's first two "cockney" books, the first of which Shelley cautions Keats from publishing, the second of which Lockhart and Croker say should not have been published. Then there are the doctors, who, though well-meaning, seem incapable of intuiting from the implications of symptoms and who diagnose from appearance and assumption and offer "cures" that are worse than the disease and in fact hasten the result. Then there is Richard Abbey, the Keatses appointed guardian, who through his thievery and knavery denies John especially his rightful claim and thus the means of independence. Then there is Brown, whose very closeness to Keats and whose on-again, off-again generosity set up expectations that perhaps no one could meet. Then there are John's brothers, Tom and George, the first of whom becomes the intimate carrier of the bacillus that ultimately infects John, the second is the brother who apparently abandons John to his final poverty. Then there is Frances Keats, the mother, whose three sons die of the disease that she dies of, having already left her children with her own mother, in effect orphaning them. Then there is the "bronchial" climate of Britain, particularly in the North, where Keats and Brown take their long walk in the summer of 1818, where cold and rain and bone-chilling damp are the norm and where they climb Ben Nevis, "where the sun on fiercest phosphor shines," like ice. Then there is Fanny Brawne, whose implicit promise of a future and a family is impossible, and at the end the mention of whose very name breaks another piece of Keats's heart. Then there is Keats himself, who surely senses what the risk is in nursing Tom (as he has nursed his mother in her last, desperate days), in always riding on the outside of the coach, in being caught in town in February without a winter coat, in a "medicinal" use of mercury, and in a hundred other large and small moments pushed too far.

When, in letters, Severn thinks and speaks of "these infernal scoundrels" and "others, besides G . . ." (meaning George), he is likely referring to more or less anonymous enemies, such as the *Blackwood's* and *Quarterly* reviewers. When, in his *Recollections*, Severn says that "I was the only personal friend present from among the little band of devoted friends whom the poet had left behind in England," he is likely referring to Brown, Haslam, the Brawnes, the Dilkes, and perhaps one or two others, including Hunt. The reference to "enemies" inscribed on Keats's tombstone derives from both his and Brown's need—particularly Brown's—to blame great insidious personified forces beyond anyone's control. The complexity of the sources building behind Keats's death is too inclusive for any of his friends to come to terms with. Severn's recovery and continued visitation of "this sacred spot . . . until the advent of the Italian summer" is testimony to not only his singular devotion but his own need for clarity concerning the winding path that has led to Keats's death in so foreign a place. In time, Severn will get back to his painting, his prizes, his cultivation of his world in Rome—almost all of it indebted to his steadfast affiliation with Keats. But that will take a while. For now, in the months following the death, Severn will try to get his strength back, try to design and erect a proper stone over the head of his friend, and try to consolidate—maybe negotiate is the better word—the various opinions of the causes of the poet's death, the importance of his life and thought, and, especially, the value of his achievement. None of this "recovery" will be easy. " 'Here lies one whose name was writ in water, *and his works in milk and water*'—this I was condemned to hear for years repeated," laments Severn, to which he adds, rather oddly, "but I should explain it was from those who were not aware that I was a friend of Keats," as if the judgment were separate from the comment.

Severn, as luck would have it, will die in Rome at eighty-six, his iron constitution unalloyed to the last. Keats, on the other hand, writes in Book IV of *Endymion*, "Yet I would have, great gods! but one short hour / Of native air—let me but die at home." Distance is one of the sources of the imagination, as what we are denied is another. The story of our lives is never, can never be, what we plan or wish for, which is why the memory of the meander that has led us here is so important. We look back at the narrative with wonder and no little confusion, as if it were a problem we could solve. Keats believes as early as February 1820 that he is through and that "if I had had time I would have made myself remember'd." He is thinking, of course, of poems, great poems, to be written not in water but on paper, of the air. But he has already written, months earlier, the last of what will, as poetry, be remembered. His story, however, in the letters will go on for another year, another kind of memory. It is Leigh Hunt to whom Keats owes much and for whom Keats feels, at different times, tremendous ambivalence: Hunt, whose florid, egocentric style set the standard for the "cockney"; Hunt, who went to prison for satirizing the Regency; Hunt, who published the liberal word of his day in *The Examiner* and *The Indicator*; Hunt, who discovered John Keats. It is Hunt who writes the most moving farewell to his friend in a letter to Severn even before he receives the actual news.

> *I hear he does not like to be told that he may get better, nor is it to be wondered at, considering his firm persuasion that he shall not thrive. But if this persuasion should happen no longer to be strong upon him, or if he can now put up with such attempts to console him, remind him of what I have said a thousand times, and what I still (upon my honour, I swear) think always, that I have seen*

> *too many cases of recovery from apparently desperate*
> *cases of consumption, not to indulge in hope to the very*
> *last. If he still cannot bear this, tell him—tell that great*
> *poet and noble-hearted man that we shall all bear his*
> *memory in the most precious part of our hearts, and that*
> *the world shall bow their heads to it as our loves do. Or if*
> *this . . . will trouble his spirit, tell him that we shall never*
> *cease to remember and love him, and that, Christian or*
> *Infidel, the most skeptical of us has faith enough in the*
> *high things that nature puts into our heads, to think that*
> *all who are of one accord in mind or heart are journey-*
> *ing to one and the same place and shall meet somehow or*
> *other again, face to face, mutually conscious, mutually*
> *delighted. Tell him he is only before us on the road, as he*
> *was in everything else; or whether you tell him the latter*
> *or no, tell him the former, and add, that we shall never*
> *forget that he was so, and that we are coming after him.*

This letter is dated March 8, just under two weeks after
Keats has passed. It will take another week for the news to reach
England. Brown will break the news to his neighbors, both new
and old—first the Brawnes, then the Dilkes. Haslam will inform
Fanny Keats. And Taylor, Keats's publisher, will place obituary
notices in the papers. Brown's personal response, as expressed
in a letter to Severn, is a bit hard to take considering the circum-
stances of Keats's departure for Italy and the near miss of hav-
ing anyone, notably Brown, accompany him. "Had I been with
him I could have borne all this with equal mind," then adds with
guilt hyperbole, the "hand of God took our friend away, and
to God, in all His behests, am I ever resigned." Then, as usual,
Brown's burden will not allow him to shut up: "I never yet lost
any one by the hand of man, though that (you will say) is still

by the will of God, but certainly with a difference,—I mean by a violent death, and know not how I could bear the loss of any one in that manner; but here, though enemies have preyed upon him, I am quite resigned, for those enemies knew not what they were doing, whose heart they were breaking." Brown doth protest too much, even in his biblical paraphrase. And he goes on and on ("I mourn for him outwardly as well as inwardly . . ."). Fanny Brawne, meanwhile, mourns in silence and by example: She becomes quite ill and, as if she were a widow, cuts her hair short and for months wears nothing but black. In May she writes Keats's sister: "All his friends have forgotten him, they have got over the first shock, and that with them is all. They think I have done the same, but I have not got over it and never shall—It's better for me that I should not forget him but not for you."

MATERIAL SUBLIME

. . .

O that our dreamings all, of sleep or wake,
Would all their colours from the sunset take,
From something of material sublime,
Rather than shadow our own soul's daytime
In the dark void of night.

1

ON JUNE 5, 1877, FIFTY-SIX YEARS AFTER KEATS'S DEATH, a General Sir Vincent Eyre writes to Lord Houghton (Richard Monckton Milnes) that he has "met with an unexpected obstacle in my efforts to carry out what seemed a very simple object; viz—that of placing in the outer wall of the house where Keats died a mural Tablet, to commemorate that Event, with a simple inscription, somewhat to the following effect:

> *In this house–died–*
> *JOHN KEATS*
> *the Young English Poet.*
> *on the 21ˢᵗ Feby. 1821.*

The permission of the owner of the house had been obtained, but that of the Municipal Syndic was also required—and was refused by him on the plea that (to use the words of my informant) *'Keats was not recognized as a SUBLIMITY!'*" Eyre's letter to Houghton is postmarked "Grand Hotel d'Aix / Aix les Bains / France," sent from such an elegant distance because of being "delayed here on my way from Rome by Lady Eyre's indisposition, which obliges her to take a course of baths." By this time Lord Houghton has published two editions of his "biography" of Keats, which includes various poems and a selection of letters, the first in 1848, the second in 1867. Eyre is viewed as the living authority on Keats, Joseph Severn notwithstanding. Yet as if Houghton is unaware of certain biographical facts, Eyre pushes on.

> *No doubt the proposed tablet to Keats would be chiefly interesting to the English and American visitors & residents in Rome—The house stands at the base of the grand flight of steps leading from the "Piazza di Spagna" to the Piazza "Trinita di Monti," and the inscription would attract the notice of all persons of those nations ascending & descending the said steps.—*
>
> *That part of Rome is chiefly frequented by the English speaking nationalities; who seldom omit to visit the grave of the deceased Poet near the Pyramid of Caius Cestius when opportunity offers. Hence, it cannot be doubted that the proposed Mural Tablet would prove highly interesting to all such persons; and the very fact of this undying interest existing in full force after the lapse of more than half a century might be safely accepted by the Syndic and his colleagues as sufficient proof of "Sublimity"—*

Eyre closes with the hope that "I am not intruding too far on your kindness in appealing thus to your powerful influence." Eyre is a retired army major-general who has spent most of his military career in India and now spends his winters in Rome. He is among those in the English community who has developed an affection for Keats—though there are still a few, even at this late date, who feel antipathy for his memory—especially Keats's emerging (soon dominating) association with this section of Rome and the Protestant Cemetery. Eyre fancies himself a latter-day Romantic, having published in 1874 *Lays of a Knight-Errant in Many Lands*—ballads, no doubt, of an autobiographical cast. The flavor of his writing can be inferred from his sonnet "Suggested by Severn's sketch of Keats on his death bed," which begins:

> 'Twas thus, amid the silent hours of night,
> The dying Poet slept, long years ago;
> Calm as "Endymion" 'neath the moon's soft glow;
> Dreaming, perhaps, of worlds more pure and bright
> Where he might lay aside his weight of woe!

And ends with the thought that, "though brief on earth his days," Keats might still "Illumine . . . our minds with his undying lays."

A "lay," derivative of "lai," is an old reference to poetry as narrative romance, ballad, or variable song composed with refrains. Eyre, for all his well-meaning Keatsian sentimentality, is typical of a certain public that responds to the tapestry in Keats during and after the long silence regarding his reputation in the decades following his death. Frankly, Eyre is only a step down from the *Eve-of St.-Agnes-, Isabella; -or-the-Pot-of-Basil*-loving Pre-Raphaelities, for whom Keats was both enchanting, ekphrastic, and, most of all, enabling. The luxury, drapery, weft, and rich weave of the texture and rhythmic structure in Keats's romances and ballads—inspired and poignant at once—are irresistible, for sure, but such qualities tend to confirm rather than challenge, reinforce rather than resist convention, and meet—in spite of counter-Victorian and post-Victorian protestations of art for art's sake—mostly middle-brow nineteenth-century expectations. Even the great Tennyson—no slouch himself at narrative and high romance (though too often seasoned with anti-Keatsian didacticism)—cannot avoid the influence of Keats's imperative sense of a closely textured tableau. Here is a moment from "In Memoriam, 95."

> *By night we lingered on the lawn,*
>   *For underfoot the herb was dry;*
>   *And genial warmth; and o'er the sky*
>   *The silvery haze of summer drawn;*
>
> *And calm that lets the tapers burn*
>   *Unwavering; not a cricket chirred;*
>   *The brook alone far-off was heard,*
>   *And on the board the fluttering urn;*
>
> *And bats went round in fragrant skies,*
>   *And wheeled or lit the filmy shapes*
>   *That haunt the dusk, with ermine capes*
>   *And woolly breasts and beaded eyes . . .*
>   *15.1–12*

It would be best if we could assign the sensual influence here to Keats's odes exclusively, without the greater notice of the brocade of the romance narratives, but Tennyson is enchanted by as much as he is interested in Keats as an abundant stylist.

Perhaps convention is the inevitable first response to genius after indifference or confusion or sheer delay of an appropriate response to the depth of the work. The badness of Eyre's bad sonnet-elegy for Keats lies primarily in his wish to turn the suffering poet into a dreamer-Endymion rather than a vital, tragic Hyperion. The "mere dreamer" is exactly the role that Keats is rejecting in his heroic confrontation with the goddess Moneta—mere dreamers, mock lyricists, and large self-worshippers. Nevertheless, whatever Eyre's motive in regarding or understanding Keats, his public mission transcends such personal limitations: The memorial plaque idea has inherent merit and will ultimately be a contributing factor in the preservation and restoration of what becomes the Keats-Shelley Memorial House at 26 Piazza di Spagna. With Lord Houghton's and generous American help, the memorial tablet is set and unveiled on February 28, 1879. According to the *London Times*, "Sir Vincent Eyre, to whose effort the erection of the tablet is due, made an admirable address . . . He spoke of Joseph Severn, . . . who would have been present had not age and infirmities rendered it impossible in such weather . . . Dr. Nevin, on behalf of his American countrymen, bore testimony to their admiration of the poet's genius and their interest in his memory—for his name was written upon their hearts."

Five months later Severn will be dead. Thirty years later, with the blessings of King Edward VII and President Theodore Roosevelt, the Memorial House will be opened as both memorial to and museum of Keats and Shelley and their era, though the project itself begins in 1903—the year of the Wright brothers— with the meeting of the minds of a group of American writers in residence in Rome. (Perhaps Keats was, at last, receiving his wish to be the first great American poet, via proxy.) The power here is the power of Keats's death—the long dying of it and the long witness of it. Keats spent just six months in the house, Shelley no time at all. Against the fact of their profound differences, Keats and Shelley become linked through the accident of having mutual friends and the coincidence of careers, then of death. Shelley had hoped that he finally would achieve the recognition that had so far eluded him with the publication of his wide-ranging elegy-celebration of Keats as *Adonais*, a poem as much about its author as it is about its stated subject. That the most accurate perception in the poem is Shelley's prediction of his own death ("I am borne darkly, fearfully, afar . . .") only adds to the irony of the linkage of the poets' names . . . competitors rather than friends.

Shelley drowns with Hunt's copy of Keats's last book opened in his pocket, the book about which he has already expressed the opinion that "*Hyperion* is very fine . . . grand poetry . . . His other poems are worth little," including, we can assume, in Shelley's view, the odes. Apparently Shelley feels that Keats has loaded too many of his rifts with too much ore, which is, of course, Keats's famous complaint against his future eulogist—not enough ore in the rifts. Strangely linked in life, now sentimentally linked in death, because memory has a gift for summary and symmetry, Keats and Shelley become, in Rome, inseparable, not unlike the way their grave sites are linked in the Protestant Cemetery, reinforced by the fact that Keats has been laid to rest next to Shelley's three-year-old son.

Mortal words and immortal words, bodies and their spirits all find their ways in time. Eyre's hopeful idea of a memorial plaque to mark the place of Keats's death will find its way. Time, the enemy, can also be a friend, given time. Decades earlier (1830), when Severn proposes a monument to Keats's memory in Rome—as if in compensation for the mistake of Keats's tombstone's indelible epigraph—Brown discourages the thought. "You ask me what shall be done with the profits of our work to poor Keats's memory," Severn writes Brown in April 1830. "Now I have thought a good deal of it, and am going to propose *that we erect a monument to his memory here in Rome.*" Severn's vision is of a "Basso Rilievo" of Keats sitting with a "half-strung lyre" caught in a tableau involving the three fates, one at his arm, one cutting a lyric string, the third, in silent speech, announcing his death. If this notion sounds mawkish, it is. Brown may have thought so: Keats's reputation is such that the timing for a memorial—less than a decade after his death—is right now inappropriate, or so he writes back to Severn. Keats's "fame," except as an example of poetic mortality, is at this moment almost nonexistent. This is in the same space of time of Fanny Brawne's oft-quoted comment (to Brown regarding a possible "biography") that in terms of the pain that Keats suffered at the end—spiritual as much as physical, emotional as much as mental—why prolong his posthumous vulnerability to criticism with more words. "The kindest act would be to let him rest for ever in the obscurity to which circumstances have condemned him." She writes this at the end of the year 1829.

Severn and Brown, in these tenuous years following Keats's passing, are no more effective on their own as keepers of the flame than they are as collaborators. After sixteen years, Brown cannot seem to find any closure on his purportive now abortive biography, perhaps because his memory and information are fragmentary, perhaps deep down because of guilt. And after only nine years, Severn, for whom "the gravestone, with its inscription, is an eye-sore to me and more," cannot get past his limited sentimental sensibility. So, whether in terms of portraiture or the proposed "half-strung lyre" of the basso rilievo memorial, Severn remains unable to separate himself from his hypernatural feelings for Keats and an objective understanding of the poet as poet. Brown and Severn will have had to pass from the scene before any perspective on Keats becomes accurate and real. All of the Keats Circle, in fact, will have to die before his work in context with his death is fully discovered and addressed. The path to immortality is not only a meander, it is episodic—if not spasmodic. Ultimately, there will be two tablets "unveiled" at what becomes the Keats-Shelley Memorial House: the first, commemorating the death of Keats, in 1879; the second, commemorating the opening of the house, in 1909—a distance of thirty years. The first tablet, the result of Sir Vincent Eyre's persistent handiwork, reads, in Italian, in white on pale blue marble, set in the pale rosso wall facing the Spanish Steps, as follows:

L'Inglese poeta Giovanni Keats
Mente meravigliosa quanto precoce
mori in questa casa
li 24 Febbraio 1821
ventesimosesto dell' eta sua

Severn sort of gets his wish of many years before, because under the plaque's inscription there is a lyre, not a broken but a whole one. This tablet and the house it memorializes become a timely realization of follow-through and understatement and no apparent agenda other than honor.

2

POSTERITY MEANS COMING AFTER, WHICH MIGHT BE READ AS not only that which follows but that which pursues. Time's arrow arcs like a rainbow into the future. The late 1870s were particularly busy years for Keats's commemorative notices—both good and bad—as well as years of factual confusion and unwanted notoriety. Besides the 1879 tablet on the house in Rome where he dies, another tablet, two years before, has been placed on the wall nearest the grave. In a letter of June 1877, Oscar Wilde asks Lord Houghton if he has "visited Keats grave since a marble tablet in his memory was put up on the wall close to the tomb. There are some fairly good lines of poetry on it, but what is really objectionable in it is the bas relief of Keats's own head—or rather a *medallion profile*, which is *extremely ugly*, exaggerates his facial angle so as almost to give him a hatchet-face and instead of the finely cut nostril, and Greek sensuous delicate lips that he had, gives him thick almost negro lips and nose." Wilde, befitting his reputation, pushes his opinion even further. "Keats we know was lovely as Hyakinthos, or Apollo, to look at, & this medallion is a very terrible lie and misrepresentation—I wish it could be removed and a tinted bust of Keats put in its place, like the beautiful coloured bust of Rajah of Koolapoor in Florence—Keats delicate features and rich colour could not be conveyed I think in plain white marble." Wilde goes on to demand that the medallion be taken down. Whether or not a colored bust along the lines of delineating the Rajah of Koolapoor is the appropriate replacement is another matter.

A month later, in July 1877, another fan of Keats writes to Lord Houghton regarding the exact location of the Hampstead address of Wentworth Place, which now, some fifty years after the drama of Keats, is apparently somewhat obscure. The writer is one Thomas Satchell, a nearby neighbor at Downshire Hill House. "My desire is to identify the house or houses in which the poet resided, for I am not satisfied with the identification of 'Wentworth place' which has been recently published . . . I trust it will not appear very extraordinary that I should desire to identify the ground whereon ('the plum tree' must have perished I fear) the Ode to a Nightingale was written and which may or may not be a portion of my own property." Satchell is confused by more than geography; he seems to think that Brawne and Brown are the same name and that Fanny B. is Charles Brown's cousin, hence confirming her residence at "the next house." Satchell's errors also have the ring of truth in that his understanding is that Keats was for a while "domesticated with her family," meaning both the Brawnes and Brown were at different times in both halves of the house—Wentworth Place—which is later called Lawn Bank before it ultimately becomes the Keats House. A commemorative tablet to Keats is attached to the property on February 24, 1896. This is 75 years after the poet's death in Rome, 101 years after his birth in old London.

The letter from Satchell reads: "The Rt: Honble: Lord Houghton D.C.L. &c &c//Downshire Hill House, Hampstead N. W, June 22nd 1878//My Lord / I take the liberty of begging your acceptance of a copy of a view of the long-lost Wentworth place (now known as Lawn Bank) which has been taken at my request by a local photographer. / That portion of the house which lies to the right of the present entrance formed the residence of Mrs. Brawne and her daughters; that to the left, of Charles Armitage Broun. / The front room, which (as appears in your biography of the poet) was occupied by Keats when 'domesticated' with Mr Broun, remains apparently in its original condition, though the interior of the house must have been subjected to considerable alteration, during the process of converting the two residencies into one for the convenience of Miss Chester, who also added the large room to the side of the house which is nearest to Wentworth House where Mr Dilke lived.— / I have the honour to be / My Lord / Your humble Servant / Tho. Satchell//P.S. / On a closer examination of the photograph I notice a mark on the house just above the string course to the left of the bedroom window, which (*ni fallor*) indicates the position of the name (*Wentworth place*) which Mr Forman has discovered to be still distinguishable under the paint & whitewash of upwards of a quarter of a century."

In October 1877, the American poet and editor Richard Henry Stoddard writes to Lord Houghton to protest "the infamy of publishing his love letters fifty six years after his death!" Stoddard is referring to Keats's often desperate, often angry, often self-abnegating letters and notes to Fanny Brawne, written between the summers of 1819 and 1820. The thirty-seven of these that have survived have been kept in packets, along with a lock of reddish hair (in a gold case), a ring set with almandine, and a minature (by Severn) of a daydreaming Keats in 1818. There are also a stack of books, among them Keats's own three publications, some Dante, Spenser, Milton, and, naturally, Shakespeare. Letters, personal items, books—these are the remnant of the Keats-Brawne romance that Fanny has held on to—in secret—her entire married life with Louis Lindon. Several years after her death, in 1865, and her husband's, in 1872, Herbert Lindon, the son, has written to the same Lord Houghton that "I have in my possession the letters addressed by Keats to my late Mother (then Miss Brawne) during the time of his illness & up to the time of his departure for Italy. I have been advised that Your Lordship may perhaps wish to purchase them & as I have no objection to dispose of them I beg, in the event of such being the case to offer them to Your Lordship." This letter is dated December 29, 1876, less than a year after Stoddard's. At this point in the crossover of the several stories of the rescue and memoralizing of Keats, converging here at the end of the 1870s, this December letter stands out for its private rather than its public nature. Because Fanny Brawne (Lindon) has never clarified her young relationship with Keats to her husband, and because Keats himself had insisted on the secrecy of their engagement, the letters and other sacred memorabilia have been kept under wraps—until, sensing her own last years approaching, Fanny reveals her lost love story to her son and daughter with the stipulation that none of her "Keatsiana" be exposed before her and her husband's death.

What is curious about Fanny's insistence on discretion is that a decade and a half earlier—1860—she writes to Charles Dilke, her mother's old friend as well as Keats's, that she "is induced to ask whether it would suit you to purchase that miniature of Mr. Keats which has been for so long a time in my possession. It would not be a light motive that would make me part with it . . ." Dilke, in these post-Keatsian decades, has become something of a collector of Keats—more like a preserver. The Lindons apparently need money, and Fanny sees selling the miniature as her best means of acquiring ready cash. The single problem is how to keep these negotiations from her husband ("I would ask you to at once remit the money to Mr. Lindon, but as he knows nothing of the transaction, I enclose a note which will explain it to him, if you will send it at the same time . . ."). The problem is finally solved through Dilke's cooperation. Now flash forward sixteen years, when Fanny's son makes his offer of the love letters to Keats's biographer, Milnes/Lord Houghton, who is preparing a new and updated edition of the *Life, Letters, and Literary Remains of John Keats.* Herbert Lindon appears bent on emptying the store of his mother's memento mori of Keats. As if taking his mother's lead while honoring her request that Louis Lindon need to have passed from the scene, Herbert waits the minimum decent interval before offering to the Dilke estate the rest of the Keatsian "relics" that his mother has left behind. (Apparently the family is still in need of money.) Prized among the collection are the letters, which Charles Dilke III is happy to buy and—having read them— place in a kind of escrow. Because of the intimate, painful, even self-destructive nature of the letters, Dilke vows to himself that they shall never see the light of publication. The problem is that there is no legal agreement drawn between Dilke and Herbert Lindon. These letters, Dilke later writes, "I certainly thought I had in a vague way bought for the purpose of preventing publication. They had been long in my possession, but the son of Fanny Brawne had reclaimed them, and I, having no written agreement, had found it necessary to give them up—although what I had bought and paid for, unless it was the right to prevent publication, I do not know." The love letters seem to have a public will of their own.

And so what is apparently given—indeed, paid for—can be legally taken back. When in 1876 Herbert Lindon proposes a second sale to Lord Houghton, having recaptured the letters, he unwittingly enhances their power, for good or ill, within the literary community. These letters will now take on a separate life, removed from the whole life of Keats's complex correspondence. Lord Houghton, who is aware of the content as well as the fact of the letters, refuses to consider them, especially because they reflect—out of context—badly on both parties and will certainly corrupt the high tone of his take on Keats in the new edition of the biography. At this moment, Herbert turns to H. B. Foreman, a well-regarded critic and reader of Keats, who agrees to edit and introduce the *Letters of John Keats to Fanny Brawne*, 1878. Years later, at public auction, the letters fetch 543 pounds; their publication has already cost Keats and Fanny a good deal of goodwill and support. Keats is reduced to "a surgeon's apprentice," who in these letters, in Matthew Arnold's words, reveals, in his "self-abandonment, something underbred and ignoble, as of a youth ill brought up." Fanny fares no better; she becomes a "piece of common clay, the unheroic Ariadne who lost her prince and lived to marry a practical being." Well, at least her son becomes a practical being, whether or not he takes after his mother. It will be another sixty years before a corrective vision—in the guise, in 1937, of Fanny Brawne's thoughtful letters to Fanny Keats—puts Keats's lover into real perspective—a young woman once greatly in love who must settle for what happiness she can find. (The secret of Keats in her life must have been a growing burden, requiring, near the end, when she tells all to her children, a certain letting go, including those correlatives of memory locked—entombed—in a box.) Keats's rescue from the response to the love letters becomes part of his reputation's continual rising and falling in the time ahead, though the permanent quality of his creative work seems even now to have begun to transcend the "vicissitudes" of the judgment of his personal liabilities. "My mistakes," Keats had said, "will be forgiven" after death. He meant his mistakes in life. He understood that there are no mistakes in art, only failures.

3

BRIC-A-BRAC, RELICS, MEMORABILIA, ITEMS AROUND WHICH has congregated an aura of light of the most personal depth and value. But what if that value becomes, on its own, not just personal, but universal? Who owns that memory then? These fragments I have shored against my ruins. The pieces and parts of Keats that each of his friends felt proprietary toward fragmented any chance of a coherent sense of his character and career in the living moment after his death. This or that group, in fact, became polarized, in spite of their mutual love of the man and admiration for his genius. These are the friends whom—on Keats's departure for Italy—Fanny Brawne had praised as "a set of friends that I did not believe could be found in the world," while writing, less than a year later, to Keats's sister that "All his friends have forgotten him, they have got over the first shock, and that with them is all." And when she adds that she has "not got over it and never shall," she is testing the truth of long promises. The personal archaeology of the soul is manifest in those few things that Keats has left her and she has held in secret all these years, until she can feel her own death coming on. What is the accumulative, acquiring power, forty years on, of a ring, a lock of hair, a miniature of vague likeness? And what of the different copies of different poems and letters and even books separated out among Brown, Severn, Reynolds, the ever-Keatsian Woodhouse, and so on—how personal, how valuable to posterity? Brown decides that Keats's brother George is a culprit, passively aligned with John's "enemies." Dilke sides with George in these years-long disputes about money and abandonment. Taylor, Keats's publisher, is to Brown not only a mere "bookseller" but unworthy of Keats. Reynolds, in his turn, wants to write Keats's biography, and should—according to Taylor, because Reynolds, not Brown, was Keats's best friend—but needs materials to be drawn from too many disparate, if not disagreeable, sources. Perhaps if Taylor himself cannot or should not write a biography, then Benjamin Bailey should. He has almost been forgotten as a member of Keats's past, but he was early on an intimate. Hunt, as a witness, no one trusts. Haydon, in his narcissism, has become Keats's antagonist. Haslam and Rice, who have no literary ambition, are those unusual kinds of friends who love without agenda. And Severn, the survivor, who outlives everyone, becomes the representative of Keats in Rome, the friend on the periphery who moves to the center but is no true writer, which he proves again and again in his miscellany of memoirs. Each of these figures, and others, has memories and Keatsian memorabilia that require coordination, which is why, decades down the road, someone such as Richard Monckton Milnes—outside the Keats circle in time and distance—will need to emerge as the collector, the gatherer, the filter of information, the arbiter of value, the editor of record.

Who among them, save Hunt—Haydon perhaps—would be remembered except for Keats? He becomes, in a way, their biographer. He is certainly the author of Fanny Brawne, who would, in order to preserve their intimacy, have him disappear, while in effect taking with him all on board. Brown, for instance, ends up stuck, apoplectic, and dead halfway around the world, buried, at fifty-five, on Marsland Hill, New Plymouth, New Zealand, in a spot later "leveled for military barracks," only to be rediscovered some eighty years after his disappearance, at which time his grandchildren erect a tombstone favored with the words "The Friend of Keats." Reynolds disappears, at fifty-eight, into dissipation and drink, "that poor baffled thing," yet he too is listed on his tombstone as "The Friend of Keats." Haydon, who disappears into larger and larger unloved epic paintings, kills himself at sixty by inaccurate gunshot and accurate knife. Haslam disappears at fifty-six, "broken by business pressure and financial straits." Rice disappears at forty, having suffered most of his life from consumption or something like its "long lingering," a condition that compromises his skill as a lawyer. Woodhouse disappears at forty-six, also of consumption. They all manage somehow to make it into middle age regardless of handicaps, bad choices, dashed hopes. George, too, makes it to middle age; Hunt and Severn, buoyant to the last, survive to old age. Fanny Brawne outlives everyone in the circle except Severn—outlives, in fact, her younger brother, Sam, who dies at twenty-four (of consumption), and her immolated mother, whose skirt catches fire from the fireplace.

Within a month of her mother's death, November 23, 1829, Fanny receives a letter of inquiry from Brown. "I am resolved to write his life, persuaded that no one, except yourself, knew him better." Brown is asking her permission to use poems and letters in his planned biography of Keats in which—without naming her—"she figured importantly." Her reply, at the end of December, is a masterpiece of indirection, focused through the lens of her long and now stated wish "that his name, his very name, could be forgotten by everyone but myself. That I have often wished most intensely. I was more generous ten years ago.

I should not now endure the odium of being connected with one who was working his way up against poverty and every sort of abuse." The fuller text of this comment is:

Hampstead Decr 29th 1829

My dear Brown

As the aggressor I am too happy to escape the apologies I owe you on my long silence not gladly to take your hint and say nothing about it. The best reparation I can make is to answer your letter today as soon as possible although I received it only this morning.

In the hours that have intervened before I sat down to answer it my feelings have entirely changed on the subject of the request it contains. Perhaps you will think I was opposed to it and am now come over to your side of the question, but it is just the contrary. Had I answered your letter immediately I should have told you that I considered myself so entirely unconnected with Mr Keats except by my own feelings that nothing published respecting him could affect me. But now I see it differently.

We all have our little world in which we figure and I cannot help expressing some disinclination at the idea that the few acquaintances I have should be able to obtain such a key to my sensations. Having said so much you will probably conclude that I mean to refuse your request. Perhaps when I assure you that, though my opinion has changed, my intention of complying in every respect with your wishes remains, you will think I am mentioning my objections to make a favor of my consent. But indeed my dear Brown if you do, you mistake me entirely. It is only to justify myself I own that I state all I think . . .

I assure you I should not have hinted that your wishes were painful to me did I not feel the suffering myself to be even alluded to was a want of pride. So far am I from possessing overstrained delicacy that the circumstance of its being a mere love story is the least of my concern. On the contrary, had I been his wife I should have felt my present reluctance would have been so much stronger that I think I must have made it my request that you would relinquish your intention. The only thing that saves me now is that so very few can know I am in any way implicated, and that of those few I may hope the greater number may never see the book in question.

Do then entirely as you please, and be assured that I comply with your wishes rather because they are yours than with the expectation of any good that can be done. I fear the kindest act would be to let him rest for ever in the obscurity to which unhappy circumstances have condemned him . . .

You can tell better than I, and are more impartial on the subject, for my wish has long been that his name, his very name, could be forgotten by everyone but myself. That I have often wished most intensely. I was more generous ten years ago. I should not now endure the odium of being connected with one who was working his way up against poverty and every sort of abuse.

To your publishing his poems addressed to me I do not see there can be any objection after the subject has once been alluded to, if you think them worthy of him. I entirely agree with you that if his life is to be published no part ought to be kept back, for all you can do is show his character. His life was too short and too unfortunate for anything else. I have no doubt that his talents

*would have been great . . . all I fear is whether he has
left enough to make people believe that. If I could think
so I should consider it right to make that sacrifice to his
reputation that I do now to your kind motives.*

*Not that even the establishment of his fame would
give me the pleasure it ought. Without claiming too much
constancy for myself, I may truly say that he is well-
remembered by me and that, satisfied with that, I could
wish no one by myself knew he had ever existed . . .*

The lawyery tone and wandering logic of this letter express, in part, Fanny B.'s grief-recovery grief experience within the parentheses of Keats's death in 1821 and her brother's and mother's deaths in 1828–29. There is a certain anger yet relief in the fact of the impersonality of a possible biography separating itself from the residual pain of Keats's continuing personal (secret) presence in her life, not to mention her reticence regarding her family tragedies. This is a letter written out of mourning, its author having already worn widow's weeds of black in her emotional isolation. As to the letter's stated content, Keats the poet is one thing, Keats the lover another, and Keats the potential husband entirely something else. Fanny argues inside this triad of Keatsian roles, then steps outside her argument to claim Keats solely for herself. The problem is that Keats, of all poets, cannot be divided between the artist and the man. ("I find that I cannot exist without poetry—") Fanny seems to know this and is willing to sacrifice the poet on the altar of the person she knew, loved, and now recognizes as both a secret and a memory. Immortality, though, is memory alive, of and on its own, present and accountable. It is a figuration, not a person. In sensing this, she wants the corporeal Keats, her Keats, to disappear, the way his friends will disappear, the way she herself will disappear, all their spirits healed by the air. Pain, over these years, has made her less "generous."

Therefore, give up those pieces of memory—that lock of hair, that ring, that small emblem of a face—into anonymous hands and let them find their own warm or cold value, depending. Let them join the posthumous world of the poems and, like the poems, take their chances.

4

IN 1917, NEAR THE CLOSE OF WORLD WAR I, IN HIS VOLUME entitled *The Wild Swans at Coole*, in a dialogic poem entitled "Ego Dominus Tuus," W. B. Yeats writes:

Hic.   *And yet*
No one denies to Keats love of the world;
Remember his deliberate happiness.

Ille. *His art is happy, but who knows his mind?*
I see a schoolboy when I think of him,
With face and nose pressed to a sweet-shop window,
For certainly he sank into his grave
His senses and his heart unsatisfied,
And made—being poor, ailing and ignorant,
Shut out from all the luxury of the world,
The coarse-bred son of a livery-stable keeper—
Luxuriant song.

Here at the true beginning of the twentieth century, almost every cliché associated with John Keats of a century before is invoked.

The sybaritic, leafy, Huntian, pre-Pre-Raphaelite bower poet; the mere dreamer, the Endymion, who thinks through his senses; the gorgeous boy-poet, "a little western flower" (Hazlitt), unable to stand up to the winds of Tory criticism. Pretty Keats, happy Keats, luxuriant Keats. Also, on the personal side, little Keats, poor Keats, "ailing and ignorant . . . coarse-bred . . . ," "With face and nose pressed" against the window-glass of a world that he can neither enter nor be admitted to—"son of a livery-stable keeper." And also the broken promise of Keats, who sinks "into his grave / His senses and his heart unsatisfied," his achievement unfulfilled, whose vision is the view of a "sweet-shop." (Byron, too, had attacked Keats's country-school classical—and class—education and its presumption on mythology.) Yeats is forgetting his own young Pre-Raphaelite nineteenth-century era of happy shepherds, Salley Gardens, and gold and silver apples. Shelley is Yeats's notion of a Romantic poet, a poet of manly politics and philosophic impact, a poet of—God forbid—"ideas."

You can see why the Victorians loved Keats. To them he offers painterly tableaux of drapery and color and sensuality and high remote romance that forgive their gray Carlylean, stoic repression. Keats gives them permission to speak of desire both exquisitely withheld and exquisitely fulfilled. What they find in him is the visual music and "luxuriant song" of the romance narratives and ballads. Those who recognize the superior strength of the odes—such as Tennyson—are in the minority, and even they draw on the poetry's perceived content: exquisite death, easeful and half-loved, or exquisite beauty, Attic shaped, coldly pastoral. Wilfred Owen, locked in the counter-reality of world war, trench war, stupid modern war, is the counterexample: He understands Keats's unique assonant music, his remarkable diction, his "style," and plays its combining qualities (sensual *and* mindful) against the grim tragedy of war. Owen makes modern irony from his

Keats. He sees, in 1917, what Yeats apparently cannot see: "Not in the hands of boys but in their eyes / Shall shine the holy glimmers of goodbyes. / The pallor of girls' brows shall be their pall . . ."; nor can Yeats see that the "mind" in Keats's work is its imagination, its edge of "fine excess," its tolerance for "light and shade," its "camelion" sense of itself as "continually informing and filling some other Body." As time passes, it will be Wallace Stevens who will realize in Keats, and in himself, the primacy and supremacy of the imagination, its commitment to beauty as a function of the act of the poem. And it will be the New Critics who comprehend in Keats—especially in the odes—the crucial distinction of the lyric poem as an ongoing contemporary experience, the experience of dynamic poetic form, what Bate calls—in Keats—"a more richly capacious form"—or form as content, structure as texture, beauty as truth.

This is the "schoolboy" Keats that Yeats should be fixed on, the young man who, in responding to the vicious reviews in *Blackwood's* and *The Quarterly* ("This is a mere matter of the moment—I think I shall be among the English Poets after my death"), writes his brother George in October 1818 that

> *I shall in a short time write you as far as I know how I*
> *intend to pass my Life—I cannot think of those things*
> *now Tom is so unwell and weak. Notwithstand your*
> *Happiness and your recommendation I hope I shall never*
> *marry. Though the most beautiful Creature were wait-*
> *ing for me at the end of a Journey or a Walk; though*
> *the carpet were of Silk, the Curtains of the morning*
> *Clouds; the chairs and Sofa stuffed with Cygnet's down;*
> *the food Manna, the Wine beyond Claret, the Window*
> *opening on Winander mere, I should not feel—or rather*
> *my Happiness would not be so fine, as my Solitude is*
> *sublime. Then instead of what I have described, there is*

a Sublimity to welcome me home—The roaring of the
wind is my wife and the Stars through the window pane
are my Children. The mighty abstract Idea I have of
Beauty in all things stifles the more divided and minute
domestic happiness—an amiable wife and sweet Chil-
dren I contemplate as a part of that Beauty, but I must
have a thousand of those beautiful particles to fill up my
heart. I feel more and more every day, as my imagination
strengthens, that I do not live in this world alone but in
a thousand worlds—No sooner am I alone than shapes
of epic greatness are stationed around me, and serve
my Spirit the office of which is equivalent to a king's
body guard—then "Tragedy, with scepter'd pall, comes
sweeping by."

There may be more than a bit of bravura here, even a plush play-fulness; there may even be—under the surface and because of Tom—a hint of fear "that I shall cease to be." But the figure drawn of a rejected domestic life has the right seasoning of the satiric; just as the configuration of solitude is sharp as well as overdrawn. Keats is speaking from a context in which he is replaying the role of nurse and witness (having sat and nursed his mother for nine years before); he has just returned from the aborted Northern tour, where he has caught the "cold" of his life; and he is dealing with reviews of his writing that will almost certainly doom its public value. Yet he offers to George that negatively capable combination of wit, seriousness, and insight that only a mind of his embrace, it seems, can. Sublimity will ultimately welcome him home. Right now his heart is full and his mind is multiple with ambition to write great poetry within the great tradition. The fact that he will fail and succeed in a way wholly different from what he intends is sim-ply how life, and art, works. His imagination is his monastery—as he will say to Shelley—and he its monk. Keats is defining here—

with a sort of buoyancy—the nature and needs of the imagination: solitude, quickness of connection, and a gift for simultaneity. And he is suggesting that, even so, the imagination does not operate in artistic or historic isolation: Its spirit is served by those—Spenser, Shakespeare, Milton—who have gone before. Schoolboy indeed; medical student turned healer-poet certainly, in a line of heritage in which the imagination and the sublime are linked with ambition, with large, great works, with truth—the tragic vision—in metaphor and myth.

Keats intuitively will, in the end, adjust the sublime equation into an equity, something more lowercase—beauty is truth, truth beauty—and find in new, expansive *lyric* forms enough spaciousness for the sublime and the imaginative balances (of light and shade) of a moral elevation. The odes will perfect this equation; the very apparent ease with which they get written is testament to the inseparability of their form and manifest content: beauty itself the sublime, the imagination itself truth. "I am certain of nothing," Keats will write Benjamin Bailey as early as November 1817, "but the holiness of the Heart's affections and the truth of the Imagination—What the imagination seizes as Beauty must be truth—whether it existed before or not." The operative words here are "whether it existed before or not"—meaning that beauty can create truth, discover it in that moment of its making; meaning "that which is creative must create itself"; meaning nothing abstract or assumed a priori to the lyric moment, realized, in the language of that language. The so-called "moment's monument" of the classic sonnet is one thing; the lyric form inventing its own enlarging landscape is another. Keats's epic expectations become sublimated—brilliantly, exquisitely—into the odal stanzas and structures that he builds from what he has learned from his masters, "endeavouring," as he writes to George—by now the spring of 1819—"to discover a better sonnet stanza than we have," and coming up with, in Bate's phrase, "a longer, more flexible form," line by line, stanza to enriching stanza. Keats, as Yeats would have it, is looking through the glass of the form of the odes and seeing cakes and candy, whereas history, posterity, immortality are seeing "Ode to a Nightingale," "Ode on a Grecian Urn," and "To Autumn" as three of the most anthologized lyric poems of tragic vision in English.

Place the central stanza of "Nightingale" beside the opening stanza of "To Autumn" and compare their confections.

I cannot see what flowers are at my feet,
Nor what soft incense hangs upon the boughs,
But, in embalmed darkness, guess each sweet
Wherewith the seasonable month endows
The grass, the thicket, and the fruit-tree wild;
White hawthorn, and the pastoral eglantine;
Fast fading violets covered up in leaves;
And mid-May's eldest child,
The coming musk-rose, full of dewy wine,
The murmurous haunt of flies on summer eves.

Season of mists and mellow fruitfulness,
Close bosom-friend of the maturing sun;
Conspiring with him how to load and bless
With fruit the vines that round the thatch-eves run;
To bend with apples the mossed cottage-trees,
And fill all fruit with ripeness to the core;
To swell the gourd, and plump the hazel shells
With a sweet kernel; to set budding more,
And still more, later flowers for the bees,
Until they think warm days will never cease,
For Summer has o'er-brimmed their clammy cells.

Late spring evening turning blue dusk into dark in the one instance; early autumn early in the day warming toward afternoon and sunset in the other instance. Both examples share, in spite of their differing perspectives (one a first-person participant, the other a third-person observer), Keats's gift for voice and visual texture, in which the play of vowels and consonants intensifies the densities of color and object. And both examples share the bower consciousness of an intimacy with the domesticated natural world, the pastoral world of lawn and kitchen garden and farmer's field. Both are a bit intoxicated, filled with the "dewy wine" and "o'er-brimmed . . . ripeness to the core" of the totality of their detail, the pressure of their vision, the abundance of what will become—in a breath, in a thought—emptiness, absence, fled, soft-dying, gone. With Keats, it is sometimes difficult to choose between the falling dark and the fallen day as the richest moment of lost time. At his best, in the odes, time is not only suspended but extended to an edge, to where the running-over almost spills.

The assonant and consonant balances in both examples do far more than franchise the beauty of Keats's language—

I cannot see what flowers are at my feet,
    - -   - -   -   - -

Nor what soft incense hangs upon the boughs . . .
   -- - - -   -   -

Season of mists and mellow fruitfulness,
  - -   - -- - -- -   -- --

Close bosom-friend of the maturing sun . . .—
  -   -   --   -   -

they are the truth of the language of the experience. Even the most cursory, superficial reading of the compounding, resonant sounds creates a received reality, a hearing just beautifully ahead of knowing. Tone is one of the terms that modernism began to use to define the inevitability of sound as sense, voice as vision, and not merely its seeming echo. Keats is arguably the first lyric poet to make a matter of the art of the poem as its ultimate subject, and the first to treat the transformation of that subject not simply as ironic but tragic. That is the truth of his language in the odes and in those telling passages in the romance narratives and of the best of the sonnets: Poetry is beauty only to the extent and power of its truth, its tragic sense of itself as a made and perishing thing. In his biography of Keats, Robert Gittings—picking up a point emphasized by Bailey concerning one of Keats's "favorite topics of discourse . . . the principle of melody in Verse"—praises the poet's "use of contrasting and linked vowel-sounds" as a way of effecting "a very subtle assonance." It is Keats's use of consonance, however, as a stay against the flow of vowels, that really grounds the substance of the music to its meaning—both its source and statement. Keats's consonants hold what his vowels would let go, the "subtle" tension of which enacts the mortality of "the wasted breath" that Yeats himself calls lyric poetry.

> *Heard melodies are sweet, but those unheard*
> *Are sweeter; therefore, ye soft pipes, play on;*
> *Not to the sensual ear, but, more endeared,*
> *Pipe to the spirit ditties of no tone:*
> *Fair youth, beneath the trees, thou canst not leave*
> *Thy song, nor ever can those trees be bare;*
> *Bold Lover, never, never canst thou kiss,*
> *Though winning near the goal—yet, do not grieve;*
> *She cannot fade, though thou hast not thy bliss,*
> *Forever wilt thou love, and she be fair!*

Only in the cold pastoral immortal world of "Ode on a Grecian Urn" could "ditties" have no tone; only there could melodies be sweeter unheard. The vision here—of a "happy melodist, unwearied, / Forever piping songs forever new; / More happy love! more happy, happy love!"—is frightening. It is what the afterlife could be like: "no change of death in paradise," writes Stevens, a place where ripe fruit never falls. "Grecian Urn" posits against the sunsetting world of "To Autumn" and the night-fragrant world of "Nightingale." The teasing eternity of the urn world, or art as the living dead, is going to be always "still to be enjoyed," frozen in its circular frieze of lovers who will forever not quite kiss and of trees that will forever not be bare. Keats's "heard" music in this poem is in a prosody of emphatic iteration and reiteration as the silent story on the urn turns and returns in front of us. Even the urn's advice, which sounds wise as it speaks to and against the meaning of mortality in Keats's other odes, contributes to the pathos of its predicament: Beauty as truth and vice versa is only a formula in such a static world, didactic in intent, reductive as rhetoric. It is a circular assertion with no linking logic of mortal imagination: an assertion not to be questioned, as if on Earth, in the flawed living world "where old age shall this generation waste," the perfection of a cold pastoral were possible, even desirable. In its arrogance the urn assumes that its marble immortality mirrors man's desired destiny, hence its wisdom is "all / Ye know on earth, and all ye need to know." The speaker of the poem is teased by this possibility to the point of seduction and believes the urn to be "a friend to man," but the poem itself—both beautiful and true—knows better.

5

T. S. ELIOT, WHO KNOWS A THING OR TWO ABOUT COLD PASTO-rals, has written that there "is hardly one statement of Keats about poetry, which, when considered carefully and with due allowance for the difficulties of communication, will not be found to be true: and what is more, true for a greater and more mature poetry than anything Keats ever wrote." This complicated opinion is both right and wrong. Keats's statements *about* poetry are brilliantly, intuitively true; his statements *of* poetry, particularly in the odes and the two *Hyperion*s, are not only true but mature in the way that tragic art must be. The same debates, speculations, interrogations that magnify the letters illuminate the best of the poetry. In both capacities they establish and perform the implicit argument between the pull of the gravity of mortality and the promise of the alchemy of art. Death may be the eternal subject, but not dying is its eternal point. It is the song of the nightingale passed on and not the nightingale itself that is that promise; it is the song of chilly spring behind the warm harvest and not the harvest itself that is that promise; it is the teasing, the temptation of the desire for eternity behind the cold pastoral and not the urn itself that is that promise. Yet it is all word of mouth nevertheless. If poetry— Keats is saying—is finally about the flesh vanishing, disappearing, turning cold—the absorbing night, the setting sun, the broken stone—it is also, in its afterlife, about the word as spirit, aspirant on the air, invisible, articulate, available. Keats's letters are the mind and heart out of which the poems—the least as well as the best—are realized. Lyric poetry, after Wordsworth and Coleridge, becomes a crucial drama of the serious, even conflicted, self. After Keats, form itself—self-reflective, self-generative—becomes integral to the acting-out of that drama. The letters are replete with how form—the poem as artifice—is inseparable from the struggle for meaning. When Eliot adds that "the general brilliance and profundity of observations scattered through Keats's letters" are "certainly the most notable and the most important ever written by an English poet," he is clearly, in part, referring to the formalist in Keats, but also to the symbolist thinker.

The now standard edition of *The Letters*, edited by Hyder E. Rollings, is a two-volume edition that covers 1814 to 1821; it was first published by Harvard University Press in 1958. One way to organize an order for the letters is through the agency of correspondents (as noted by Gittings in his introduction to the Oxford edition *Selected Letters*): early, sort of trying-out "principles of poetic composition" letters to Bailey and Reynolds; the great travel letters of the Northern tour written primarily to Tom; the meandering journal-length letters to George and his wife in America; and the painfully mortal, lovesick notes and letters to Fanny Brawne in the last phase. The two-volume idea, however, suits a different paradigm, bridged by the fact of the long-suffering "plaguy" sore throat, a complaint that ends the first volume and begins the second. Whereas the first volume represents the robust, thinking, speculative Keats, the Keats espousing theory and artistic worry, the Keats of the "walks in the north" with Brown, ending with the abrupt return to Hampstead and Tom's death, the second volume of the letters shows the reflective, ailing, and ultimately dying Keats, the Keats of the great poems, the isolated Keats, Keats in love, and the Keats excused to Italy. You could make a highlight essay of the assertive, speculating, symbolist Keats as drawn from the first volume.

Does Shelley go on telling strange Stories of the Death of kings? Tell him there are strange Stories of the death of Poets— . . . *several things dovetailed in my mind, & at once it struck me, what quality went to form a Man of Achievement especially in Literature & which Shakespeare possessed so enormously—I mean* Negative Capability, *that is when man is capable of being in uncertainties, Mysteries, doubts, without any irritable reaching after fact & reason* . . . *We hate*

poetry that has a palpable design upon us—and if we do not
agree, seems to put its hand in its breeches pocket . . . Now it
appears to me that almost any Man may like the Spider spin
from his own inwards his own airy Citadel—the points of
leaves and twigs on which the Spider begins her work are few
and she fills the Air with a beautiful circuiting; man should
be content with as few points to tip with the fine Webb of
his Soul and weave a tapestry empyrean—full of Symbols
for his spiritual eye, of softness for his spiritual touch, of
space for his wandering of distinctness for his Luxury—
. . . I think Ethereal things may at least be thus real, divided
under three heads—Things real—things semireal—and
no things—Things real—such as existences of Sun Moon
&Stars and passages of Shakespeare—Things semireal real
such as Love, the Clouds &c which require a greeting of the
Spirit to make them wholly exist—and Nothings which are
made Great and dignified by an ardent pursuit . . . What a
happy thing it would be if we could settle our thoughts, make
our minds up on any matter in five Minutes and remain con-
tent—that is to build a sort of mental Cottage of feelings
quiet and pleasant—to have a sort of Philosophical Back
Garden, and a cheerful holiday-keeping front one— . . .
I live in the eye; and my imagination, surpassed, is at rest
. . . As to the poetical Character itself, (I mean that sort of
which, if I am any thing, I am a Member; that sort distin-
guished from the wordsworthian or egotistical sublime; which
is a thing per se and stands alone) it is not itself—it has no
self—it is every thing and nothing—It has no character—it
enjoys light and shade; it lives in gusto, be it foul or fair,
high or low, rich or poor, mean or elevated—It has as much
to delight in conceiving an Iago as an Imogen. What shocks

the virtuous philosopher, delights the camelion Poet . . . A
poet is the most unpoetical of any thing in existence; because
he has no Identity—he is continually informing—and fill-
ing some other Body—

Although the second volume of *The Letters* enacts much of
the "light and shade" enjoyed in discussion in the first, it repre-
sents more shade than light. The much-analyzed comparison of
"human life to a Large Mansion of Many Apartments," in a May
1818 letter to Reynolds (I, 275–83)—"I will put down a simile
of human life as far as I now perceive it"—with its "Chamber
of Maiden-Thought" meditation, becomes in the second volume
the deeper, darker consideration of the "Soul as distinguished
from an Intelligence" or "Call the world if you Please 'The
vale of Soul-making,' " as explored in a spring journal-letter of
1819 (II, 58–109) to George and Georgiana. Keats, in the second
instance, is struggling ("I can scarcely express what I but dimly
perceive . . .") to define identity. "I will call the *world* a School
instituted for the purpose of teaching little children to read—I
will call the *human heart* the *horn Book* used in that School—and
I will call the *Child able to read, the Soul* made from that *school*
and its *hornbook*. Do you not see how necessary a World of Pains
and troubles is to school an Intelligence and make it a soul?"
The house-of-many-mansions analogy in the first instance—the
"Many Apartments"—is a construct of the allusive mind. The
valley-of-the-shadow analogy in the second volume is existential
experience drawn from proved-on-the-pulses feeling. The letters
in the first half of the Rollins edition are about being schooled,
schooling of all kinds, particularly medicine and poetry; the let-
ters in the second half are about learning in "a World of Pains
and troubles," particularly love and the prospect of death. The
enthusiast tone of the first volume is replaced by a preoccupation

with illness and indolence—indeed, a saturation: On February 4, 1819 (II, 37), Keats states—and understates—that "I have not been entirely well for some time"; on February 4, 1820 (II, 250–51), he writes a note to Fanny Brawne to the effect "That they say I must remain confined to this room for some time," having, the night before, coughed up the signature "arterial blood" that is his "death warrant"; on February 4, 1821, he is close to dying, and in nineteen days he will (II, 375–76)—"Last night I thought he was going—I could hear the Phlegm in his throat," Severn writes to Haslam.

Yet in spite of the unfolding self-narrative of his illness, his frustration in love, and the perceived failure as poet, Keats, in the second volume of *The Letters*, can on occasion be upbeat, especially when writing to his sister. Within a month (late July to late August 1819), he will say to Fanny Brawne that "I have two luxuries to brood over in my walks, your Loveliness and the hour of my death. O that I could have possession of them both in the same minute. I hate the world: it batters too much the wings of my self-will, and would I could take a sweet poison from your lips to send me out of it," while chanting to Fanny Keats that "I enjoy the Weather I adore fine Weather as the greatest blessing I can have. Give me Books, fruit, french wine and fine whether and a little music out of doors, played by somebody I do not know . . . and I can pass a summer very quietly without caring much about Fat Louis, fat Regent or the Duke of Wellington." And earlier, the month he begins his intense and complex sequence of the spring odes (April 1819), he writes his sister that he hopes she has a "good store of double violets—I think they are the Princesses of flowers and in a shower of rain, almost as fine as barley sugar drops are to a schoolboy's tongue. I suppose this fine weather the lambs tails give a frisk or two extraordinary—when a boy would cry huzza and a

Girl Square—the first time I do I will remember your Seals—I
have thought it best to live in Town this Summer, chiefly for
the sake of books, which cannot be had with any comfort in the
Country—besides my Scotch journey gave me a doze of the
Picturesque with which I ought to be contented for some time.
Westminster is the place I have pitched upon—the City or any
place very confined would soon turn me pale and thin—which
is to be avoided. You must make up your mind to get Stout this
summer—indeed I have an idea we shall both be corpulent old
folks with triple chins and stumpy thumbs—" This same warm
April of the odes is the month that Keats crosses paths with
Coleridge on the Heath, the meeting from which Coleridge
later claims the conclusion that there was death in Keats's hand-
shake.

Then there are the spring odes themselves, and *The Fall of
Hyperion* and then "To Autumn," all written with this living,
dying hand. The letters beginning in January 1819, contrary
to Eliot's contrary opinion, start to speak to a new, sometimes
unsettling, darker, richer take on actual as well as imaginative
experience. Tom has just died, George is gone off to the mid-
dle of nowhere, and Keats is recognizing the risk to his health
compounded by his "Scotch journey" and is becoming aware
of a necessary ambivalence regarding Fanny Brawne: He has
too little future to offer her. Sometimes "I think if I had a free
and healthy and lasting organization of heart and Lungs—as
strong as an oxe's—so as to be able to bear unhurt the shock
of extreme thought and sensation without weariness, I could
pass my Life nearly alone though it should last eighty years.
But I feel my Body too weak to support me to the height; I am
obliged continually to check myself and strive to be nothing"—
so Keats writes to Reynolds at the end of the summer of 1819,
the season between the spring odes and "To Autumn." Keats's

enormous sense of absence, separation, and alternating intensity and indolence are of course connected to his sense of his vulnerable health, but even more to his "knowledge enormous" of the degree to which "The Soul is a world of itself and has enough to do in its own home." This vision of self-containment, even isolation, the soul itself as a world to be filled, may in the abstract sound Blakean. For Keats, though, it is a world not only to be filled but realized, returned, transformed into a work of art as an independent entity outside the self, rescued from chaotic quotidian life—made into an art self-standing, as if it were a world, too, which, according to Keats, it is. However "accidental" their making, the odes and the best passages in the *Hyperion*s lift the lyric poem past the limitations of common narrative and image, practicable form and paraphrasable content to the sublime status of an object created "that must create itself"— or one that seems to have created itself—not as a cold pastoral but one of holistic, discrete integrity, confirmed but without conforming to singular resonant emotional experience. Keats's inherent modernism is inseparable from this insight of the necessary distance between maker and the made, the sublimity of the poem as something other from the "egotistical sublime" of the poet.

In his long winter-into-spring journal letter to George, Keats notes on April 30, 1819, that "The following Poem—the last I have written is the first and the only one with which I have taken even moderate pains—for the most part dashed off my lines in a hurry—This I have done leisurely—I think it reads the more richly for it and will I hope encourage me to write other things in even a more peacable and healthy spirit." Keats is, as we know, talking about the "Ode to Psyche," the first of the great odes. "You must recollect that Psyche was not embodied as a goddess before the time of Apulieus the Platonist who lived after the Augustan age, and consequently the Goddess was never worshipped or sacrificed to with any of the ancient fervor—and perhaps never thought of in the old religion—I am more orthodox than to let a hethen Goddess be so neglected—" He then fair-copies the entire poem for George's perusal, though later he will take further pains and rewrite "more richly" the achieved whole poem we have now, whose last stanza reiterates that

> *Yes, I will be thy priest, and build a fane*
>   *In some untrodden region of my mind,*
> *Where branched thoughts, new grown with pleasant pain,*
>   *Instead of pines shall murmur in the wind;*
> *Far, far around shall those dark-cluster'd trees*
>   *Fledge the wild-ridged mountains steep by steep;*
> *And there by zephyrs, streams, and birds, and bees,*
>   *The moss-lain Dryads shall be lull'd to sleep;*
> *And in the midst of this wide quietness*
>   *A rosy sanctuary will I dress*
> *With the wreath'd trellis of a working brain;*
>   *With buds, and bells, and stars without brain,*
> *With all the gardener Fancy e'er could feign,*
>   *Who breeding flowers, will never breed the same:*
> *And there shall be for thee all soft delight*
>   *That shadowy thought can win,*
> *A bright torch, and a casement ope at night,*
>   *To let the warm Love in!*

Dream and myth—two of Keats's symbolist standbys—dominate this poem, which is a passionate retelling of the Psyche-Cupid legend: soul and sex completely entwined, "calm-breathing on the bedded grass; / Their arms embraced, and their pinions too." Keats opens the poem asserting that either he "dreamt today" or "wander'd in a forest thoughtlessly," which comes to the same thing. The thoughtless qualification is important because, by the end of the poem, thought itself, as rational consciousness, has a priori been replaced by "some untrodden region of my mind," meaning not only the dream part but where the involuntary imagination does its work as a "working brain"—the brain conceived as a kind of grand, inclusive bower. Keats is claiming the legend, in other words, as a source for how the imagination operates and for what constitutes—in this case—the baseline material it needs in order to create. He builds his "fane," his symbolist temple, in the richest possible terms, both majestic and small. In fact, in the sequence of detail the information dresses down from a region of pines and wind and "wild-ridged mountains" to zephyrs, birds and bees to "moss-lain Dryads" to the garden scale of a "rosy sanctuary" of flowers and an open castle window. All this is worked out in the secret mind of imagination, in a rhyming language that juxtaposes the archaic "fane" with a modern "brain." Keats invents in this ode what he will explore in the others: an interior, intimate sublime whose world and dimensions are the mind made multiple but whose first source is loss, longing, desire at the lip. "Their lips touch'd not, but had not bade adieu"—this frozen, ambiguous moment will be echoed throughout the odes: in the "Bold Lover" who, "winning near the goal," can never kiss; in the question "Do I wake or sleep?"; in the "Joy, whose hand is ever at his lips / Bidding adieu"; in figures, shades, and shadows passing on another urn, "masque-like figures . . . Phantoms" drawn "from my idle sprite." Keats's magnificent grasp of ambient texture—of the stationing, stasis, and paralleling of color and sound and compounding particulars—and ambivalent tone—"in the very temple of the Delight / Veiled

Melancholy has her sovran shrine"—define the complex lyric imperative that he discovers in lieu of his failure to complete a tragic epic. He pours the preparation for the epic gesture into the smaller yet capacious vessel of the ode.

6

THIS, THEN THAT. IN HIS SOMEWHAT WANDERING *LIFE AND Letters of Joseph Severn* (1892), William Sharp cites a letter to Severn from one Alfred Domett, whom he characterizes as a "poet-traveller and colonist." There is no date attached to the letter, though by inference it seems to fall into the late 1870s, just before Severn's death in 1879. Like a select few other literary peripheral figures of the day, Domett is in search of whatever Keatsiana he can find, even though at this moment Keats remains the author—according to Sharp—of "rarely sought verses." Domett is further unique, however, in that among "my friends in New Zealand (where I passed thirty years of my life) was, and *is*, a Mr. Charles Brown—son of Charles Armitage Brown, who emigrated with his only son to that colony about the year 1839 or 1840, and died at New Plymouth there a few years afterwards." (Carlino and his father were both, in different ways, looking for new opportunities in a faraway place while hoping to allay old failures. Carlino ultimately became Superintendent of the Province of New Plymouth; his father quickly became disillusioned with his new choice and broke down, bit by piece.) Domett's particular interest is "in a sketch in Indian ink" that Carlino has passed on to him ("ten or fifteen years ago"): "a portrait of poor Keats, the poet on his death-bed; at the foot of which

is written: 'Copied from a drawing by Joseph Severn, 28th
January, 1821, 3 o'clock morning, drawn to keep me awake.'
This, as Charles Brown told me, was done by his father, the
intimate friend, as you know, of Keats."

Domett's ignorance here comes off as condescending,
especially in his use of the word *intimate*, because intimate is
exactly what Severn's role as nurse and moral support becomes
in Keats's last months. Brown's "intimacy" with Keats, on the
other hand, amounts to an almost professional relationship:
"landlord," provisional friend, traveling companion, sometime
caregiver, would-be biographer, and finally—though it may
sound harsh—betrayer. The question of the deathbed draw-
ing focuses the Keats story precisely. Domett's letter to Severn
continues.

> *The copy, I think, bears the evident marks of being
> most truthfully and carefully executed; and seems to
> prove that the original must also have been a most
> truthful and striking likeness of the "poor glorious"
> being it represented. For besides its obvious resem-
> blances to the published portraits of Keats, it shows all
> the affecting changes in the lineaments of the coun-
> tenanse which the disease of which he died must have
> produced. The face is wasted and thin; the tangled hair
> thrown about the brow in locks which look damp and
> straightened a little out of their natural curl by mid-
> night perspirations. The expression, as he is asleep,
> is resigned and tranquil; and but for this, the portrait
> would be intensely painful to contemplate. Indeed, it
> is almost so, in spite of this; and, with the words at the
> foot of it, makes the most pathetic piece of drawing I
> have ever seen either on canvas or paper.*

It is important to remember that Domett is talking about a copy—Brown's apparent rendition of, likely, Severn's finest, most spontaneous work of art—of the dying Keats's sweat-soaked head—done no doubt to keep Severn awake, but also done under the tremendous duress of days without much sleep, days of enormous stress, days of grief and the expectation of his friend's imminent death. Brown doubtless copied a published version of Severn's original sketch, unless he had the original at hand once he arrived to join Severn in Rome long—but not too long—after Keats had died.

Among the many ironies here is the fact that, though an amateur, Brown has proved himself to be an excellent draftsman, as witness the best portrait ever done of the living Keats by Brown at Shanklin. Now he has demonstrated, according to Domett, his "copying" skills once again, fair-copyist of Keats's poems that he is. Domett's descriptive reading of the copy-drawing is acute in its insight into the power of the original as created, via verisimilitude, in Brown's secondary version. Why would Brown copy as well the script under the drawing that is so profoundly authored by Severn, notably the phrase "drawn to keep me awake"? The lack of use of quotation marks by Brown sends us back to the end of "Ode on a Grecian Urn"—"Beauty is truth, truth beauty,— that is all / Ye know on earth, and all ye need to know"—and the question of who is speaking, who belongs to these words. Who is the "me," the ignorant reader asks? "The words just alluded to, which I have copied exactly as they stand, seem to render necessary the inference that Mr. Brown *made the copy* at 3 o'clock in the morning to keep *himself* awake. Charles Brown (Jun.) could not tell me much about it; but as far as I remember now, seemed to think that the last words were written by yourself on the original portrait. But as they are all in precisely the same hand, and as there are no inverted commas or other mark to distinguish the first words ('Copied from a drawing by Jos. Severn') from those which follow, I cannot but conclude that Mr. Brown (Chas. A.) was himself watching by Keats's bedside when he made this copy, and perhaps relieved yourself, for a short time, in the performance of that last painful act of friendship."

There is no record of Severn's response to this remarkable conclusion. He undoubtedly in late life was past caring for such pointless, mistaken, and presumptuous speculation. But from the perspective of how life sometimes plays out—by accident, error, and false assumption—it is probably fitting that someone could come to the conclusion, based on false clues and falser assumptions, that Brown, who should have been at Keats's side on the *Maria Crowther* and the slow *vettura* and the small coffin of his bed, was in person there at the end with Severn, offering him relief. Severn himself had spent his posthumous Keatsian life copying Keats, in drawing after painting after miniature, trying to bring him back to life, copy him back to life. So why not Brown: Why not make Keats reappear by the proxy of a copy? What is a poem, after all, but the proxy of a copy of itself, with written authorization, sent into the future? Brown, too, had cared for Keats right after the first, nearly fatal hemorrhage; he had supported Keats in nearly every possible way; personally, financially, artistically he was there when George was not. He had been, surely, the surrogate older brother. And he had listened, had heard Keats often when no one else would or could. His very presence in Keats's life presupposed that he would be the companion on the last, fateful journey. Yet at the critical moment, Brown fails; he manages to miss the moment. (As Dilke notes: "Keats died Feby 1821 and Brown started for Italy in July or August 1822! fifteen or sixteen months after he was dead!" And again, as Brown himself writes Keats on December 21, 1820: "So you still wish me to follow you to Rome," "and truly

I wish to go,—nothing detains me but prudence. Little could be gained, if any thing, by letting my house at this time of year, and the consequence would be a heavy additional expense which I cannot possibly afford,—unless it were a matter of necessity, and I see none while you are in such good hands as Severn's.") Yet in spite of Brown's failure of friendship, Alfred Domett has good—if presumptuous—reason to believe that Brown was with Severn at Keats's bedside in those final weeks—mostly because, in a more perfect story, he should have been. As these things go, however, Domett's late inquiry to an aging Severn seems sent into the void.

> *As the fact (if it be one) of Chas. A. Brown's having attended Keats at all during his last illness, is not mentioned in any life I have seen of the Poet—and especially not alluded to by Lord Houghton in his Memoir, it occurred to me that the best way would be to apply for this information directly to the source from which it could most certainly and conclusively be obtained.*

Severn apparently never answers, and Brown by now is long gone.

7

WRITTEN IN STONE, WRITTEN ON PAPER, WRITTEN IN WATER, written on air. How little survives us but words and words on words. The regretted words on Keats's tombstone have survived not only mockery ("I was a great sufferer, after the death of Keats, from the scorn and sneers passed upon his memory . . . Even the pathetic line on his tomb, 'Here lies one whose name was writ in water,' was particularly made the object of ridicule. 'Here lies one whose name was writ in water *and his works in milk and water.*' ") but gravity, as the "head-stone, having sunk twice, owing to its faulty foundation, has been twice renewed by loving strangers, and each time, as I am informed, these strangers were Americans." (On February 8, 2006, close to 185 years after Keats has been buried in the "Cemetery of Poets," the *International Herald Tribune* reports that "this precious bit of paradise is decaying . . . Many of its important monuments are crumbling like the bones they mark, damaged by pollution and years without archaeological maintenance. The landscape is overgrown, waterlogged by poor drainage . . . 'It looks romantic and lovely, but the stones are falling apart,' said Valerie Magar, a conservation specialist at the United Nations International Center for the Study of the Preservation and Restoration of Cultural Property.")

In his various memoir prose, Severn, nearing eighty, adds that Keats's own words—his poems—have survived in spite of "the changes in the changing world, sometimes for the worse, sometimes for the better, but always an intellectual lottery in which the world delights." Robert Gittings, in his introduction to his version of *Selected Letters*, speculates that Keats's immortal phrase " 'Negative Capability' may have been invented or misread by Jeffrey"—that is, John Jeffrey, Georgiana's husband after George, who badly "transcribed" much of Keats's correspondence with his brother. The implications of this possible invention speak powerfully to the lottery that Severn suggests immortality is—and to the vulnerability of anything written in stone or on paper. One is reminded of F. Scott Fitzgerald's definition of negative capability in his essay "The Crack-Up": that the test of a first-rate intelligence is the ability to hold opposing ideas in the mind at the same time yet retain the ability to function. The dialectic of mortality/immortality is itself perhaps an example of—because we are dealing in words, regardless of their source—negative capability, of living eternally in doubt and uncertainties, alive, so to speak, among the ambiguities of a possible afterlife. The title of the only prose that Severn published in his lifetime, "On the Vicissitudes of Keats's Fame" (the *Atlantic Monthly*, April 1863), was originally proposed as "On the Adversities of Keats's fame"; vicissitudes and adversities both imply tension, opposition, the pull of mortality inherent within the concept and the chanciness of immortality, the fragile, lucky, deferred thing that immortality is.

Then there is the palimpsest itself that is a poem: How many tries, how many erasures, how many traces are necessary to bring the best words in their best order to the surface of the impure page? Keats wrote fast and revised faster. In every case (with the possible exception of "La Belle Dame sans Merci"), the revision, word to word, lifts the text from something less extraordinary. In "Ode to a Nightingale," the restored pronominal adjective "My" rescues "heart" from the generality of an allusion to poetic history, just as the substitution of the adjective "drowsy" for "painful" allows "pain" to become a verb—"My heart aches and drowsy numbness pains, My sense. . . ." In "To Autumn," florid, inert writing is quickly crossed out ("While bright the Sun slants through the husky barn"; "Spares for some slumberous minutes the next swath") in favor of some of the most transparent writing in English ("Spares the next swath and all its twined flower"). In "Ode to Psyche," the point of departure for the great odes, it is "by my own eyes inspired," not by "clear eyes"; and at the end of the poem, "A bright torch, and a casement ope at night" is meant "To let the warm Love in," not to let the "Warm Love glide in." The odes are everywhere enriched with such changes, changes

made on paper that has somehow survived human hands pass-
ing them along, mortal hands in mortal time. Brown's claim that
Keats wrote "Nightingale" in one long morning sitting under a
plum tree in the garden of Wentworth Place is subjective at best;
his further claim that "When he came into the house, I perceived
he had some scraps of paper in his hand, and these he was quietly
thrusting behind the books" is likely memory heavily edited or
misread. But to add that the "writing was not well legible; and it
was difficult to arrange the stanzas on so many scraps" is to imply
coauthorship, even with Keats's "assistance." Brown here seems
to be assuming control of an assumed artistic chaos, an authority
over the "scraps" of authorship. But Brown aside, the real story
is the paper itself, and how after a "false start on sheet two, Keats
wrote two and half stanzas on sheet one. He then wrote the next
two and a half on sheet two, turning it upside-down to avoid the
false start. Stanzas six and seven were written on the verso of sheet
one, and he then returned to the verso of sheet two to write stanza
eight." These are small sheets (8 by 4¾ inches), sent by Keats to
his friend Reynolds, who passed them on to his sisters, who willed
them to a nephew, an artist named Towneley Green, whose death
in 1900 occasioned their sale to the Marquess of Crewe, who in
1933 offered them to the Fitzwilliam Museum, Cambridge.

"Ode on a Grecian Urn" was copied by Keats's brother
George, from manuscript, into a notebook of other fair-copied
Keats poems. (George, remember, has returned to England in
January 1820 to try to raise money enough to save himself from
complete bankruptcy.) Within a month the notebook is on its way
to America, where it remains in possession of the Keats-Jeffrey
family until George's grandson, John Gilmer Speed, borrows,
on a permanent basis, the notebook as a source for his edition of
The Letters and Poems of John Keats (1883). The notebook, with
the "Urn" inside, turns up next in 1891 in Melbourne, Australia,

where it is purchased by Edward Jenks, Professor of Law, who sells it two years later to a Bernard Quaritch, who sells it in yet another two years to the British Museum as part of its *Additions to the Manuscripts*. Gittings, who is the scholar of these paper trails, says of "Ode to Psyche" that

> *Keats drafted the Ode to Psyche on a single sheet of the white wove paper known as "Bath," that is a large size of note-paper, eight by fourteen inches when flat, and folding into four pages of approximately eight by seven. It was a paper which he himself described in his letters as used by "Boarding schools and suburbans in general," and though he employed it often for his own letters, it may reflect here the extra care he thought he was taking over this poem. On 4 May 1819, he gave this draft to his friend J.H. Reynolds, who kept it until his own death in 1852. Reynolds appears to have let it out of his sight only twice, once to Richard Woodhouse, who made a copy of it at some unspecified date, and, years later on 2 July 1847, to Richard Monckton Milnes for the preparation of his Keats biography.*

Gittings then follows a trail similar to that of the "Nightingale" ode. On Reynolds's death, "Psyche" passes to his sisters, who bequeath it to Towneley Green, after whose demise it comes up for sale in 1901 at Sotheby's (for eighty-six pounds), disappears for a while, "until 1909 it was acquired by the Pierpont Morgan Library from an unknown source."

Nothing but paper passed along with the breath of its words alive with fire. Scraps of paper, scraps of words written in fire. As if written by "the bright Hyperion," "whose flaming robes" stream out "beyond his heels . . . / as if of earthly fire," to scare away "the meek ethereal Hours." "On he flared," writes

Keats, who is himself on fire in Haydon's portrait of his young fierce profile in *Christ's Entry into Jerusalem*. In the pantheon of that portion of the wall-size painting, where Keats is just above Wordsworth, who in prayerful reverence is flanked to his left by Voltaire and Newton, even the air that these luminaries occupy looks kindled, pocked with flame. But those last days, those last meek hours in Rome, in the small rectangular bedroom that had for six months surrounded his life, in this now cold space suspended above the warm flow of the Spanish Steps, Keats's diminished profile and wasting body seemed to have taken over, and what was left of Keats seemed to be melting, disappearing before Severn's eyes. The night sweats and constant evacuations were only part of it. The fire that was Keats, the breath to feed it, was going. Still, in Severn's middle-of-the-night deathbed portrait, the face of Keats—through its calm and utter sleep-set exhaustion—seems intensely if darkly alive, potentially mobile, angular, and, if wasted, expressively there. Fire as the figure of the spirit, fire to think by, fire to heal the soul, fire for the bread of the body. Keats had reprised each of these phases these last months. "Small busy flames play through the fresh-laid coals, / And their faint cracklings o'er our silence creep / Like whispers of the household gods that keep / A gentle empire o'er fraternal souls"—so Keats had written as part of a birthday poem for Tom. Then Severn, like a brother, years later keeping watch: "I have sat up all night— I have read to him nearly all day, and even in the night—I light the fire—make his breakfast, and sometimes am obliged to cook—make his bed, and even sweep the room. I can have these things done, but never at the time when they must and ought to be done . . . what engages me most is making a fire—I blow—blow for an hour—the smoke comes fuming out—my kettle falls over on the burning sticks—no stove—Keats calling me to be with him—the fire catching my hands and the door-bell ringing."

The one ringing the doorbell the day after Keats dies is likely the Roman maskmaker Gherardi, who takes a cast of Keats's bone-white face as the death mask. This matrix of the mask is soon passed on to John Taylor, Keats's publisher, and in 1865 is purchased by Lord Houghton, Keats's first biographer, after which it seems to get lost. This face of a sleeping Keats is fired like pottery, like porcelain, stronger than the face that Severn has only a few weeks before drawn in stoic suffering. It is a face fixed in transition, truly frozen in time. "On Saturday a gentleman came to cast the face, hand, and foot," remembers Severn. "On Sunday his body was opened; the lungs were completely gone." There is a moment, about a page long, in a wonderful little book put together by the Romantic scholar Neville Rogers (*Keats Shelley & Rome: An Illustrated Miscellany*, 1949) that has this to say about the "alleged" death mask of John Keats:

> In 1948 a lively interest in the Keats world was aroused by the discovery of this cast of the death mask; although why it should have been regarded as a discovery is in itself a minor mystery. The cast, advertised for many years in the trade catalogue of a London firm at trifling cost, appears to have entirely escaped the attention of Keats scholars. When it was brought to my notice I could recall only one possible example which appeared in the Browning Sale Catalogue, 1913, as item 1394 "a plastered Death Mask of Keats". I have, however, since come to the conclusion, from a description of it by Browning in a letter to the Storeys (see Browning to his American Friends, *edited by Gertrude Reese Hudson, Bowes & Bowes, p. 6)* as "my cast from the face of Keats,

*such a beautiful and characteristic thing" that this was the life
mask so often misdescribed.*

The author here is Dorothy Hewlett, an early biographer of
Keats. The vexed question of the life/death masks, she reports,
comes down to "measurements taken with the craniometer" of
two other castings "by Professor F. Wood Jones, F.R.S., of the
Royal College of Surgeons who, together with T.B. Layton,
D.S.O., M.S., of Guys," examines both. Their opinion is that
"there is nothing incompatible with both masks being of the same
man, living or dead."

A death mask becomes a life mask "misdescribed"—or is
it the other way around?—while two other castings belong to
the same Keats "living or dead." Surely this is fire alive in two
worlds at once or the fire that lives between worlds, the mor-
tal and immortal. Is Keats's face in the mask that Haydon casts,
almost to the day that he paints Keats's fiery profile in *Christ's
Entry*, the same, almost identical face that Gherardi casts the day
after Keats dies—after six months and more of wasting disease,
starvation diets, and severe depression? How could a healthy,
living Keats and a long-suffering dead Keats have more than less
the same fired face in a mask? Or are we being asked to see with
the wishful eyes of a beholder, one who would have Keats alive
in death? Yet there are obvious, if subtle, differences between
Haydon's mask and Gherardi's mask having primarily to do with
the weight of the face, the content of flesh. The "death" mask is
clearly closer to the bone, and the more compelling for it; the life
mask shows a trace of a smile. Those who would have the masks
as merely different castings of the same source are looking for
mortal fire or fearing the transforming power of fire from what
we sometimes dramatically call the other world. There are five
years between the life and death castings, with later confirmation

of each in Brown's beautiful 1819 Shanklin drawing and Severn's beautiful 1821 deathbed portrait. The two sketches separate the two worlds; the two masks, supposedly the most accurate kind of renderings, bring them together, perhaps because of their presumed objective reading of the subject. The face under the face of the referred-to death mask feels, not surprisingly, more alive than the 1816 living casting. It feels more alive because of the force of life, the five more years behind it: the five years of medical training, the years of losing brothers and Fanny Brawne, the years of the struggle to become "among the English Poets," the years of slowly succumbing to consumption, the year of "marching up against a Battery . . . This Journey to Italy." Experience, inhabiting experience, obviously marks a difference between the life and death masks, while their similarities derive from the one being implied in the other, the living haunting the dead. That is what finally the Professors of Faces are saying: Keats is the same man, the same face, living or dead—just as the meaning behind immortality is life, vital mortal life, not simply life not-dead. And more life, more elemental experience, especially in one so young, means twice alive.

By 1809 Keats's fevered mother has returned to Edmonton and the home she abandoned five years earlier. She is thirty-three years old and dying of consumption. She is doubtless a broken woman, now bedridden. Keats, at fourteen, will become her nurse, companion, and willing servant. He cooks for her, gives her her medicine, reads to her, sits up with her sometimes through the night, all of which ministration takes place in a small, confined, almost airtight room. Almost nine years later, having completed his medical training at Guy's Hospital, he will be many months into his nursing of Tom, who by the autumn of 1818 is falling away before Keats's eyes. This time Keats is more vulnerable to "the family disease": He has just gotten back from his aborted walking tour of the North with Brown, fairly sick himself with a serious sore throat. Again the confinement room is small, with the windows closed to keep out the damp, dangerous night air. The two brothers together in close daily, deadly quarters, September through November, will signal the end for one and the beginning of the end for the other. This fraternal image will be repeated two years later in Rome, except that Keats will be the patient and iron Severn will act as nurse, companion, and witness. For six months Severn will keep watch, most of it in the now famous tiny bedroom in which Keats dies above Piazza di Spagna. Sometimes the window is open, sometimes Severn—from December onward—carries Keats into the larger living space within their apartment for a change of scene, a change of air.

The Italians, unlike the English, know about air, its possible lethal, invisible qualities. The Campagna in summer has taught them that: insect air, evil air, malaria. All the while, it is not the sweet-sour odors or noises off the street but heat from light that causes them to close their blinds and often their windows. They suspect that whatever phthisis or consumption is, it is in the air and thus in the clothes, the furniture, the wall coverings, the books. Six Anglo-trained doctors cannot diagnose correctly Keats's pulmonary condition, though the wasting illness is responsible for at least 25 percent of all deaths reported. Until his body is opened and the lungs' black cavity is revealed, James Clark, a communicable disease specialist, is still not sure as to Keats's cause of death. But the Italians know or know enough to know that Keats's living and dead body carries and communicates something dangerous, as contagious as fire. Yet fire is also a purifier, a chastisement to evil air. No sooner is Keats buried than the "brutal Italians" do "their monstrous business." According to Severn, "vile indiscriminating Roman law required that all the furniture should be burned, and the rooms refurnished and everyway restored." The "burning of the furniture in the death-room" becomes not only an exemplary bonfire, visible from Keats's window, in the middle of the popular Piazza di Spagna, but a symbolic burning and purifying of Keats's absent body. For Keats, though, the Keats who forever matters, this fire, this purging of the body of the spirit, has already happened. It happened somewhere back there in lost time, perhaps the autumn of 1819, when the last great lines get written, or perhaps the autumn of 1820, when he sails into the unknown and the known, when he disappears into the sublimity of his words.

SELECTED BIBLIOGRAPHY

À Brassard, Nigel. *Keats in Rome: A Posthumous Existence*. Cirencester, England: Letter Press of Cirencester, 2003.

Adami, Marie. *Fanny Keats*. New Haven, Connecticut: Yale UP, 1938.

Ash, Russell, and Bernard Higton, eds. *Spirit of Place: Rome*. New York: Arcade–Little, Brown, 1991.

Barnard, John. *John Keats*. New York: Cambridge UP, 1987.

———, ed. *John Keats: The Complete Poems*. New York: Penguin, 1973.

Bate, Walter Jackson. *The Burden of the Past and the English Poet*. 1970. Cambridge, Massachusetts: Harvard UP, 1991.

———. *From Classic to Romantic: Premises of Taste in Eighteenth-Century England*. 1946. New York: Harper & Row, 1961.

———. *John Keats*. Cambridge, Massachusetts: Belknap–Harvard UP, 1963.

———, ed. *Keats: A Collection of Critical Essays*. Englewood Cliffs, New Jersey: Prentice-Hall, 1964.

Bertoneche, Caroline. "John Keats, Joseph Severn and the Fanny Brawne Episode." *Keats-Shelley Review* 15 (2001): 22–32.

Beyer, Werner W. *Keats and the Daemon King*. New York: Oxford UP, 1947.

Blunden, Edmund, ed. *Selected Poems of John Keats*. London: Collins, 1955.

Bridges, Robert. *A Critical Introduction to Keats*. London: Humphrey Milford–Oxford UP, 1929. Vol. 4 of *Collected Essays Papers &c. of Robert Bridges*. 5 vols. 1927–1930.

Briggs, Harold E., ed. *The Complete Poetry and Selected Prose of Keats*. New York: Modern Library, 1951.

Brock, Russell Claude. *John Keats and Joseph Severn: The Tragedy of the Last Illness*. London: Keats-Shelley Memorial Association, 1973.

Brown, Charles Armitage. *Life of John Keats*. New York: Oxford UP, 1937.

Brown, Sue. "Fresh Light on the Friendship of Charles Brown and Joseph Severn." *Keats-Shelley Review* 18 (2004): 138–48.

Burr, David Stanford, ed. *The Love Poems of John Keats: In Praise of Beauty*. New York: St. Martin's, 1990.

Bush, Douglas. *John Keats: His Life and Writings*. New York: Macmillan, 1966.

Bushnell, Nelson S. *A Walk After John Keats*. New York: Farrar & Rinehart, 1936.

Cacciatore, Vera. *A Room in Rome*. 1970. New York: Keats-Shelley Memorial Association, 1973.

Carstairs, Charlotte. *Notes on Selected Poems of Keats*. York Notes series. Essex, England: Longman-York, 1983.

Clark, Tom. *Junkets on a Sad Planet: Scenes from the Life of John Keats*. Santa Rosa, California: Black Sparrow, 1994.

Colvin, Sidney. *John Keats*. London: Macmillan, 1917.

Cook, Elizabeth, ed. *John Keats: The Major Works*. New York: Oxford UP, 1990.

Cook, Olive. *Constable's Hampstead*. 2d ed. London: Carlile House, 1978.

De Man, Paul, ed. *John Keats: Selected Poetry*. New York: Signet Classics, 1966.

Di Almeida, Hermione. *Romantic Medicine and John Keats*. New York: Oxford UP, 1991.

Dickstein, Morris. *Keats and His Poetry: A Study in Development.* Chicago: University of Chicago, 1971.

Dubos, René and Jean. *The White Plague: Tuberculosis, Man, and Society.* 1952. New Brunswick, New Jersey: Rutgers UP, 1987.

Edgcumbe, Fred, ed. *Letters of Fanny Brawne to Fanny Keats 1820–1824.* New York: Oxford UP, 1937.

Ellman, Richard, and Charles Feidelson, Jr., eds. *The Modern Tradition: Backgrounds of Modern Literature.* New York: Oxford UP, 1965.

Erlande, Albert. *The Life of John Keats.* Trans. Marion Robinson. New York: Jonathan Cape & Harrison Smith, 1929.

Evans, Gareth. "Poison Wine—John Keats and the Botanic Pharmacy." *Keats-Shelley Review* 16 (2002): 31–55.

Franklin, John Curtis. "Once More the Poet: Keats, Severn, and the Grecian Lyre." *Keats-Shelley Review* 18 (2004): 104–22.

Garrett, John. *Selected Poems of John Keats.* London: Macmillan, 1987.

Garrod, H. W. *Keats.* New York: Clarendon–Oxford UP, 1926.

Gates, Barbara Timm, ed. *Journal of Emily Shore.* Charlottesville, Virginia: University of Virginia, 1991.

Gee, Christina M. *Keats House, Hampstead: A Guide.* 8th ed. London: London Borough of Camden, 1980.

Gittings, Robert. *John Keats.* 1968. New York: Penguin, 1979.

———. *John Keats: The Living Year.* 1954. London: Heinemann, 1978.

———, ed. *Letters of John Keats.* 1970. New York: Oxford UP, 1982.

———, ed. *The Odes of Keats & Their Earliest Known Manuscripts in Facsimile.* Kent, Ohio: Kent State UP, 1970.

Goellnicht, Donald C. *The Poet-Physician: Keats and Medical Science.* Pittsburgh, Pennsylvania: University of Pittsburgh, 1984.

Graham, William. *Last Links with Byron, Shelley, and Keats.* London: Leonard Smithers, 1898.

Graham-Campbell, Angus. " 'O For a Draught of Vintage': Keats, Food and Wine." *Keats-Shelley Review* 17 (2003): 42–60.

————. "Where Byron Stayed in Rome: The 'Torlonia Letter' Rediscovered." *Keats-Shelley Review* 18 (2004): 102–3.

Groom, Bernard, ed. *Selections from Keats*. Rev. ed. London: Macmillan, 1959.

Guide to the Keats-Shelley Memorial House. Rev. ed. London: Keats-Shelley Memorial Association, 1988.

Harris, Judith. *Signifying Pain: Constructing and Healing the Self through Writing*. Albany: State University of New York Press, 2003.

Hecht, Anthony. "Keats's Appetite." *Keats-Shelley Review* 18 (2004): 68–88.

Hewlett, Dorothy. *A Life of John Keats*. London: Radius-Hutchinson, 1970.

————, ed. *Keats at Wentworth Place: Poems Written December 1818 to September 1820 by John Keats*. London: London Bureau of Camden, 1971.

Heys, Alistair. "Dialectic and Armistice: Dylan Thomas's Reception of Keats." *Keats-Shelley Review* 18 (2004): 217–38.

Hilton, Timothy. *Keats and His World*. New York: Viking, 1971.

Hirsch, Edward, and Jim Pollock, eds. *Complete Poems and Selected Letters of John Keats*. New York: Modern Library, 2001.

Hobsbaum, Philip. "Keats's Theory of Poetry." *Keats-Shelley Review* 18 (2004): 38–50.

————. Rev. of *John Keats: The Major Works* ed. by Elizabeth Cook, *The Cambridge Companion to Keats* ed. by Susan J. Wolfson, and *How to Study Romantic Poetry (Second Edition)*. *Keats-Shelley Review* 16 (2002): 169–74.

Hughes-Hallet, Penelope. *The Immortal Dinner: A Famous Evening of Genius & Laughter in Literary London, 1817*. Chicago: New Amsterdam, 2000.

Hunt, Leigh, ed. *Brothers in Unity: Lord Byron and Some of His Contemporaries*. Philadelphia: Carey, Lea & Carey, 1828.

Jack, Ian. *Keats and the Mirror of Art*. New York: Clarendon–Oxford UP, 1967.

Jones, Leonidas M., ed. *The Selected Prose of John Hamilton Reynolds*. Cambridge: Harvard University Press, 1966.

Kaplan, Louise J. *The Family Romance of the Impostor-Poet Thomas Chatterton*. New York: Atheneum, 1987.

Kenyon, Katharine M. R. *Keats in Winchester*. Rev. ed. London: Keats-Shelley Memorial Association, 1965.

Kucich, Greg. "A Lamentable Lay: Keats and the Marking of Charles Brown's Spenser Volumes." *Keats-Shelley Review* 3 (1988): 1–22.

Lehmann, John. *Three Literary Friendships*. New York: Holt, Rinehart and Winston, 1983.

Levine, Philip, ed. *The Essential Keats*. New York: Ecco, 1987.

Lipking, Lawrence. *The Life of the Poet: Beginning and Ending Poetic Careers*. Chicago: University of Chicago, 1981.

Lowell, Amy. *John Keats*. 2 vols. Boston and New York: Houghton Mifflin, 1925.

Marsland, Clive. Rev. of *John Keats* by Stephen Hebron, *John Keats: The Poems* by John Blades, and *Victorian Keats: Manliness, Sexuality, and Desire* by James Najarian. *Keats-Shelley Review* 17 (2003): 146–52.

McGann, Jerome J., ed. *Byron: A Selection of His Finest Poems*. New York: Oxford UP, 1994.

Michelin London: Tourist Guide. 3d ed. Harrow, Middlessex, England: Michelin Tyre Public Ltd. Co., 1983.

Michelin Rome: Tourist Guide. 2d ed. Harrow, Middlessex, England: Michelin Tyre Public Ltd. Co., 1992.

Miller, Luree. *Literary Villages of London*. Washington and Philadelphia: Starrhill, 1989.

Monkhouse, Cosmo. *Life of Leigh Hunt*. London: Walter Scott, 1893.

Morpurgo, J. E., ed. *Keats: A Selection of His Poetry*. Baltimore: Penguin, 1953.

Motion, Andrew. *Keats*. New York: Farrar, Straus and Giroux, 1997.

Murchie, Guy. *The Spirit of Place in Keats*. London: Newman Neame, 1955.

Murry, John Middleton. *Keats*. Rev. ed. New York: Noonday, 1955.

Olshansky, David. "A Comparative Analysis of Sensation and Reflection Within John Keats's 'Ode to a Nightingale.' " *Keats-Shelley Review* 17 (2003): 27–33.

Page, Giorgio Nelson, ed. *The Protestant Cemetery in Rome (Il Cimitero Acattolico di Roma): A Guide for Visitors*. Rome: Grafica S. Giovanni, 1986.

Park, Hye-Young. "Beyond Formalism: The Problem of Keatsian 'Self.' " *Keats-Shelley Review* 15 (2001): 118–32.

Parson, Donald. *Portraits of Keats*. New York: World Publishing Company, 1954.

Peare, Catherine Owens. *John Keats: A Portrait in Words*. New York: Dodd, Mead & Company, 1960.

Plumly, Stanley. *Argument & Song: Sources & Silences in Poetry*. New York: Handsel, 2003.

———. "A Commentary." *Singular Voices: American Poetry Today*. Ed. Stephen Berg. New York: Avon, 1985.

The Pre-Raphaelites. London: Tate Gallery Publications Department, 1984.

Quigly, Isabel, ed. *Shelley: Poems*. New York: Penguin, 1956.

Raleigh, Walter, ed. *Poems by John Keats*. London: George Bell & Sons, 1901.

Raymond, Ernest. *Two Gentlemen of Rome: The Story of Keats and Shelley*. London: Cassell, 1952.

Richardson, Joanna. *The Everlasting Spell: A Study of Keats and His Friends*. London: Jonathan Cape, 1963.

———, ed. *Keats and His Circle: An Album of Portraits*. London: Cassell, 1980.

———. *The Life and Letters of John Keats*. London: The Folio Society, 1981.

Rogers, Neville, ed. *Keats Shelley & Rome: An Illustrated Miscellany*. 1949. London: Johnson, 1970.

Rollins, Hyder Edward, ed. *The Keats Circle: Letters and Papers, 1816–1878*. 2 vols. Cambridge, Massachusetts: Harvard UP, 1948.

————, ed. *The Letters of John Keats 1815–1821*. 2 vols. Cambridge, Massachusetts: Harvard UP, 1958.

Rollins, Hyder Edward, and Stephen Maxfield Parrish. *Keats and the Bostonians*. Cambridge, Massachusetts: Harvard UP, 1951.

Rosenthal, Elisabeth. "A Cemetery of Poets Is in Crisis in Rome." *New York Times*, 8 Feb. 2006, late ed.: E1+.

Rossetti, William Michael. *Life of John Keats*. London: Walter Scott, 1887.

Ryan, Robert M., and Ronald A. Sharp, eds. *The Persistence of Poetry: Bicentennial Essays on Keats*. Amherst, Massachusetts: University of Massachusetts, 1998.

Schwartz, Lewis. *Keats Reviewed by His Contemporaries*. Metuchen, New Jersey: Scarecrow, 1973.

Scott, Grant F., ed. *Selected Letters of John Keats*. Rev. ed. Cambridge, Massachusetts: Harvard UP, 2002.

Scudder, Horace E., ed. *The Complete Poetical Works and Letters of John Keats*. Cambridge ed. Boston and New York: Houghton Mifflin, 1899.

Scully, James, ed. *Modern Poetics*. New York: McGraw-Hill, 1965.

Sharp, Ronald A. *Keats, Skepticism, and the Religion of Beauty*. Athens, Georgia: University of Georgia, 1979.

Sharp, William. *The Life and Letters of Joseph Severn*. London: Sampson Low, Marston & Company, 1892.

Siraisi, Nancy G. *Medieval & Early Renaissance Medicine: An Introduction to Knowledge and Practice*. Chicago: University of Chicago, 1990.

Skues, G. E. M. *Itchen Memories*. 1951. London: Andre Deutsch, 1984.

Sperry, Stuart M. *Keats the Poet*. 1973. Princeton, New Jersey: Princeton UP, 1994.

Stillinger, Jack, ed. *John Keats: Complete Poems*. Cambridge, Massachusetts: Belknap–Harvard UP, 1978.

————, ed. *John Keats: Poetry Manuscripts at Harvard, A Facsimile Edition*. Belknap–Harvard UP, 1990.

————, ed. *The Letters of Charles Armitage Brown*. Cambridge, Massachusetts: Harvard UP, 1966.

————, ed. *The Poems of John Keats*. London: Heinemann, 1978.

————, ed. *Twentieth Century Interpretations of Keats's Odes*. Englewood Cliffs, New Jersey: Prentice-Hall, 1968.

Stone, Brian. *The Poetry of John Keats*. New York: Penguin, 1992.

Sullivan, K. E., ed. *Keats: Truth & Imagination*. New York: Gramercy–Random House, 1999.

Todd, Pamela, ed. *When the Night Doth Meet the Noon: Poems by John Keats*. London: Pavilion, 1996.

Trilling, Lionel, ed. *The Selected Letters of John Keats*. New York: Farrar, Straus and Young, 1951.

Varriano, John. *A Literary Companion to Rome*. New York: St. Martin's Griffin, 1991.

Vendler, Helen. *The Odes of John Keats*. Cambridge, Massachusetts: Belknap–Harvard UP, 1983.

Wade, Christopher. *The Streets of Hampstead*. Rev. ed. London: High Hill–Camden History Society, 1984.

Walker, Carol Kyros. *Walking North with Keats*. New Haven, Connecticut: Yale UP, 1992.

Walsh, John Evangelist. *Darkling I Listen: The Last Days and Death of John Keats*. New York: St. Martin's, 1999.

Walters, Roger. "Keats and Cyclothymia." *Keats-Shelley Review* 3 (1988): 70–76.

Ward, Aileen. *John Keats: The Making of a Poet*. Rev. ed. New York: Farrar, Straus and Giroux, 1986.

————, ed. *The Poems of John Keats*. Norwalk, Connecticut: Easton, 1980.

Watts, Cedric. *A Preface to Keats*. New York: Longman, 1985.

Weiskel, Thomas. *The Romantic Sublime: Studies in the Structure and Psychology of Transcendence*. Baltimore: Johns Hopkins UP, 1976.

Wellens, Oskar. "Keats in the Netherlands: A Survey of His Dutch Translations and Editions." *Keats-Shelley Review* 16 (2002): 61–73.

Wellesley, Dorothy, ed. *Keats*. The English Poets in Pictures Ser. London: William Collins, 1941.

Wells, Walter A., ed. *A Doctor's Life of John Keats*. New York: Vantage, 1959.

Whitman, William B. *Literary Cities of Italy*. Washington and Philadelphia: Starrhill, 1990.

Willis, Mark. "In Search of Mr Keats." *Keats-Shelley Review* 17 (2003): 136–45.

Wolfson, Susan J., ed. *The Cambridge Companion to Keats*. New York: Cambridge UP, 2001.

Woof, Robert, and Stephen Hebron. *John Keats*. Grasmere, England: Wordsworth Trust, 1995.

Wordsworth, Jonathan, Michael C. Jaye, and Robert Woof. *William Wordsworth and the Age of English Romanticism*. New Brunswick, New Jersey: Rutgers UP, 1987.

LIST OF ILLUSTRATIONS

On He Flared; Pencil drawing of John Keats by Charles Brown, 1819. Courtesy of the National Portrait Gallery, London.

Cold Pastoral; Deathbed portrait of John Keats by Joseph Severn, 1821. Courtesy of the British Library / HIP / Art Resource, NY.

This Mortal Body; Detail of Haydon's *Christ's Entry into Jerusalem*: the figures in the foreground are, from left to right, Wordsworth, Voltaire, and Sir Isaac Newton; John Keats is immediately above Wordsworth. Courtesy of Eugene H. Maly Memorial Library, The Athenaeum of Ohio. Photograph by Matthew Lee.

A Dreaming Thing; Portrait of John Keats by William Hilton. Courtesy of the National Portrait Gallery, London.

Physician Nature; First miniature portrait of John Keats by Joseph Severn, 1818 or 1819. Courtesy of the National Portrait Gallery, London.

Season of Mists; Drawing of Keats's head by Benjamin R. Haydon, 1816. Courtesy of the National Portrait Gallery, London.

Material Sublime; *John Keats* by T. Sampson, 1828, after the *Life Mask of Keats* by Benjamin R. Haydon, 1816. Courtesy of the National Portrait Gallery, London.

INDEX